REGIONALISM AND REVISION

1200–1650

REGIONALISM AND REVISION

THE CROWN AND ITS
PROVINCES IN ENGLAND
1200–1650

Edited by

Peter Fleming, Anthony Gross
and J. R. Lander

THE HAMBLEDON PRESS

LONDON AND RIO GRANDE

Published by The Hambledon Press 1998
102 Gloucester Avenue, London NW1 8HX (UK)
PO Box 162, Rio Grande, Ohio 45674 (USA)

ISBN 1 85285 157 0

A description of this book is available from
the British Library and from the Library of Congress

Typeset by Carnegie Publishing Ltd, Chatsworth Rd, Lancaster
Printed on acid-free paper and bound in
Great Britain by Cambridge University Press

Contents

Preface   vii

Acknowledgements   ix

Abbreviations   xi

1   Regionalism and Revision   1
Anthony Gross

2   The Significance of the County in English Government   15
J.R. Lander

3   A Crisis of the Knightly Class? Inheritance and Office among the Gentry of Thirteenth-Century Buckinghamshire   29
Anne Polden

4   Mid Thirteenth-Century Reformers and the Localities: the Sheriffs of the Baronial Regime, 1258–1261   59
H.W. Ridgeway

5   The Commons and the Early Justices of the Peace under Edward III   87
Anthony Verduyn

6   The Dissolution of St Augustine's Abbey and the Creation of the Diocese of Bristol   107
J.H. Bettey

7   Sir Thomas Cheyne, Lord Warden of the Cinque Ports, 1536–1558: Central Authority and the Defence of Local Privilege   123
Peter Fleming

8   Purveyance and Politics in Jacobean Leicestershire   145
Richard Cust

Index   163

Preface

For the last thirty years historians of later medieval and early modern England have explored regional communities in the hope of developing insights into the nature of pre-modern political society. The county provided many of these historians with their principal focus, since it was assumed to be the most likely framework within which could be forged not only local administrative and political associations but also social and cultural identities. However, in recent years this assumption has been called into question – not least by some of the leading exponents of county studies themselves.

The following essays address many of the issues at the heart of the debate over local society. Fundamental to these studies is the question of the nature of relations between centre and periphery. To what extent could local communities be seen as independent of central government – in whose interests the counties were originally created as administrative, military and fiscal units; or were not only local political institutions but also local identity and *mentalité* largely the product of metropolitan imperatives? Are we correct in seeing institutional principle as the root of local solidarities, or were relations with the Crown and its sometimes overweening officers grounded in more pragmatic and immediate concerns, so that faction-fighting and opportunism, rather than ideology, were the usual causes of conflicts between 'court' and 'country'? And what of 'county society'? How strongly did the 'county gentry' identify themselves with 'their' county, as opposed to seeing themselves as actors on a regional or even national stage? The interests of landed society could not neatly dovetail with county boundaries, nor was the county the only territorial unit around which local loyalties and identity could coalesce. Apart from the parish and subdivisions of the county such as hundreds and lathes, there were socio-political organisations and administrative entities whose territorial limits developed with little heed of county boundaries. Should we not expect noble affinities, dioceses or jurisdictional liberties to have played an important part in the determination of a sense of local belonging.

The study of county society was largely pioneered by historians of the seventeenth century, whose ideas and approaches influenced the study of local society in earlier centuries. This volume, in bringing together work across a broad chronological sweep, demonstrates the essential long-term continuity within local and regional society. However, while acknowledging the artificiality of the divide between late medieval and early modern times, these essays also explores the fluidity of contemporary conceptions of 'the county'. The county, along with a range of other administrative units, is principally useful to historians as a means of pinpointing people in their historical context, because it sets limits of time and place. But since the meaning of the county, as contemporaries understood it, is intangible and evanescent, the county study may all too readily present a paradox: having set individuals within a convenient context, we find that we comprehend them no better for having done so. By addressing the multiple identities of local community, this volume offers a valuable corrective to those approaches which assume that local solidarities were homogeneous and unifocal throughout England and across the centuries, whether these characteristics are supposed to have been based on the county community, the noble affinity or the demands of the centre.

Acknowledgements

The publication of this book has been assisted by a grant from The Scouloudi Foundation in association with the Institute of Historical Research.

This book has its origins in a conference, 'English Provincial Society and its Institutions, *c*. 1250-1650: Authority, Representation and Community', held at Bristol Polytechnic (now the University of the West of England) in 1990, in collaboration with CORAL, who gave valuable financial support.

Abbreviations

APC	*Acts of the Privy Council*
BIHR	*Bulletin of the Institute of Historical Research*
BL	British Library
CCR	*Calendar of Close Rolls*
CKS	Centre for Kentish Studies, Maidstone
CPR	*Calendar of Patent Rolls*
CSPD	*Calendar of State Papers, Domestic*
DNB	*Dictionary of National Biography*
EHR	*English Historical Review*
ESRO	East Sussex Record Office
FA	*Feudal Aids*
HJ	*Historical Journal*
HL	Huntingdon Library
HMC	Historical Manuscripts Commission
LRO	Leicestershire Record Office
LP, Henry VIII	*Letters and Papers, Foreign and Domestic, of the Reign of Henry VIII*
PH	*Parliamentary History*
PRO	Public Record Office
RP	*Rotuli Parliamentorum*
TRHS	*Transactions of the Royal Historical Society*
VCH	Victoria County History

1

Regionalism and Revision

Anthony Gross

It has become commonplace for historians of pre-modern Europe to think in terms of 'small worlds':[1] a series of regional societies which, to a very great extent, functioned independently of one another.[2] This concept has proved most effective when applied to remote valleys in the Mediterranean and the Pyrenees by some of the best-known studies of the *Annales* school.[3] In the context of English historiography, the regional dimension has raised important conceptual issues, particularly in the study of southern and central England, where regional identities need to be carefully reconciled in historical explanations with the existence of a powerful central authority and the absence of major geographical obstructions. In these conditions the prevalence of the regional *mentalité* and the forms in which it crystallised were always likely to be difficult to assess.[4]

This task has been made more difficult by the nature of the available evidence, which is composed largely of legal and governmental records compiled under the auspices of the crown and divided according to the traditional pattern of local administration, that is to say into the counties. This arrangement of the evidence had a decisive effect on the development of local studies. The records of king's bench, the pipe and memoranda rolls all bear marginal tabulations which had a comforting solidity for young historians who had abandoned the security of the single estate in search of a less tangible entity. As they searched for the focus of regional solidarity, the county quickly claimed primacy. By 1974 there seemed little doubt that 'in late Tudor and Stuart England most people who could think politically regarded themselves as members of a county community ... which stood

[1] I am extremely grateful for the insights and evidence contributed to this introduction by Professor J. R. Lander and Dr. Peter Fleming.

[2] The phrase is suggested by W. Davies, *Small Worlds: The Village Community in Early Medieval Brittany* (London, 1985).

[3] Most notably in F. Braudel, *The Mediterranean and the Mediterranean World in the Age of Philip II*, trans. S. Reynolds (2 vols, London, 1972–3).

[4] See especially R. Frame, *The Political Development of the British Isles, 1100–1400* (Oxford, 1990), pp. 7–19.

apart from, sometimes even in opposition to, the greater but remoter community of the nation'.[5]

Fuller reflection has brought some disillusion with the regional approach and in particular with the county as a focus of study. In the early 1980s, having accumulated a welter of monographs and doctoral theses, early modern historians began to question the validity of what had been done. Clive Holmes in particular identified a 'County Community School' which had paid far too little attention to the degree to which 'national religious and constitutional issues' framed the political culture of the localities.[6] As the syntheses produced by Stuart scholars gradually carried the debate into more abstract issues, medieval historians, whose ventures into local history lagged several years behind their early modern counterparts, enjoyed certain advantages in setting out a theoretical base for their subject. For one thing, they had been able to watch the debate prompted by the work of their sixteenth- and seventeenth-century colleagues. Even more important, it was inherent in the medievalists' brief to search for origins both of a gentry identity and of the sense of community within the counties. This aspect of the task instilled a degree of theoretical rigour and helped to spark an important debate about where the focal points of regionalism really lay.

For some, like Michael Bennett writing of Cheshire and Lancashire at the end of the fourteenth century, the county has retained its cardinal significance. Bennett justifies this position by giving his counties an importance beyond institutional form, attempting to show that they provided the chief arena for social interaction among the local gentry. At the same time, Bennett found that some relationships, particularly those of commerce, the church and military service, transcended county boundaries, incorporating even quite humble families into a regional society which embraced the whole of the north west.[7] For other medievalists the strength of cross-county ties calls the very significance of the county community into question. Susan Wright's fifteenth-century Derbyshire gentry chose friends who held lands close to their own. The result was a network of small gentry associations which made the county and its boundaries almost irrelevant. Nigel Saul finds a similar model serviceable for fourteenth-century Sussex, where in his view 'the familiar picture of a county community may have to be discarded ... in favour of that of a county of communities'.[8] Topography is increasingly seen as an important element in fashioning these patterns of association below the level of the county. Even in south-east England, where there are no

    [5] A. Hassell Smith, *County and Court: Government and Politics in Norfolk, 1558–1603* (Oxford, 1974), p. 108.

    [6] C. Holmes, 'The county community in Stuart historiography', *Journal of British Studies*, xix (1979–80), p. 73.

    [7] M. J. Bennett, *Community Class and Careerism: Cheshire and Lancashire Society in the Age of Sir Gawain and the Green Knight* (Cambridge, 1983), pp. 5–41.

    [8] N. A. Saul, *Scenes from Provincial Life: Knightly Families in Sussex, 1280–1400* (Oxford, 1986), p. 60.

major geographical obstructions to communication, the contrasting physical environments of Weald and Downland led, in Peter Fleming's view, to the development of distinctive communities at the levels of both the gentry and their humbler neighbours.[9] In this region settlement or investment in land by Londoners also seems to have helped to forge patterns of association, an urban dimension to the social intercourse of the countryside which may have been present elsewhere in England on a smaller scale in the hinterlands of county towns.

A rather different attempt has been made to undermine the concept of the medieval county community by importing Clive Holmes's constitutionalism from the seventeenth century. Those who employ such terminology need to think very carefully about its meaning in a society where the ideologies of Calvin and Beza had not yet transformed the Thomist hypothesis of justified resistance to tyranny into a practical creed that would test the inviolability of dynastic monarchy. Even among those who are prepared to entertain the concept of constitutionalism in pre-Reformation society, many admit that, as a formative element in political life, it was no more than a tender sapling. Next to it was the vigorous growth of locally based affinities, which sometimes cut across the administrative structure of the counties while still reinforcing the centripetal division characteristic of the kingdom.[10] None of this is to deny that there are good reasons for suggesting that the county aristocracies were underpinned on a national, and to some extent on a supranational scale, by a common *mentalité* which can easily be forgotten if too great an emphasis is placed on local solidarities.[11] It was a related consideration, the spread of standard English in the fifteenth century, which encouraged David Morgan to set an elegant *terminus ad quem* for local studies, in the 'hope that having with much profit gone into provincial society, we may in due course, laden with our booty, consider getting out'.[12] But this somewhat premature recall to barracks raises some important questions about why the troops were dispatched into the shires in the first place. Was it to load ourselves with precious data that would make it possible to redefine history from the centre? If so, this goes

---

[9] P. W. Fleming, 'The character and private concerns of the gentry of Kent, 1422–1509' (unpublished University of Wales Ph.D. thesis, 1985), pp. 148–54. See also A. E. Everitt, *The Community of Kent and the Great Rebellion* (Leicester 1966), pp. 22–7.

[10] J. R. Lander, 'Family, "friends" and politics in fifteenth-century England', in R. A. Griffiths and J. Sherborne (ed.), *Kings and Nobles in the Later Middle Ages* (Gloucester, 1986), p. 37.

[11] The recognition of such a *mentalité* does not support the use of terminology indicative of constitutionalism, which according to the most cogent recent definition 'signifies advocacy of a system of checks upon the exercise of political power': H. A. Lloyd, 'Constitutionalism', in J. H. Burns (ed.), *The Cambridge History of Political Thought, 1450–1700* (Cambridge, 1991), p. 254. For a discussion of the role of 'constitutionalism' in medieval local studies, M. C. Carpenter, 'Fifteenth-century English politics', *HJ*, xxvi, 4 (1983), pp. 963–7.

[12] D. A. L. Morgan 'The individual style of the English gentleman', in M. Jones (ed.), *Gentry and Lesser Nobility in Late Medieval Europe* (Gloucester, 1980), p. 27.

far towards explaining why vital concepts of regional identity were so vaguely delineated at the outset and why the resulting debate has lacked clear and accepted terms of reference.

All too often gentry scholars address one another at cross-purposes. Take, for example, the number of gentry in a county. On this most basic issue scholars, influenced by changes in social function (particularly the expanding personnel of local office) and perhaps even more by changes in social nomenclature, have reached conclusions which differ so widely that it is difficult to account for the disparity through geographical variations. Some historians of the middle ages evaluate populations of gentry at between one and two hundred for each county.[13] But other estimates are substantially higher. In Lancashire and Cheshire, Bennett found 600 gentry families and, although he believes the concentration of gentry in this part of the country to have been abnormally high, a similarly large population of gentry has been found in Kent for the same period.[14] Despite the considerable dispute over the number of knights in Elizabethan England, there is general agreement that the period saw a major expansion in the numbers of gentry as a whole, a process which was monitored rather than controlled by the College of Arms. Even in counties where the gentry were already numerous by the fifteenth century, substantial growth is apparent by 1600. Studying Kent for the seventeenth century and using the title of gentleman as his mark of qualification, Everitt calculated between 800 and 1000 gentry. In Norfolk in 1580 there were at least 424 gentry and some 641 in Yorkshire in 1603.[15]

For both the early modern and medieval periods, scholars have sought to deal with these unwieldy numbers by dividing the 'county gentry' from the mass of the 'parochial gentry'. But, as Christine Carpenter has recognised, it has proved problematic to differentiate the gentry elite in any one county.[16] Attempts to do so have indeed only created a new layer of statistical difficulty, as historians have been forced to use subjective criteria to approach the task. This is seen most strikingly in Saul's groundbreaking study of Gloucestershire, where known retainers and participants in military campaigns are used to compose a universal index of the elite so that the same retainers and soldiers can be assessed as proportions of the resulting total.[17] It is difficult to produce a balanced sample, let alone a comprehensive roll

[13] N. A. Saul, *Knights and Esquires: The Gloucestershire Gentry in the Fourteenth Century* (Oxford, 1981), pp. 33–34; S. M. Wright, *The Derbyshire Gentry in the Fifteenth Century*, Derbyshire Record Society, viii (1983), p. 4.

[14] Bennett, *Community, Class and Careerism*, pp. 83–4; P. W. Fleming, 'Charity, faith and the gentry of Kent', in A. J. Pollard (ed.), *Property and Politics: Essays in Later Medieval English History* (Gloucester, 1984), pp. 36, 54.

[15] D. M. Palliser, *The Age of Elizabeth: England under the Later Tudors, 1547–1603* (London, 1983), p. 70.

[16] M. C. Carpenter, 'Gentry and community in medieval England', *Journal of British Studies*, xxxiii (1994), pp. 340–380.

[17] Saul, *Knights and Esquires*, pp. 48–51, 97, 270–92.

call. Even the use of contemporary lists of local landowners, a dispiritingly scarce resource for the medieval period, is fraught with difficulty. How far do we make adjustments for bias generated by the purpose for which the list was drawn up or for omissions caused by dynastic minorities or human error? This high degree of subjectivity has led scholars to produce numerical estimates of the 'county gentry' so disparate that the variations cannot be accounted for by regional differences. Susan Wright and Nigel Saul, writing of medieval Derbyshire and Gloucestershire respectively, give an estimate of about fifty families which can be classed as county gentry.[18] For fifteenth-century Kent on the other hand, a figure of one hundred is suggested, but with an upper echelon of twenty dominant families.[19] For Nottinghamshire in the same period Simon Payling takes this concept of an elite within the elite even further, reducing his focus of interest to 'the dozen or so wealthiest county families'.[20] Despite these wide differences between various numerical estimates of the gentry, no attempt has been made to reconcile them or explain the disparity. With so little correspondence between the statistical samples chosen by historians, it is difficult to pursue themes in gentry history over more than a single century. Everitt's claim that the horizons of the gentry were limited to the locality and incorporated little knowledge of national issues is likely to seem absurd to the medievalist who has watched a wide spectrum of the provincial gentry campaigning in France or repre-senting the county in parliament, until it is remembered that two centuries earlier many of Everitt's eighty gentry would, at best, have been classed as yeomen. The difficulty encountered in taking account of changes in nomen-clature which did not always reflect alterations of social function and behaviour is clearly evident. Yet even if we could identify an acceptably constant grouping of provincial lesser lights with relatively limited horizons, we should not be tempted to assume that the county was the focus of their loyalty. For, as Lander points out in this volume, those with limited horizons were normally restricted to a region far smaller than the county as a whole.

While the growing popularity of the county as a tool of analysis has not provided any clear route out of this statistical maze, the notion of an elite has at least permitted some useful lateral thinking. In particular, scholars can no longer apply the shorthand terminology of county and community without questioning its validity. That does not mean, however, that we should go to the extreme marked out by Christine Carpenter, who has hinted that we must ban that vexed word 'community' from all academic writing.[21] Above all, we do not need to accept her distillation from the social scientists which instructs us that the county and its community can be defined only as an

---

[18] Ibid., p. 34; Wright, *Derbyshire Gentry*, p. 5.

[19] Fleming, 'Charity, faith and the gentry of Kent', pp. 36, 54.

[20] S. Payling, *Political Society in Lancastrian England: The Greater Gentry of Nottinghamshire* (Oxford, 1991), p. vii.

[21] Carpenter, 'Gentry and community', p. 340.

'organic unity ... sealed in a harmonious hierarchy' and demonstrated only through the detailed prosopographical assessment of social connections.[22] The point is that, in seeking out the various factors which helped to form and sustain local elites, historians have begun to see the county less as an identifiable body of persons with ascertainable characteristics than as a volatile concept which took on a variety of institutional forms and which had a dynamic influence on men's lives. There is still further to go in this direction. If put to the question, almost all historians would acknowledge that community itself resides not in any distinct, identifiable and interconnected body of persons but rather in the connection and identity which bonded those individuals together.

The 'community' is, nevertheless, still too frequently concretised into a list of persons or families the extent of whose bonding can be defined according to the range of their social contacts and the extent of their harmonious consensus. Charles Moreton's attempt to describe the fifteenth-century Norfolk of the Townshends shares Carpenter's scepticism towards the concept of community but uncritically assumes that community should be defined in just this way.[23] Eric Acheson's study of Leicestershire slides into the same error. He rightly sees the danger that the county may assume a greater significance in the historian's thinking 'than it in fact possessed for the knights and esquires of the time'.[24] He astutely casts doubt on J. E. A. Joliffe's assertion that 'common obligation created a common outlook'.[25] He then gives the game away by proposing to address the question of whether the gentry considered themselves members of the community of the shire by determining 'the associations forged among the gentry', principally land transactions.[26] No doubt this approach is pragmatic, in that it facilitates the statistical analysis of various forms of behaviour, but while it predominates it is scarcely surprising that the essence of community remains hard to isolate. We cannot trick our way around the problem simply by describing the essential as the feeling of bonding experienced by those within our postulated communities. Self-perception is evanescent. It is difficult to use as a tool of social analysis in the present, let alone at a distance of more than five hundred years. Furthermore, we cannot assume that bonds of community were always consciously perceived as such. Discord and violence must have been disruptive, where they occurred, they also played their part in sharpening and intensifying the moral and cultural conventions which lent cohesion to the social fabric.[27]

Alongside these theoretical debates, strides continue be made in

---

[22] Ibid., p. 352.

[23] C. E. Moreton, *The Townshends and their World: Gentry, Law, and Land in Norfolk, c. 1450–1551* (Oxford, 1992), pp. 80–1, 195–6.

[24] E. Acheson, *A Gentry Community: Leicestershire in the Fifteenth Century, c. 1422 – c. 1485* (Cambridge, 1992), p. 77.

[25] Ibid., p. 78.

[26] Ibid., p. 79.

[27] See for example J. G. Bellamy, *Bastard Feudalism and the Law* (London, 1989), pp. 34–56.

investigating the impact which the county's institutional functioning made on peoples' lives. While Simon Payling, in particular, has done much to add to the substantial corpus of work available in this area, it remains as important as ever to gather information about the county's action as a focus for the defence of private interests and as a channel for the distribution of responsibilities and rewards. Ann Polden's essay in the present volume takes up the challenge in an earlier period by examining the contribution which the benefits available from service to the crown made to the evolution of the gentry elite in thirteenth-century Buckinghamshire. The point is reinforced on a national scale by H. W. Ridgeway's study of the sheriffs established by the baronial reform movement of Henry III's reign.

The issues raised by Polden and Ridgeway remind us that earlier generations of medievalists, Tout, Morris, Cam and their contemporaries, resolved questions of the county's identity by grounding their analyses solidly in its administrative aspect. There was initially good reason for broadening this definition to try to take fuller account of sentiments and cultural influences which may have coalesced around the core of the administrative function. But with the weakening of the administrative emphasis the meaning of the county comes to rest on a gamut of volatile social bonds. The ten knights of Payling's Nottinghamshire elite whose arms were used to decorate the windows of the archbishop of York's great hall at Southwell in about 1450 may, arguably, have regarded themselves as the representatives of an estate within the county, rather than the embodiment of the county as a whole. But even if the ten did envisage themselves as the political sum of their shire, the 229 men who attested the Nottinghamshire election in 1449 could have said the same about themselves with no less justification. In fact Payling's conclusion, that the knights on the Southwell window derived their sense of corporateness from their joint responsibility for local government, shows that it was the administration which provided the common denominator between these two disparate expressions of county identity.[28] Even those who do not wish to go as far as J. R. Lander in doubting the county's role in the formation of public opinion, or the existence of any social body which can accurately be called the county, must take account of the point that it was not until 1647 that the term was first used to describe the whole population of the shire and then in the context of resistance to royal taxation. They should also bear in mind the importance of the county surveys and developments in map-making which took place at the end of the sixteenth and the beginning of the seventeenth centuries. If, as one of Camden's near contemporaries noted, before that time the counties of England had scarcely known each other then their ignorance must have placed a check on their individuation.[29] The medieval shires could conceive of themselves as

---

28 Payling, *Political Society*, p. 218.
29 Bishop Gibson prefacing an edition of Camden's *Britannia*, cited by Palliser, *Age of Elizabeth*, p. 8.

communities, but there was little information on which to base a sense of differentiation from other counties or as they were often called 'countries'. Our own knowledge of how local identity was understood before the seventeenth century is correspondingly thin, though Jack Straw's confession that the rebels of 1381 had planned to give each county its own 'king' certainly suggests a notion of local solidarity and relation to the wider kingdom very different to that promulgated from the centre.[30] On the other hand, it is only the central government's notion of the county as a body associated by common rights and obligations that reaches us with any clarity.

Of the three meanings which Lander finds ascribed to the word 'county' at different historical periods it is therefore certainly the first, 'a territorial unit of defence, justice and administration' which will best repay the attention of historians of the pre-modern period. This should by no means be taken to advocate a return to narrow institutional history which abandons the trend towards prosopography or the recent emphasis on *mentalité*. For it does not ignore the possibility that the counties, once given concrete form by the influence of the centre, provided foci around which cultural and social expressions of local solidarity could coalesce. At the same time, a definition of the county which superficially appears reductionist may actually bring us much closer to the medieval perception. Although some counties centred on ancient Saxon kingdoms, their institutional development owed most to the administrative needs of the tenth-century English kings. The fiscal administrators of the post-conquest Anglo-Norman regime recognised in the shire, and its chief official the *vicecomes* or sheriff, the most effective structure with which to obtain funds for continental wars. When the crown extended its command over resources by instituting a system of representation, in the thirteenth and fourteenth centuries, the same local units came naturally to hand. Even if we suppose that an indigenous and long-standing sense of community preceded and acted alongside the central government's policies of management and exploitation, the pressures exerted by the crown were so insistent that any preexistent concept of the county must have undergone radical redefinition. For this reason it may be productive, when considering local usages of the terminology of community, to bear in mind the possibility, even the probability, that these developed not autonomously but in reaction to definitions which originated at the centre.

This was certainly the case in the celebrated incident of 1450 when the sailors aboard the *Nicholas of the Tower* mimicked the attitudes of parliamentary impeachment by declaring that they had executed the duke of Suffolk on behalf of the 'community of the realm'. The shipmen's statement, nowadays quoted with increasing frequency, that 'they did not know the said king [Henry VI] but they well knew the crown of England' and that 'the aforesaid

---

[30] E. M. Thomson (ed.), *Thomas Walsingham, Chronicon Angliae*, Rolls Series, lxiv (London, 1874), p. 309.

crown was the community of the said realm and that the community of that realm was the crown of the realm' only goes to show how thoroughly the lessons taught by kings since Edward I had been learned.[31] In the Carlisle parliament of 1307, as in the Remonstrance of 1297, criticism or requests could be addressed to the king in the name of the 'community of the land'. But the future belonged to the king's preferred formula employed in the *Confirmatio cartarum* of 1297.[32] By speaking of community of 'the realm' as opposed to that 'of land' the jurists incorporated the community within the orbit of the crown. By 1450 the perceived unity and indivisibility of that orbit was such that even those who refused to acknowledge the grandson of a usurping king could express their opposition only within its terms of reference.

Two remarkable legal cases from the early fourteenth century allow us to see more clearly how such an interraction between centre and localities developed a conceptual and linguistic framework and give a strong hint of the determining and initiating roles played by the crown and its agents. Staffordshire and Warwickshire had responded to an investigation into concerted tax abuse by adapting the language of the royal jurists in seeking mitigation of the penalty imposed for underassessment. The Staffordshire taxers claimed that they had always trusted to the common profit of the entire county ('omnino fiebant ad communem utilitatem totius comitatus'), while those of Warwickshire asserted that they had allowed the concealments and embezzlements for the benefit of themselves and the whole community ('concelamenta et disportaciones in taxacionibus predictis omnino cedebant ad commodum ipsorum et totius communitatis').[33]

What was understood by the reference to community in these proceedings? The conception certainly appears to be a more inclusive one than the county gentry elite recently defined by some fifteenth-century scholars. In Stafford-shire there were no less than ninety-two men who assumed responsibility for the county's fine of 340 marks, most of whom were of modest status. In addition, they asked that the burden fall entirely on them, completely sparing the sub-taxers themselves who were men of small means (*minus potentes*) and that within their own ranks the sum be distributed according to their rank (*habito respectu statum eorum*). Idealists may be tempted to assume that these demands reflect an entrenched sense of community in these localities and, however surprisingly, a progressive attitude to the burden of fiscal exactions, requiring those most able to pay to pay most. Sceptics might reply

---

[31] R. L. Virgoe, 'The death of William de la Pole', *Bulletin of the John Rylands Library*, xlvii (1964–5), pp. 489–502.

[32] M. Prestwich, *English Politics in the Thirteenth Century* (London, 1990), p. 143; idem, *Edward I* (London, 1988), pp. 434–5.

[33] G. Wrottesley (ed.), 'Extracts from the Plea Rolls of the reign of Edward III', *Staffordshire Historical Collections* (formerly the William Salt Archaeological Society), ix, p. 95; W. F. Carter (ed.), *The Lay Subsidy Roll for Warwickshire of 6 Edward III*, Dugdale Society, vi (1926), pp. 96–9.

that since the low assessments had originally been made in return for bribes, the negotiations are less likely to represent a strong indigenous sense of community than a crude though startling attempt by minor local officials to coopt the terminology of national taxation as an excuse for their peculation.[34]

Neither of these explanations is entirely convincing. It is more persuasive to ascribe the greater share of the initiative in formulating these concepts of local solidarity and custom to the itinerant justices. To do so explains why the pleas in mitigation advanced in Staffordshire and Warwickshire were so similar, even displaying a significant degree of shared terminology (it is difficult to ascribe the common use of the term *omnino* here to coincidence). The justices had a clear motive for encouraging such a resolution to these cases. The admission that the evasion had been undertaken on behalf of the counties as a whole enabled them to ensure that the crown received its due by ammercing those counties rather than fining the sub-taxers as individuals. The requirement that in Staffordshire the fiscal burden should fall on those best able to bear it may be satisfactorily explained in the same way. It is therefore likely that the justices, having uncovered the transgressions, offered a prepared formula by which reconciliation with the crown could be achieved. The guiding principle was a concretised county community responsible to central authority and able to bear the requisite financial burdens. Such an approach would of course have been impossible in the absence of some existing local sentiment. It should not necessarily be assumed that that amounted to anything constant or coherent.

Yet while it is extremely plausible that local perceptions of the county community were subject to conditioning from the centre which was continuous, though variable in intensity, we should not underestimate the degree to which the county became the chief focus for provincial politics. While the idea that the county courts were anvils of public opinion may attribute too much cogency to the localities, an examination of the court's authority explains why it exerted a magnetic draw over the shire notables. For one thing it returned MPs, the most effective carriers of petitions.[35] The court also gave the sheriff a rare opportunity to target enemies or hardened offenders by instituting processes of appeal, which faced the accused with outlawry in the event of non-appearance.[36] Similarly we should understand the sheriff's importance in local society less through his role as an interlocutor between the centre and a self-contained community and more in terms of his own need to balance the rewards of office against his fiscal responsibility. It is the second interpretation of the office which brings us closest to

---

[34] Wrottesley, 'Extracts', p. 95.

[35] J. R. Maddicott, 'The county community and the making of public opinion in fourteenth-century England', *TRHS*, 5th series, xxviii (1978).

[36] A. J. Gross, 'The king's lordship in the county of Stafford, 1312–22', *Midland History*, xvi (1989), pp. 34–6.

the string of sheriffs who visited the Fleet prison by reason of the bad debts of office. The experience of such men reminds us of the extent to which the politics of the county, the invention and tool of royal government, remained continuous with those of the centre.[37]

The essays in this volume explore the dimensions of this theme. One of the most important advances is in the study of the justices of the peace: for so long a cornerstone both for those historians who sought to establish the notion of semi-autonomous communities operating 'self-government at the king's command' and for others who were inclined to portray the Tudor monarchy as reliant upon gentry who were independent of magnate influence.[38] Lander showed recently that the late fifteenth-century kings trusted the justices less than has previously been supposed. The central government altered their powers in accordance with what it perceived as its own advantage, curtailing their independence by ensuring that magnates and judges regularly oversaw the work of the commissions. A careful eye was also kept on the personnel of the commissions, a concern also reflected in the purges of Elizabeth's reign.[39] Anthony Verduyn has been able to take these issues back to the very creation of the justices and has produced related conclusions. The justices of the peace did not come into being because of consistent pressure from local communities, which wanted to manage their own judicial affairs, but as a result of shifts in policy by the central government which was finding it difficult to maintain order. 'Local opinion', concludes Verduyn, 'was more inclined to be guided by the actions of the king and council than to challenge them.'

Ridgeway shows that conclusions drawn from a study of the justices of the peace in the fourteenth century may also be applied to the sheriffs of the thirteenth. Ridgeway goes a long way towards dispelling the belief that the baronial movement of 1258 to 1261 offered a genuine and sustained response to demands for reform in the localities, by changing all the sheriffs and making concessions to calls for elected officials. As soon as it was safe to do so, the regime dropped some of the less practicable stipulations of the Provisions of Oxford. This was possible because the complaints had been prompted not by constitutional principle but by the excessive demands and financial pressures which Henry III's regime had piled onto the sheriffs and their counties before 1258. Where conflicts over rights did arise, they often took their origins from family rivalries stimulated by the central government's distribution of offices. According to Richard Cust, this was still the case in

[37] W. M. Ormrod, *The Reign of Edward III: Crown and Political Society in England, 1327–1377* (London, 1990), pp. 156–7. The concept of a continuity between local and central politics was suggested to me by Professor R. R. Davies, but I may here have given it a slant that he would not entirely accept.

[38] A. B. White, *Self-Government at the King's Command* (Minneapolis, Minnesota, 1933).

[39] J. R. Lander, *The English Justices of the Peace, 1461–1509* (Gloucester, 1989), pp. ix–x, 1–12, 108–44; A. G. R. Smith, *The Emergence of a Nation State: The Commonwealth of England, 1529–1660* (London, 1984), pp. 116, 138.

the early seventeenth century, when the dispute over the crown's rights of purveyance did much to set the political climate. In Leicestershire the issue of purveyance was used as a weapon by a clutch of families alienated by the reservation of key local offices to the earl of Huntingdon. It was factional rivalry which spilled over into constitutional debate and not vice-versa.

If common feeling within the counties was nurtured by the administrative framework, we should also consider other local administrative structures which may have generated their own community solidarities. After all, a map of later medieval political and administrative units could not appear as other than a palimpsest of overlapping jurisdictions. It may even be that the county's emergence as the all-purpose focus of local community feeling took place from the mid sixteenth century onwards, when this melange of liberties and smaller jurisdictions was being reduced to greater uniformity by the centre. In this case, it would be two-dimensional and teleological to apply these conditions to the earlier period. Irrespective of this, it is significant that in the essays of both J. H. Bettey and Peter Fleming, where the concentration does shift from the county to other institutions of locality, the substantive issues remain very much the same. Thus Bettey explores the doubts as to whether the initiative for the establishment of the diocese of Bristol came from Bristol itself, motivated by civic pride; or, as is perhaps more likely, from central government, anxious to establish centres which could quell dissent. In the event the turbulent career of the first bishop, Paul Bush, demonstrates the extent to which careers in the church stood at the discretion of the central government. Deprived of his position as abbot by the Dissolution, he was appointed bishop of Bristol before finally resigning that position because his married status was unacceptable to the Marian regime. Although the Reformation had created an unprecedented opportunity for reshaping the structure of the provincial church, neither of the key constituents of its policy – the close control of personnel and the use of the ecclesiastical establishment to maintain order – was new. The medieval English kings had jealously preserved their de facto right to nominate to English bishoprics and, as far back as the reign of Edward II, the crown had systematically planted the cathedral chapters with its supporters as a means of maintaining a strong presence in the shires.[40]

Peter Fleming's study of the Cinque Ports emphasises the liberty's role as an administrative and jurisdictional unit which cut across county boundaries. Despite the considerable distances which separated some of its members, it managed to maintain a sense of solidarity in the face of, indeed to some extent because of, outside pressures. The liberty, and in consequence the sense of common feeling which was integral to it, was created and then sustained as a result of the needs of the crown. According to the analysis presented here, the nature of the Cinque Ports is encapsulated by the

[40] J. S. Roskell, 'A consideration of certain aspects of the English *Modus tenendi parliamentum*', *Bulletin of the John Rylands Library*, i (1967–8), pp. 411–42.

Janus-faced character of their lord warden: on the one hand the liberty's spokesman in its relations with the outside world, on the other the creature and representative of the central administration.

It is not only the constant presence of such characteristics which has encouraged the growing emphasis on relations between centre and periphery as opposed to regional studies undertaken for their own sake. It is entirely compatible with the determination of scholars to shed the restriction of narrow and artificial definitions of lordship and community which do not begin to reflect the complexity of the medieval and early modern world view. As a development in historiography it also responds to current concerns by focusing on the early development and potency of the centralising influence which is one of the chief characteristics which differentiates England from its neighbours. The influence of this experience on responses to recrudescent centrifugal forces, and to the emergence and consolidation of political entities greater than the nation state, is certain to attract increasing interest. The essays in this volume help to set an agenda which future contributors to the field of local studies may seek to redefine but which they will be unable to ignore.

2

The Significance of the County in English Government

J. R. Lander

The mere repetition of words can be deceptive. The continuous use of a single word often conceals tremendous, even fundamental changes in the form and function of an institution which it purports to describe. Witness the term 'parliament': a mutation from any kind of discussion or conversation to an assembly of feudal or other tenants; to a meeting of aristocrats, prominent landowners, lesser landowners, citizens and burgesses from small towns; to one mainly elected from the upper ranks of landed society; and finally to a democratic forum.

The meanings of the word 'county' have been almost equally diverse at different periods: (1) a territorial unit of defence, justice and administration; (2) the population of the territorial unit in general; and (3) more particularly the area's social elite and its ruling families. Moreover, as the major unit of local government, the county has had to reconcile two conflicting roles: at one and the same time it has been a unit for control and exploitation by the central government and a unit of almost autonomous action and protective of the interests of its inhabitants, with a kind of balance of power fluctuating between them.

An institution prominent from Anglo-Saxon times, its traditional boundaries are still recognisable today in spite of the very considerable administrative readjustments of 1974. Again until the county councils' acts of 1888 and 1894, which introduced elected governing bodies for the first time, it had generally been ruled by a small (though constantly fluctuating) group of elite families. From the late fourteenth century the governing groups consisted of various combinations of magnates, gentry, clerics and lawyers, appointed through a wide variety of influences, whose predominance extended well into the present century in spite of the late nineteenth-century acts. The self-consciousness and the political sophistication of these groups increased with the passage of time and during long periods they entered into phases of acute tension with the central government: a state of affairs with which we are all too familiar today.

I think it may well be significant that the first example in the *Oxford English Dictionary* of the meaning of the word 'county' as the population of the shire occurs rather late, in the context of 1647 and of resentment against taxation.[1] It occurred after at least three decades during which increasingly acute tensions over military demands, religious practices and central directions on social policy, as well as abnormally heavy taxation, had distinctly soured relationships between the central government and the local establishments: a major stage, perhaps, in the development of the self-consciousness of the county communities resisting what they regarded as ill-informed, misguided and incompetent interference in local affairs. Indeed, according to one seventeenth-century historian the whole business was a completely confused hit-and-miss shambles.[2]

One has to recall that the very diverse origins of the shires (small kingdoms in East Anglia and the south; military and defensive units in the midlands; later imitative units imposed upon the far north and as late as 1536 in Wales), resulted in variety: in size, in legal and economic institutions, and to some extent in social structure. The uniformity so cherished by modern bureaucrats did not exist.

It is generally maintained that the development of English government was unique in Europe, summed up many years ago by A. B. White in the words 'self government at the king's command'.[3] Late Anglo-Saxon England had maintained something of a unity that had been almost completely shattered elsewhere in Europe. Moreover, unlike the higher aristocracies of the Continent, English magnates never held large compact blocks of territory. With estates widely scattered through many areas, they never dominated the equivalent of entire provinces, thus inhibiting the development of provincial loyalties comparable in strength to those of France, Germany and Italy. These two factors in combination, assisted by the small size of the country, enabled the Anglo-Norman and Angevin kings to establish the earliest centralised government in northern Europe, equalled elsewhere only in the Norman kingdom of Sicily. It was perhaps based on units potentially freer of aristocratic dominance than elsewhere. Yet at the same time this achievement was flawed by a defect which profoundly affected its future course. Centralisation was premature, in that it preceded the development

[1] It occurs in Clarendon's famous *History* under the year 1647 as a protest against billeting: 'The counties throughout the kingdom were so incensed ... that they refused to suffer the soldiers to be billeted on them' – in other words in local protests against exploitation by the central government. Local recalcitrance was, of course, notorious during the 1640s and 1650s. For a balanced view see D. Hirst, *Authority and Conflict: England, 1603–1658* (London, 1986), pp. 44, 54, 191, 224, 235, 245, 260, 282–4. The meaning of 'county' as the county gentry or county families collectively according to the *OED* occurs for the first time only as late as 1886 in Mrs Oliphant's *Poor Gentlemen.*

[2] The deficiencies and inadequacies of the central government in the early seventeenth century are encapsulated in the statement that 'policy' tended to be merely ad hoc responses to whatever happened to land on ministers' desks (normally petitions from interested parties), and consistency was lost both in a fog of ignorance and amid the often conflicting cries of vested interests, while even if a policy was declared, lack of personnel and information limited enforcement: Hirst, *Authority and Conflict*, pp. 27–9, 43ff, 148–9.

[3] A. B. White, *Self-Government at the King's Command* (West Port, reprint of original of 1933).

of an adequate literate civil service and the ability to pay for one. Therefore kings had to rely upon local, half-voluntary, half-compelled response to execute their orders. Moreover, their financial inability to pay a professional staff continued, except on a very small scale, for centuries after the necessary personnel had become available.[4] Historians have noted the acute tensions this generated. J. E. A. Joliffe analysed a bitter conflict between the arbitrary will of the king (often outrageously unjust and tyrannical) and the stultifying traditional inertia of the local feudal communities.[5] More recently, Dr M. T. Clanchy has expressed the view that the extension of royal justice could actually increase the levels of immemorial corruption, the curse of local government everywhere.[6]

Conflict was thus endemic. Clashes between the centre and the localities resound across the ages: from local wails about William the Conqueror and his notorious agent, Picot the wicked sheriff of Cambridge; the sheriff of Nottingham of Robin Hood fame (to whichever century he may belong); the wails of Elizabethan and early Stuart governments against the negligence and inefficiency of the justices of the peace; the achievement, according to Sidney and Beatrice Webb, of almost complete autonomy by the shires in the eighteenth century; in the nineteenth the clash between the fanatical and tactless Sir Edward Chadwick, trying to eradicate the consequent incompetence; to the immense differences of opinion in our own day between Mrs Margaret Thatcher of Westminster and the likes of Mrs Margaret Hodge of Islington.[7] All of which, perhaps, raises a rather cynical reflection. In

---

[4] The problem was then compounded by competing demands for patronage, i.e. nobles demanding a share of the royal patronage for their own followers: J. P. Dowson, *A History of Lay Judges* (Cambridge, Massachusetts, 1960), p. 127; J. R. Lander, *The Limitations of English Monarchy in the Later Middle Ages* (Toronto, 1989), pp. 22–3.

[5] J. E. A. Joliffe, *Angevin Kingship* (London, 1955), Introduction, chapters 3 and 4 and Recapitulation. See especially, for example, the case of Arnold of Lisieux, pp. 20 n. 3, 103–4, 107.

[6] 'It might even be argued that royal power contributed to disorder and corruption and that the judicial authority of the crown was a public nuisance.'; M. T. Clanchy, 'Law, government and society in medieval England', *History*, lix (1974), p. 78. Dr Maddicott has amply illustrated the notoriety of the corruption of the royal justices in the fourteenth century, J. R. Maddicott, *Law and Lordship: Royal Justices as Retainers in Thirteenth- and Fourteenth-Century England*, Past and Present Supplement, iv (1978). There may have been some improvement in the fifteenth century, for after the reign of Henry IV there are no known complaints about the judges, J. G. Bellamy, *Crime and Public Order in England in the Later Middle Ages* (London and Toronto, 1973), pp. 14–16.

[7] E. g. G. C. F. Forster, 'The North Riding justices and their sessions, 1603–1625', *Northern History*, x (1975), pp. 110–15. 'The century and a half lying between the dismissal of the Stuarts and the Reform Parliament constitutes, for the historian of the internal administration of England and Wales, a period of extraordinary significance. For the first, and perhaps for the last, time in English history, the national government abstained from intervention in local affairs, practically leaving all the various kinds of local bodies to carry out their several administrations as they chose, without central supervision or central control': S. and B. Webb (ed.), *English Local Government from the Revolution to the Municipal Corporations Act* (9 vols, London, 1906–9), i, p. vi.

government, is one limited group of vested interests inevitably followed by another, equally lax or corrupt (or both), and did this happen in the later middle ages?[8]

With this background in mind, how far by the late fourteenth and fifteenth centuries had the shire court developed as a unit both of local government and of public opinion? I rather doubt a recent view which postulates that by the third quarter of the fourteenth century the shire court was already a forum for a kind of public opinion. It seems to me that the duration of its sittings, level and type of attendance, and the logistics of its organisation make this view at least somewhat implausible. Although the court in most areas met every forty days, it always met in the same town, much to the inconvenience of the public from the more distant parts, especially in a large county where the shire town was not centrally situated. Dr Maddicott has inferred that the normal attendance at these frequent assemblies was about 150.[9] But who attended, and how influential they were, are very different matters. Other evidence suggests that those present were there mostly to pursue their own affairs, and that such people were hardly men of great influence.

Dr R. C. Palmer, working mainly on Cheshire records, considers that the judgements of the court had slipped from the hands of the traditional suitors, fairly prominent men who owed suit by tenure. Such men had been quite content to see the tiresome and time-consuming legal business, which was, after all, the main function of the court, taken over by the stewards and other officials of local lords, constituting a small and increasingly legally qualified professional class who were sustained by fees from other professional work: 'The actual functioning of the county court was dominated by the barons through their legal experts. The normal meetings, therefore, had strictly limited functions and a limited personnel'.[10]

Speculation apart, however, there is only one piece of direct evidence for attendance at one of these 'normal' sessions. It occurs in the Paston Letters, in the context of a petition of 1424 against Walter Aslak, commenting on the great fear of violence at the shire court in Norwich, 'beyng there thanne

[8] See the statement of R. W. Kaeuper, 'Law and order in fourteenth-century England: the evidence of special commissions of Oyer and Terminer', *Speculum*, liv (1979), pp. 734–84.

[9] J. R. Maddicott, 'The county community and the making of public opinion in fourteenth-century England', *TRHS*, 5th series, xxviii (1978), pp. 27–43. See also the same author's 'Parliament and the constituencies, 1272–1377', in R. G. Davies and J. H. Denton (ed.), *The English Parliament in the Middle Ages: A Tribute to J. S. Roskell* (Manchester, 1981), pp. 61–87.

[10] Dr Palmer has shown that the suitors of the court (owing suit by tenure) had been drawn from the upper ranks of tenants. As early as the first half of the thirteenth century they had to be distrained to enforce attendance. Nor did they attend every session. Their attendance was generally required only twice a year and by 1300 even this obligation had been allowed to lapse: R. C. Palmer, *The County Courts of Medieval England, 1150–1350* (Princeton, 1982), chapter 3, especially pp. 87–8. Also for the majority of the population the jurisdiction of the hundred courts and the manorial courts may have been of greater day-to-day significance than that of the shire courts.

a grete congregation of poeple by cause of the seyd shire'. This was obviously an *ex parte* statement describing a violent feud, and suspicions of rented mobs cannot be ruled out.[11] Moreover, there is evidence of violence at other meetings: in August 1461, for example, when one of Sir John Howard's men attacked John Paston the eldest with a dagger.[12]

Certainly county courts at election times present a different picture. As Dr Virgoe has shown, indentures of return made to Chancery indicate numbers of up to a thousand in the larger counties.[13] These were only the attestors of the election returns and the crowds there gathered must have been greater. There were certainly many there who were not legitimate voters: those followers who rode in with magnates and gentry, sometimes with sinister intent. As there were no electoral registers, it was impossible accurately to identify genuine freeholders and reject others. Interference could be blatant. A Derbyshire jury indicted Henry, Lord Grey of Codnor, of bringing 200 men to Derby on 24 June 1433 with the intention of hindering the shire election: rented mobs again.[14]

What questions were likely to be raised in these larger assemblies, and how could they be discussed? Fundamental questions of government policy (matters of state as they were later known) obviously could not be. Unlike today, government policies were unveiled only after the assembly of parliament, not on the hustings. Questions of policy surely entered only after the Reformation, when ideological issues were introduced into English politics for the first time. On the other hand, could matters affecting the shire itself receive anything like full discussion?

J. G. Edwards demonstrated that by far the greater majority of elections were uncontested. The gentry regarded contests as undesirable. When a contest did take place, procedures for decision, in a crowd assembled in the open air, were by modern standards rough and ready and crude, wide open to manipulation and violence. Generally, dominant groups agreed on the choice of the knights of the shire beforehand, with the role of the assembled electors limited to acclamation.[15]

I suggest that the same considerations apply to any possible formulation of petitions on local matters. The logistics of these large, noisy, open-air assemblies were more suitable for demonstrations, favourable or hostile, than for rational, detailed discussions; so that just as the MPs were generally chosen by small groups beforehand and acclaimed in the shire court, such

---

[11] J. Gairdner (ed.), *The Paston Letters* (Edinburgh, 1910), i, pp. 13–18. For a full discussion see R. Virgoe, 'Aspects of the county community in the fifteenth century', in M. Hicks (ed.), *Profit, Piety and the Professions in Later Medieval England* (Gloucester, 1990), pp. 8–9.

[12] *The Paston Letters*, ii, p. 42.

[13] Virgoe, 'Aspects of the county community', pp. 8–9.

[14] S. M. Wright, *The Derbyshire Gentry in the Fifteenth Century*, Derbyshire Record Society, viii (1983), p. 130.

[15] G. Edwards, 'The emergence of majority rule in English parliamentary elections', *TRHS*, 5th series, xiv (1964), pp. 175–96.

considerations are even more plausible for the formulation of any significant proposals made on local affairs. If particular proposals were put forward in petitions to be sent to the central government, they must surely have been formulated by particular interest groups who were for the time dominant and, as Dr Maddicott himself suggested, drafted by local lawyers and by implication presented for acclamation.[16] It is surely difficult to envisage detailed rational discussion by a large crowd in a market place.

It has sometimes been implied that quarter sessions became a focus of county loyalty. Once again I remain sceptical. Quarter sessions were run mainly by the gentry: but in this context who were the gentry? Can we, in fact, plausibly speak of the gentry as a homogeneous group showing common attitudes and sentiments, producing a consensus that might be called a county opinion? Dr Virgoe has recently shown that for certain of the Norfolk gentry 'country', a word denoting their own locality (and then far more commonly used than 'county'), had strong emotional associations, but, from lack of evidence, he was forced to leave open the question whether lower sections of the population in any way shared their sentiments.[17] Once again words are a stumbling-block. Can we equate 'country' with 'county', and can we really treat the gentry as a single homogeneous group sharing the same attitudes and sentiments? The gentry (possibly about 2 per cent of the population at this time), in spite of extensive kinship networks, were far from being a homogeneous, countrywide group.[18] Their thickness on the ground varied from area to area as did their wealth: some so poor as to be hardly distinguishable from the more prosperous yeomen, others as rich as some of the lesser barons; some with no more than parochial interests, others with influence over a large part of the shire or even in several shires.

Resistance to royal centralisation of local government personnel had been prolonged and successful, especially as regards the sheriffs. This desire had also extended to the commissions of the peace. Under Richard II the commons had wished to restrict membership of the commissions to a small number of the upper ranks of the gentry.[19] Such men quickly recoiled from

[16] Maddicott, 'County community', pp. 37–8.

[17] Virgoe, 'Aspects of the county community', pp. 4ff. Speculation about the composition of the community of the shire is also relevant for earlier centuries, H. M. Cam, *Law-Finders and Law-Makers* (London, 1962), pp. 170–2. Dr A. Gross has, in fact, suggested to me that the use of the word county itself may well be anachronistic at this period.

[18] A. J. Pollard, 'The Richmondshire community of gentry during the Wars of the Roses', in C. Ross (ed.), *Patronage, Pedigree and Power in Later Medieval England* (Gloucester and Totowa, 1979), pp. 37–59. Although very closely related, their interests were so localised that Dr Pollard claims they were hardly aware of a wider Yorkshire.

[19] Public pressure in the thirteenth century had forced the abandonment of powerful curialist sheriffs in favour of local gentlemen, and in the later fourteenth century the commons successfully insisted that the shrievalties, like a number of other local offices, should be held for one year only, thus frustrating the establishment of what the government probably regarded as the next best thing to a completely centralised bureaucracy, the development of a local corps of more or less professional bureaucrats over-devoted from the local point of view to the central

the strenuous activity which this limitation involved. The commissions steadily increased in size until they included men from almost all levels of the gentry, the quite obscure as well as the rich. Yet the increase in size was not accompanied by any increasing devotion to duty, as reflected in attendance at quarter sessions. In some counties sessions were held in different towns. In Kent, for example, two were held at Canterbury and two at Maidstone. In other shires there was a complicated system of adjournments from town to town and they were not always attended by the same people.[20] Some indeed may have attended only those meetings nearest their own residences. I suggest that attendance was far too thin for quarter sessions to have become an alternative to the shire court as a focus for the formation of a public opinion. Negligence was widespread. In the whole of Norfolk under the Yorkists, less than half (46 per cent) of the commissions claimed payments for attendance, and the average number claiming payments for each year for which there are records was only 13.2 or about 21 per cent.[21] Moreover this is a collective figure for the whole year, not for individual meetings. The only two surviving pieces of direct evidence for single sessions (from other shires) support this contention of low levels. In a session at Cambridge in 1464, for example, only five out of a total gentry membership of twenty were present.[22] At the Southampton (Hampshire) session at Winchester in December 1474, only three of the local gentry turned up as against three peers, and the son of one of those peers, and two royal officials.[23]

The gentry had various reasons for desiring to be on the commissions: by the late fifteenth century it may have become a question of prestige, although far less creditable emotions were at play. Whatever the reasons,

government and over-ready to exploit their neighbours on its behalf: H. M. Cam, 'Cambridgeshire sheriffs in the thirteenth century', in her *Liberties and Communities in Medieval England* (Cambridge, 1944) pp. 27–48; D. A. Carpenter, 'The decline of the curial sheriff in England, 1194–1258' , *EHR*, xci (1976), pp. 1–32; R. Virgoe, 'The crown and local government: East Anglia under Richard II', in F. R. H. Du Boulay and C. M. Barron (ed.), *The Reign of Richard II: Essays in Honour of May McKisack* (London, 1971), pp. 218–22; J. R. Lander, *The Limitations of English Monarchy in the Later Middle Ages* (Toronto, 1989), pp. 28 ff.

[20] Dr Virgoe informs me that in Norfolk in the 1440s and the 1450s quarter sessions were held mainly in Norwich, often in Lynn and occasionally in Walsingham, Dereham and Swaffham, but it is not clear whether in the smaller places there were completely separate sessions or just adjournments from Norwich and Lynn. Dr Virgoe tells me that matters seem to have been similar in Suffolk. Also in Derbyshire, 'The county town of Derby is not centrally placed and the justices moved their sessions around the county. For example, between October 1440 and April 1441 justices sat at Whitwell, Chesterfield, Derby, Belper and Ashbourne, perhaps by adjournment, perhaps by holding sessions in addition to the statutory quarterly meeting', Wright, *Derbyshire Gentry*, p. 98.

[21] J. R. Lander, *English Justices of the Peace, 1461–1509* (Gloucester and Wolfeboro', 1989), pp. 68–71. For difficulties in the use of figures for claims for payment, see ibid., pp. 58–61.

[22] PRO, Ancient Indictments, bundle 8, printed in I. D. Thornley, *England under the Yorkists* (London, 1920), pp. 160–2.

[23] B. H. Putnam, *Proceedings before the Justices of the Peace in the Fourteenth and Fifteenth Centuries: Edward III to Richard III* (London, 1938), p. 274.

once appointed many were far from zealous, particularly some of the greater gentry. The Paston Letters make it amply clear that the Pastons and their friends were at times extremely anxious to secure the appointment of their cronies, and to exclude others who were not well-disposed to them, with the laudable object of furthering their own interests and doing down their opponents; yet once appointed they were by no means assiduous in their attendance at quarter sessions. Some of the richer gentry were amongst the worst attenders.[24] Sir Edward Bedyngfeld, on the Norfolk commission from 1480 to 1496, claimed payment for attendance for only eight days out of a possible thirty-nine between 1480 and 1485. Under Henry VII his record was even worse, with only one out of 109 days.[25]

As earlier with the shire courts, this meant that at least in some areas a certain type of professional element took over. During the minority of Henry VI, in the West Riding of Yorkshire most of the gentry JPs came from the middle rank families; generally they were office-holders on the duchy of Lancaster estates. The major families do not seem to have been at all interested.[26] At about the same time a similar phenomenon was apparent in Derbyshire.[27] Under Henry VII, Southampton seems to have been more or less well controlled by the bishop of Winchester, whose hand-picked officials, mostly lawyers and of the quorum, dominated quarter sessions.[28] Possibly, even probably, therefore, in some parts of the country at least, the brunt of the work in quarter sessions was borne by a few members of the middling and lower ranks of the gentry, many of whom were also professional lawyers and holders of other well-paid offices. Two possible hypotheses emerge: as earlier in the shire courts, there may have been a stronger professional element than a long tradition has maintained; and the effective units of local cooperation and sentiment may have been sub-sections of the shire rather than the shire itself.

So the two major assemblies, the shire court and quarter sessions, were far from ideal venues for the formation of any coherent county opinion, owing to lack of any great enthusiasm for attendance. Neither was the general background favourable. In spite of their sentiments about their

---

[24] *The Paston Letters*, Introduction, p. 24, i, p. 189; PRO, pipe rolls, E 327/314, sheriff's accounts. See also Lander, *English Justices of the Peace*, pp. 44–45.

[25] PRO, E 327/326, 327, 331.

[26] C. Arnold, 'The commission of the peace in the West Riding of Yorkshire, 1437–1509', in A. J. Pollard (ed.), *Property and Politics in Later Medieval England* (Gloucester and New York, 1984), pp. 121, 126. By the reign of Henry VII, however, families of higher status and greater wealth were more interested: Arnold, 'Commission', p. 132.

[27] Wright, *Derbyshire Gentry*, pp. 96–9.

[28] In contrast in neighbouring Surrey, lacking the control of any dominant magnate, the JPs were a quarrelsome and faction ridden set. Lawyers again, but this time lawyers of fairly low status, formed the bulk of the quorum, though their attendance at quarter sessions was no better than that of the rest, and the shire appears to have been ill-run compared with Southampton. I owe the information on these two counties to Professor W. B. Robinson of Southeastern Louisiana University.

'country', the Pastons and their friends were a quarrelsome and violent lot. Other counties show a hardly greater degree of amity. A significant minority of the JPs were up to their necks in crime.[29] In the later middle ages, partly owing to the deplorable state of the law of real property and the survival of an immemorial tradition of self-help, riot was particularly an avocation of the gentry, a common adjunct to litigation. Dr J. G. Bellamy has even gone so far as to refer to a perpetual state of land war, though this may be something of an exaggeration.[30] Yet record evidence from county after county indicates tension and hostility between leading families, from Shropshire (under Henry V and Edward IV) to Derbyshire and Norfolk. Dr S. M. Wright claims that feelings amongst the Derbyshire gentry were limited, individualistic rather than 'communal', possessing no more than 'a community attitude to law and order, with a combination of expedients for its maintenance'. Even so by the 1490s and the early 1500s some of the premier families of the county were amongst the most criminal. Conditions were little better in neighbouring Nottinghamshire.[31]

Such conditions were hardly conducive to widespread cooperation amongst the gentry at the level of the county's formal institutions. Dr Wright again and Dr Saul think that in Derbyshire and Gloucestershire the majority of the gentry (even those on the commissions of the peace) did not participate actively in local government, while others took only the most limited part.[32] Dr Gross has informed me that similar factors prevailed in Staffordshire, where possibly no more than about 30 per cent participated, and not all of those at any one time.[33] Therefore various strands of evidence (admittedly somewhat localised) point to a strong probability that the formal administration of the county lay in a small corps of interested and experienced

---

[29] Lander, *English Justices of the Peace*, pp. 93–8.

[30] J. G. Bellamy, *Bastard Feudalism and the Law* (London, 1989), pp. 6, 8, 12, 34–56.

[31] T. B. Pugh, *Henry V and the Southampton Plot of 1415* (Gloucester, 1988), p. 143. Dr Pugh also states his opinion that 'All Henry V achieved after a vigorous attempt at law enforcement was to confine the chronic state of disorder in the realm within acceptable limits'. See also G. L. Harriss, 'The king and his magnates' in idem, *Henry V: The Practice of Kingship* (Oxford, 1985), pp. 56, 67–72; E. G. Kimball (ed.), *The Shropshire Peace Rolls, 1400–1414* (Shrewsbury, 1959); E. Powell, 'Proceedings before the justices of the peace at Shrewsbury in 1415: a supplement to the Shropshire peace roll', *EHR*, xcix (1984), pp. 535–50; *CPR, 1416–22*, pp. 97–99; E. F. Jacob (ed.), *Register of Henry Chichele, Archbishop of Canterbury, 1414–1443*, Canterbury and York Society (1938–47), ii, p. 678. In the 1460s two prominent JPs, Roger Kynaston and his stepson, Lord Straunge, were attacking each other with armed gangs in the course of a prolonged dispute over a family property settlement: J. R. Lander, 'The Yorkist council, justice and public order: the case of Straunge versus Kynaston', *Albion*, xii (1980), pp. 1–22; Wright, *Derbyshire Gentry*, pp. 119, 141, see also chapter 9 generally; S. J. Payling, 'Law and arbitration in Nottinghamshire, 1399–1461', in J. Rosenthal and C. Richmond (ed.), *People, Politics and Community in the Later Middle Ages* (Gloucester and New York, 1987), pp. 140–60.

[32] N. Saul, *Knights and Esquires: The Gloucestershire Gentry in the Fourteenth Century* (Oxford, 1981), pp. 147–67; Wright, *Derbyshire Gentry*, p. 94.

[33] Dr Gross has also kindly allowed me to use his unpublished London Ph.D. thesis 'Adam Peshale: a study of the gentry society of fourteenth-century Staffordshire' (1989).

gentry, mostly legally trained, who almost formed, in effect though not in name, an official class of semi-professionals.[34] So much at this stage for amateur, unpaid 'government at the king's command.'

I am well aware that this essay is raising more questions than it answers, in particular, about a 'county opinion'. Most probably there is no general answer for the whole country. It is necessary to stress once again the lack of any uniform development. In some shires a strong community sense may have developed by the end of the fifteenth century, and the greater gentry may have shown a strong interest in appointment to the commission of the peace. In other counties gentry rivalries and/or greater magnate dominance may have prevented such a consummation. Even so the full development of a self-conscious county community in any active, positively political sense may well have been delayed until the later sixteenth and seventeenth centuries. It may also have been more closely associated with new tendencies in national politics and with the assizes rather than with quarter sessions: witness the new seventeenth-century meaning of the word 'county' earlier discussed, and the late seventeenth- and early eighteenth-century development of social occasions and seasons in the assize towns, architecturally demonstrated in the building of grand and elegant assembly rooms.

It may be that with our modern experience in mind we tend to lay too great a stress on formal institutions. A recent author has suggested that during the high middle ages kings had raised greater expectations than their successors could satisfy. By devoting too great a proportion of their resources to warfare (one of their two major functions), these successors were unable to give adequate attention to the other, the supervision of justice and public order.[35] It indeed seems possible to claim, first, that governments had raised greater expectations than they could satisfy, as the formal institutions which they had created were inadequate and may have become even more so with time;[36] secondly, that means of enforcement were every-

---

[34] Dr Virgoe also states that in Norfolk by the 1450s, 'Although ... there was rather greater attendance, there remained a small core, most of them lawyers, who did the majority of the judicial work of the commission', R. Virgoe, 'The crown, magnates and local communities in England and France in the fifteenth century', in J. R. L. Highfield and R. Jeffs (ed.), *The Crown and Local Communities in England and France in the Fifteenth Century* (Gloucester, 1981), p. 78.

[35] R. W. Kaeuper, *War, Justice and Public Order: England and France in the Later Middle Ages* (Oxford, 1989); this consideration runs throughout the argument of the book but especially pp. 13ff. As mentioned earlier (see above p. 17) Dr M. T. Clanchy went even further and suggested that royal justice actually increased corruption.

[36] Dr Gross has suggested to me that checks on the activities of the gentry and of local administration had seriously diminished with the end of the general eyre. The assize judges were not an adequate substitute and the sheriff and JPs to a large extent controlled, and could frustrate, the flow of information to the centre. On the other hand the arbitrary financial transactions of the eyre had been notorious, e.g. Roger of Hovendon, *Chronica*, ed. W. Stubbs, Rolls Series (4 vols, 1868–71), iv, pp. 62–6. For the declining efficiency of the central courts, M. Blatcher, *The Court of King's Bench, 1450–1550* (London, 1978), pp. 47ff. Things were made

where inadequate; and thirdly, that the local ruling classes were everywhere distinctly two-faced in their attitudes, excoriating the courts while rushing into litigation.[37] They stand accused of condemning in others the corruption which they blatantly practised themselves, complaining endlessly about 'lack of governance' (the favourite fifteenth-century winge) but at the same time opposing any extension of the powers of the crown, especially if this involved higher taxation and the intrusion of outsiders into the shire to exercise a greater degree of control over local affairs.[38]

It has now become apparent that over the centuries inadequate state institutions have in practice functioned in parallel with less formal bodies which have supplemented their inadequacies. Examples spring to mind: patron-client relationships in the ancient world; lordship in England from Anglo-Saxon times onwards; the peace-keeping leagues of the Holy Roman Empire; private charity perhaps more significant than the poor law from Elizabethan to late Victorian times; in the eighteenth century the private provision of public services, water supplies, street lighting, paving, turnpikes when quarter sessions and the somewhat somnolent municipal corporations failed to supply such amenities; the black markets relieving the clapped-out official industries of the former communist states; and, in the last few years, the revival of arbitration in several western countries.[39]

In fifteenth-century England informal relationships seem to have been almost as significant as formal institutions, and there was a kind of atavistic reaction to types of self-help.[40] This parallel system was perhaps better fitted to the age's social and emotional needs. One aspect of the prevalent violence was the need for reconciliation. Medieval justice was much less punitive in intention than modern justice. It aimed rather for the reconciliation of

worse by the complete lack of a police system and fifteenth-century reluctance to dismiss officials of any kind: see Lander, *English Justices of the Peace*, chapter 5, and the references there given.

[37] C. M. D. Crowder, 'Peace and justice around 1400: a sketch', in *Aspects of Late Medieval Government and Society: Essays Presented to J. R. Lander* (Toronto, 1986), pp. 53–82.

[38] Lander, *English Justices of the Peace*, chapter 5. See also M. Condon, 'Ruling elites of the reign of Henry VII', in C. Ross (ed.), *Patronage, Pedigree and Power in Later Medieval England* (Gloucester and Totowa, 1979), pp. 124–5, for the strong influence of certain royal officials in some counties. A considerable number of statutes on public order passed under Henry VII were valid only for a limited number of years or until the next parliament. See also Chief Justice Finieux's remark, 'The prince's prerogative and the subject's privileges are solid felicities together and but empty notions asunder. That people is beyond precedent free and beyond comparison happy who restrain not the sovereign's power so far as to do them harm, as he hath none left to do them good': Lander, *The Limitations of English Monarchy*, pp. 52, 82; S. B. Chrimes, *Henry VII* (London, 1972), chapter 8; J. R. Lander, *Government and Community: England, 1450–1509* (London, 1980), p. 335.

[39] For this last point see *The Times*, 5 October 1990, p. 3.

[40] E.g. in addition to arbitrations discussed below the collection of benevolences and personal judicial tours by Edward IV: H. L. Gray, 'The first benevolence', in A. E. Cole, A. L. Dunham and N. S. B. Gros (ed.), *Facts and Factors in Economic History Presented to J. F. Gay* (Harvard, 1932), pp. 90–113; J. G. Bellamy, 'Justice under the Yorkist kings', *American Journal of Legal History*, ix (1965), pp. 135–55.

opponents than for clear-cut adversarial verdicts. The mass and the confessional, for example, both laid strong emphasis on reconciliation. Arbitration became a key factor in this situation. Age-old and different traditions of arbitration (classical, barbarian, Christian and feudal) across the centuries had reinforced each other. In the face of the weakness, even the decline, of the law courts, there was a notable revival of arbitration, by magnates and their councils, by groups of gentry themselves, and in towns through religious and trade guilds. Professor Ralph Griffiths has pointed out that this tendency had gone so far that a more or less 'standardised form of agreement had been evolved for use by panels of arbitrators in several parts of the country with a tariff of compensation reminiscent of the Anglo-Saxon blood feud'. Moreover, many of the lawyer JPs who were so prominent in quarter sessions were also conspicuous in 'love days' and arbitrations.[41]

To attempt some kind of conclusion. The shire was certainly a most important unit of administration and justice, but its official organs had to be supplemented by more informal arrangements working in parallel, and its reputation with the central government was not high. Government control and supervision were inadequate and attempts to improve them sporadic and short-lived. Local sentiment was certainly strong: counties cherished their local customs and strongly held that only local landowners of some standing should represent them in parliament. Yet I doubt if even the gentry as a group, let alone together with the lower ranks of society, could formulate any type of public opinion. They were too diverse in wealth and influence. The horizons of many, if not most, of the lesser gentry, in spite of a good deal of intermarriage between them, were generally limited to contacts with those in their own parts of the shire. Quarrels and faction were as prominent as cohesion and unity. What little evidence there is suggests that only a small minority took an active part in county administration. Small groups competed for temporary dominance and to do down others, often with

---

[41] R. A. Griffiths, 'Public and private bureaucracies in England and Wales in the fifteenth century', *TRHS*, 5th series, xxx (1980), pp. 128–9. See the sixteenth-century *The Institution of a Gentleman*, published in 1553, 'To bee a justice of peace in the cuntrye, as a staye for symple men & helper of theyr causes by way of arbitrement, or otherwise to end their contentions, and stynt theyr stryves, it is a goodly ministration and office for a gentleman wherein a man may doe muche benefite to the commonwealth & perches great loue among his neighbours': Bodleian Library, Oxford, MS Douce G. 89, quoted from G. W. Bernard *The Power of the Early Tudor Nobility: A Study of the Fourth and Fifth Earls of Shrewsbury* (Brighton and Totowa, 1985), p. 194. For wide evidence on the theme of justice and reconciliation in the later middle ages, see E. Powell, 'The restoration of law and order', in Harriss, *Henry V*, pp. 57–99; J. J. Scarisbrick, *The Reformation and the English People* (Oxford, 1984), p. 44; J. Bossy, 'Essai de la sociographie de la messe, 1200–1700', *Annales*, xxxvi (1981), pp. 44–70; idem, 'The mass as a social institution, 1200–1700', *Past and Present*, c (1983), pp. 29–61; R. B. McRee, 'Religious gilds and the regulation of behaviour in late medieval towns', in Rosenthal and Richmond (ed.), *People, Politics and Community*, pp. 113–14. See also C. Rawcliffe, 'Parliament and the settlement of disputes: arbitration in the later middle ages', *PH*, ix (1990), pp. 316–42, and the numerous references there given.

considerable violence involved in the process. Ideological divisions had not yet developed. Normally pressures from the central government were not yet strong enough, as they later became under Henry VIII and under the early Stuarts, to unite significant numbers in opposition to it, though this could happen when a particular monarch like Richard III tried to introduce too many 'foreigners' into a county establishment.[42] The conditions and logistics of the greatest assemblies, the meetings of the county courts at election times, were really inimical to any kind of discussion or to anything but the crudest elucidation of opinion on any topic. Quarter sessions were certainly too poorly attended by the gentry, especially the greater gentry, to provide an adequate substitute. I doubt if at this period there was anything like a county community capable of formulating coherent public policies on anything much except opposition to outside interference, aside from small groups protesting to the government against what they regarded as the nefarious activities of other groups, as happened in Norfolk on the accession of Edward IV.[43] Finally, a major consideration which is all too depressingly familiar today: is conflict between central and local government endemic, always latent but liable to break out at any time because different interest groups place so great a variety of conflicting demands upon it?

[42] A. J. Pollard, 'The tyranny of Richard III', *Journal of Medieval History*, iii (1977), pp. 147–66.
[43] J. R. Lander, *Crown and Nobility, 1450–1509* (London, 1976), pp. 163–4.

3

A Crisis of the Knightly Class? Inheritance and Office among the Gentry of Thirteenth-Century Buckinghamshire

Anne Polden

Much has been written about the economic health of the 'knightly class' in the thirteenth century.[1] The number of belted knights contracted but, as Treharne pointed out, their social status probably went up as a result of the Barons' Wars, their growing involvement in local government and the emergence of parliament.[2] What, however, of the rest? Did a significant number fail to maintain their standard of living, or indeed their knightly status, because they were unable to cope with the effects of high prices consequent on the inflation of 1180–1220, which continued at a lower level for the rest of the century?[3] Verdicts based on local studies have been mixed, with P. R. Coss arguing that there were real problems, especially for the smaller landholders and those with small demesnes, while others, including King and Carpenter, are more sceptical.[4]

The question of economic and social mobility retains its importance: in his recent work on Warwickshire Coss rejects the idea of a 'decline of the gentry' but none the less maintains that the vicissitudes of the knightly class between 1180 and the Barons' Wars 'are symptomatic of something more than the rise and fall of landed families to a degree which was normal in

---

[1] See especially R. F. Treharne, 'The knights in the period of reform and rebellion, 1258–67', *BIHR*, xxi (1946–8), pp. 1–12; M. M. Postan, *Cambridge Economic History of Europe* (2nd edn, Cambridge 1966), i, pp. 590–5, idem, *The Medieval Economy and Society* (London, 1972), pp. 158–65; R. H. Hilton, *A Medieval Society: The West Midlands at the End of the Thirteenth Century* (London, 1966), pp. 49–55; E. King, 'Large and small landowners in thirteenth-century England', *Past and Present*, xlvii (1970), pp. 26–50; P. R. Coss, 'Sir Geoffrey Langley and the crisis of the knightly class in thirteenth-century England' *Past and Present*, lxviii (1975), pp. 3–37; D. A. Carpenter, 'Was there a crisis of the knightly class in the thirteenth century? The Oxfordshire evidence', *EHR*, ccclxxvii (1980), pp. 721–52; J. F. Newman, 'Greater and lesser landlords and parochial patronage in Yorkshire in the thirteenth century', *EHR*, xcii (1977), pp. 280–308.

[2] R. F. Treharne, 'Knights in the period of reform'.

[3] For the inflation, P. D. A. Harvey, 'The English inflation, 1180–1220', *Past and Present*, lxi (1973), pp. 3–30.

[4] Coss, 'Sir Geoffrey Langley', pp. 27–9, 34; King, 'Large and small landowners', pp 45–50; Carpenter, 'Crisis of the knightly class', pp. 745–6, 748–51.

feudal societies'.[5] This essay examines economic and social mobility within a group of Buckinghamshire families during the thirteenth and early fourteenth centuries, with respect not only to the extent of upward and downward movement, but also to the factors precipitating these changes in status. In particular, consideration is given to the relative importance of various factors internal to the county, relating to the circumstances of the families themselves. These include their initial economic standing, patterns of inheritance, the role of family dispositions, disputes and the importance of marriages to heiresses. Set against these is the influence of external factors, such as the rising costs of knighthood, office-holding in central and local government, and royal favour or displeasure.

The sample initially consisted of eighty-nine jurors (representing eighty-seven families) sitting on grand assize juries and forest inquisitions in the county in the 1220s.[6] One juror has been omitted because his involvement in Buckinghamshire affairs was minimal: he was essentially a Northumbrian knight.[7] Another fourteen had to be omitted because no coherent picture of their lands or histories could be constructed from the evidence.[8] This is unfortunate because they were probably all very minor landowners whose omission inevitably means that this group is underrepresented in the sample.[9] The final group therefore comprises seventy-two families.[10]

[5] P. R. Coss, *Lordship, Knighthood and Locality: A Study in English Society, c. 1180–c. 1280* (Cambridge, 1991), p. 304.

[6] *Curia Regis Rolls*, x, no. 16, xi, no. 37; J. G. Jenkins (ed.), *Calendar of the Roll of the Justices on Eyre, 1227*, Buckinghamshire Archaeological Society, vi (1942), nos 132, 134, 138, 142, 143, 256, 310; PRO, C47/11/1/14 and 15.

[7] Hugh de Eure: see *A History of Northumberland*, issued under the direction of the Northumberland County History Committee (Newcastle, 1893–1940), v, pp. 23, 26, 27, vi, p. 19, for Hugh and his Northumbrian estates.

[8] Ralph Baret; Richard de Beauchamp; Humphrey Carun; William fitz Luke of Drayton; Paris of Edgcott; Oliver of Edlesborough; Oliver fitz Philip; Alexander Ash; Simon fitz Hamo; Ralph Hampden; Ralph Pitstone; Nicholas de St Germain; William Neirenuit; Stephen Warmeston. Four of these knights were probably relatives of other better-documented members of the group. Simon fitz Hamo was probably a member of the family holding the Wolverton barony and therefore a relative of Robert fitz Alan, a cadet of that family: I. J. Sanders, *English Baronies: A Study of their Origin and Descent, 1086–1327* (Oxford, 1960), p. 100; VCH, *Buckinghamshire*, iv, pp. 506–8; G. R. Elvey (ed.), *Luffield Priory Charters*, Buckinghamshire Archaeology Society, xv, xviii (1968, 1975), pp. ii, xxxix–xliii, lix, lxxii. Richard de Beauchamp was the uncle of William de Beauchamp: VCH, *Buckinghamshire*, iii, p. 341; Elvey, *Luffield Priory Charters*, ii, nos 547–52. Ralph de Hampden was presumably a relative of Alexander de Hampden: VCH, *Buckinghamshire*, ii, pp. 287–8; J. G. Jenkins (ed.), *The Cartulary of Missenden Abbey*, Buckinghamshire Archaeological Society, ii, x, xii (1938–46), appendix 6, pp. 245–49. William Neirenuit was presumably a relative of Miles Neirenuit: VCH, *Buckinghamshire*, ii, p. 250, iii, p. 408, iv, p. 74.

[9] Richard de Beauchamp, the only one about whose estate something is known, apparently had three virgates, in Thornborough, held for 1/10th of a fee's service of the Wolverton barony, which he had granted away for homage rent and a down payment of two silver marks before 1214, Elvey, *Luffield Priory*, ii, nos 552, 657.

[10] Attention has been confined in most cases to the fortunes of the senior line. The exceptions

Classifying these into four groups according to the number of manors held, there were ten knights, each with four or more manors (Group One), thirty-four knights, each with two or three manors (Group Two), nineteen knights, each with one manor of three hides or more, or one fee or more if hidage is unknown (Group Three) and nine knights, each with a manor of under three hides or a fractional fee where hidage is not known (Group Four).[11] This accords fairly well with Carpenter's figures for Oxfordshire

to this are the Siffrewasts and the Nierenuits, where division of lands in the thirteenth century led to the establishment of two equally important branches, both of which have been followed through.

[11] I have followed Carpenter's method of classification here, although it is not always completely straightforward or satisfactory since, even in a highly manorialised county like Buckinghamshire, the definition of a manor is sometimes difficult. Problems of evidence sometimes mean that references to small land portions may conceal something more substantial.

Group One (knights with four or more manors although some of these might be enfeoffed): Thomas de Doynton (or fitz Geoffrey); Otto fitz William; Henry de Nafford; Miles Neirenuit; Amory de Noers; Henry de Scaccario; Richard de Siffrewast; Simon de Turville; Humphrey de Visdelou; Ralph de Wedon.

Group Two (knights with two or three manors): the Barrys; William de Beauchamp; William de Blackwell; Simon de Blosseville; Gilbert de Bolbec; Robert de Broughton; Robert de Chetwood; William de Clinton; Ralph Dairel; Robert Damory; William le Dun; Walter Duredent; William fitz Ellis; Ralph fitz John (Ralph held by the right of his wife parts of several manors but the inheritance of John Bidun had been divided between five co-heiresses so the estates were small, Sanders, *Baronies*, p. 128); Walter de Fulbrook (the Fulbrooks later quitclaimed land in the Claydons to Thomas Valognes. Despite a paucity of earlier references this has been considered as a manor for the purposes of classification because of the large quantities of land involved: see below, n. 87); Richard de Grenville; Alexander de Hampden; Walter de la Haye; William de Houghton; Ralph de Langport; Hervey Malet, whose family's main estate lay at Quainton, but a charter of Robert Malet probably dated 1242–3 granted 200s. of yearly rents in Cambridgeshire and Huntingdonshire to his brother-in-law Lawrence de Broke, G. H. Fowler and J. G. Jenkins (ed.), *Early Buckinghamshire Charters*, Buckinghamshire Archaeological Society, iii (1939), p. 41; G. Lipscombe, *The History and Antiquities of the County of Buckingham* (London, 1831–47), i, pp. 392–3. The land probably lay in part at least in Clinton (Cambridgeshire): *Rotuli hundredorum*, ii, p. 440. Although no other references have been found it has been considered as a manor here because of its size; John Maunsel; Thomas Maunsel; William fitz Reginald de Morton; Ralph Passelewe; Robert Purcell; Ralph de Puttenham; William Russel; Hamon de St Fey; Osbert de Saunderton; Richard de Stoke; Ralph de Tothill; Richard de Turri; Roger de Verly.

Group Three (knights with one manor of three hides or more, or one fee or more if hidage is unknown): William de Beachampton; Robert de Bracy; Ralph de Carun; Simon de Curtfalun; William Darches; William de Emberton; Robert fitz Alan; Robert fitz Nigel; Richard fitz Osbert; William Fraxino; Luke de Keynes; Richard fitz Walter de Morton; Fulk de Rycote; Roger de Stanford; William de Upton; Peter de Oving; Robert de Valognes; Hugh de Vavassur; Walter de Woughton.

Group Four (knights with one manor of under three hides or a fraction of a fee): Richard de Bataille; John de Burton; Andrew le Corp; John de Cowley; William de Hareng; Ralph de Langetot; Ralph Malet; Simon de Olney; Roger de Wavendon.

Knights have been classified according to what they held up to 1230. While limitations of space make it impossible to provide full references, these can be compiled from the sources listed in this and other notes to this essay.

and with Hilton's conclusion for the west Midlands, that most knights held two or three manors.

In this essay these jurors are referred to as knights, though whether in fact all knightly jurors *were* belted knights in the early thirteenth century remains uncertain. Quick and Coss have argued that they were, against Palmer's view that even grand assize jurors could be recruited from amongst the substantial freeholders.[12] Certainly some of these grand assize jurors were very poorly endowed indeed, but these may well have been the descendants of the minor knights of the twelfth century who are called *milituli* and *militi rustici* in the *Dialogue of the Exchequer* and the chronicles.[13] For present purposes this question is of limited importance, since it can safely be assumed that these families were of the highest standing in the county, excluding the magnates – the gentry in other words – whether they were knights or not.

Then there is the question of to what extent those knights identified themselves or were identified by others solely or primarily with Buckinghamshire, or whether the county classification is an artificial one imposed largely by the arrangement of government records. The debate continues among historians as to the nature, existence and development of the county as a political and social reality – a 'county community' – rather than simply as an administrative unit used by the crown. Many historians are persuaded that, by the fourteenth century at least, a shire community did exist in the form of a group of wealthier 'county gentry' families much involved in county administration and with close political, social and business ties with each other.[14] However, in some counties it appears that greater significance attached to more local loyalties based on patterns of landownership in the shire, or on its subdivisions (such as the Sussex rapes or the Kentish lathes).[15] Payling's study of Lancastrian Nottinghamshire clearly identifies an elite gentry group monopolising major offices and parliamentary representation, but he expresses considerable doubts about whether they, or the lesser gentry below them, had any real cohesiveness or sense of community as a group.[16] Coss goes further: he argues that to stress the county as the main principle of cohesion in the

---

[12] J. Quick, 'The numbers and distribution of knights in thirteenth-century England: the evidence of the grand assize lists', in P. R. Coss and S. Lloyd (ed.), *Thirteenth-Century England*, i (Bury St Edmunds, 1986), pp. 114–15; P. R. Coss, 'Knighthood and the early thirteenth-century county court', in P. R. Coss and S. Lloyd (ed.), *Thirteenth-Century England*, ii (Bury St Edmunds, 1988), pp. 45–57.

[13] Of the hundred knights on panels or in the grand assize in Warwickshire, 1220–32, one third were obscure or had minor interests in the county. Coss concludes that 'the *militulus* was clearly alive and well in early thirteenth-century England', Coss, 'County court', pp. 53–4. For a more extended treatment of this issue see too P. R. Coss, *Lordship, Knighthood, and Locality*, chapter 8.

[14] C. Given-Wilson, *The English Nobility in the Late Middle Ages* (London, 1987), pp. 74–8.

[15] Ibid.; N. Saul, *Scenes from Provincial Life* (Oxford, 1988), p. 60.

[16] S. Payling, *Political Society in Lancastrian England: The Greater Gentry of Nottinghamshire* (Oxford, 1991), pp. 86, 216–20.

thirteenth century is anachronistic, and that a reevaluation of the role of alternative *loci* of social power, especially the honour, is overdue.[17]

By the early fourteenth century there does seem to have emerged a core group of Buckinghamshire gentry, whose families had been of knightly status a century earlier.[18] By contrast, the county's knightly jurors of the 1220s were a heterogeneous group, covering a very wide spectrum of landholding wealth, and the extent to which their lives were bound up with the county clearly varied enormously. Just under two-thirds of these families were predominantly or solely Buckinghamshire landowners, while a third had significant holdings elsewhere, mainly in contiguous counties and especially in Oxfordshire, Bedfordshire and Northamptonshire. A few of the major knights held lands further afield.[19]

Of course, a scatter of manors over several counties was common among the wealthier gentry and did not preclude identification with one, usually the county of residence. But it should be noted that a number of the 'Buckinghamshire gentry' served on grand assize juries and held office in other counties during the century.[20] Three of these families provided Oxfordshire sheriffs and four other families provided sheriffs for Cambridgeshire/Huntingdonshire, Northamptonshire, Warwickshire/Leicestershire and Berkshire.[21] Nor do all these families appear to have held office exclusively in just one county (even if that county was not Buckinghamshire).[22]

---

[17] P. R. Coss, *Lordship, Knighthood and Locality*, p. 5.

[18] Ibid., pp. 307–10, for a recent treatment of the origins of the gentry.

[19] Knights holding only in Buckinghamshire: Bataille, Beachampton, Blackwell, Bracy, Broughton, Burton, Corp, Curtfalun, Cowley, Darches, Emberton, fitz Alan, fitz Nigel, fitz Walter, Fraxino, Fulbrook, Hareng, Ralph Malet, Olney, Oving, Passelewe, Stanford, Saunderton, Upton, Valognes, Wavendon, Woughton. Knights primarily concerned with Buckinghamshire (those who lived in the county, whose outside landed interests were small or where they and their predecessors only appeared on Buckinghamshire juries): Barrys, Beauchamp of Drayton, Blosseville, Bolbec, Chetwood, Carun, Dun, Duredent, fitz Osbert, fitz Reginald, Grenville, Hampden, Keynes, Langport, Langetot, Hervey Malet, Stokes, Turri, Vavassur, Wedon. Knights with more substantial interests elsewhere: Clinton, Dairel, Damory, Doynton, fitz Ellis, fitz John, fitz William, Haye, Houghton, John Maunsel, Thomas Maunsel, Nafford, Neirenuit, Noers, Purcel, Puttenham, Russel, Rycote, St Fey, Scaccario, Siffrewast, Tothill, Turville, Verly, Visdelou.

[20] As far as jury service is concerned, six of these knights (Damory, fitz Ellis, Fraxino, Purcell, St Fey and Rycote) served in Oxfordshire in the 1220s and are dealt with in Carpenter, 'Crisis of the knightly class', as well as this study.

[21] Damory, Rycote and Purcel, Houghton; Noers; Olney; Scaccario, PRO, *Lists and Indexes*, ix, pp. 6, 12, 92, 107, 145.

[22] For example, the Noers family were escheators, justices, coroners and subsidy assessors in Buckinghamshire during the course of the century as well as providing a Northamptonshire sheriff in 1307: *CPR, 1216–25*, p. 568; *CPR, 1225–32*, pp. 152, 156, 211, 220; *CPR, 1292–1301*, p. 104; *CPR, 1324–27*, pp. 101, 116; *CCR, 1231–34*, p. 131; *Parliamentary Writs*, i, pp. 27, 64, ii, pt i, pp. 694, 699, 713, 721; H. E. Salter (ed.), *The Boarstall Cartulary*, Oxford Historical Society, lxxxviii (1930), p. 182; PRO, Just 1/63, m. 55; Just 1/66, m. 1. In addition, Robert Barry, John de Chetwood, John de Olney and John de Siffrewast all represented in various parliaments both Buckinghamshire and another county in which they had lands, see below.

Perhaps it would be dangerous to deduce too much in the way of developing county community feeling here, even by the end of the period under discussion. As for the early thirteenth century, it has not been possible on the basis of surviving evidence to prove that all the grand assize jurors had a primary identification with the county, or any link with it other than the possession of landed interest there, although it is known that the great majority of them had much stronger ties than this.

Before moving on to the fortunes of the families, let us look briefly at the county itself. Buckinghamshire lay in the most heavily manorialised part of the kingdom.[23] It is well watered with a number of rivers (the Ouse, Colne and Thames), and the Thames gives it good communications with London. Although wealth and productivity varied – the Burnham plateau in the south with its gravel soils was a poor region for agriculture – it mostly provided good farming land. Primarily arable and especially wheat producing, it also had a fair amount of dairying, stock-raising and some sheep.[24]

Buckinghamshire was also a region dominated by small landowners. There were only four baronies and two probable baronies with *caputs* in the county, and the largest of these, the Giffard honour of Long Crendon (given as 97½ fees in 1166), was subdivided by the thirteenth century.[25] Tracing the descent of the seven Domesday lay lordships comprising ten or more Buckinghamshire manors reveals that by the thirteenth century only the Wolverton honour of Manno le Breton was undivided and in the hands of a resident family.[26] Indeed the holders of this small honour (only fifteen fees in 1166) were apparently the only lords of baronial status residing in the county on a regular basis in the thirteenth century.[27] There were magnates with extensive estates in Buckinghamshire – most prominently the Clares who inherited half the Giffard honour – but they had other baronies with *caputs* elsewhere and seem to have taken little direct interest in the county.[28] The most important lordship for the purposes of this study is the honour of Wallingford (Berkshire) which was held by Henry III's brother, Richard, earl of Cornwall, and from 1272 by Richard's son Edward, who died without heirs in 1300.[29] Richard also held the honour of Berkhamsted which included about a dozen Buckinghamshire manors and the

[23] E. A. Kosminsky, *Studies in the Agrarian History of England in the Thirteenth Century* (Oxford, 1956), p. 69.

[24] VCH, *Buckinghamshire*, i, pp. 397–404.

[25] Sanders, *Baronies*, pp. 50–1, 62–4, 98, 100, 116–17, 128.

[26] J. T. Sheahan, *The History and Topography of Buckinghamshire* (London, 1862), p. 25; Sanders, *Baronies*, p. 13; VCH, *Buckinghamshire*, i, pp. 207–228.

[27] For this family see also Elvey, *Luffield Priory*, ii, pp. xxxix–xlvii, lxxii.

[28] The lack of magnate influence in the county proved an enduring feature. In the early sixteenth century, the gentry are calculated to have held 57.6 per cent by value of all lay owned land, and peers only 6.3 per cent, J. Cornwall, 'The early Tudor gentry', *Economic History Review*, 2nd series, xvii (1964–5), pp. 456–77.

[29] Sanders, *Baronies*, p. 93.

six manors which had belonged to Roger de Iveri in 1086.[30] Together these baronies made him one of the major, if non-resident, landholders in the county, and twelve of the knights in this study were the earl's tenants.[31] There were no great ecclesiastical landlords: as the Victoria County History says, 'The religious houses of Buckinghamshire, although fairly numerous, were for the most part small and insignificant', and none of them goes back beyond the late eleventh century.[32]

The fragmentation of feudal tenures and the consequent weakening of ties between lords and tenants is a feature of thirteenth-century social development generally, but this landholding pattern in Buckinghamshire may have exaggerated it. Only a few of the jurors in the sample group seem to have had close connections with their feudal lords.[33] The only magnate known to have had other than purely tenurial connections with more than one of these Buckinghamshire knights was the earl of Cornwall. Richard de Turri was constable of Wallingford and the earl's steward in the 1230s, also appearing as attorney of the earl and a witness to his charters in the 1250s.[34] Fulk de Rycote and Robert Malet were both stewards in the 1270s and also witnessed charters.[35] The Damorys also served the earl of Cornwall for two generations, Robert Damory being granted an estate by the earl in the 1280s.[36] Finally, Stephen de la Haye was called a yeoman of the countess

---

[30] Sheahan, *History and Topography*; Sanders, *Baronies*, pp. 9, 14.

[31] Barry (VCH, *Buckinghamshire*, iv, p. 285); Damory (VCH, *Oxfordshire*, v, p. 286); Darches (VCH, *Buckinghamshire*, iv, p. 111); fitz Ellis (ibid., p. 81); Hervey Malet (ibid., p. 94); Stanford (ibid., iii, p. 94); Neirenuit (ibid., p. 408, ibid., iv, p. 74); Purcel (VCH, *Oxfordshire*, vi, p. 263); Rycote (*The Book of Fees, Commonly Called Testa de Nevill, 1189–1293*, 2 vols in 3, London, 1920, 1923, 1931, nos 446, 555; *Rotuli hundredorum*, ii, p. 757); Scaccario (ibid., pp. 464, 467, 470, 556); Valognes (VCH, *Buckinghamshire*, iv, p. 102); Wedon (ibid., iii, p. 392; iv, p. 365).

[32] VCH, *Buckinghamshire*, i, p. 346.

[33] Walter de Fulbrook was jointly accused of disseisin with Geoffrey de Lucy in 1212 and served with him in 1225, while Andrew le Corp accounted for Northumberland on behalf of his lord Robert fitz Roger who was the sheriff, and witnessed a charter of John fitz Robert, for whom Henry his son acted as attorney in 1223: *Curia Regis Rolls*, vi, pp. 367–8, xi, no. 186; *CPR, 1216–25*, p. 535; H. E. Salter (ed.), *The Cartulary of Oseney Abbey*, Oxford Historical Society, lxxxix–xci, xcvii–xcviii, ci (1928–9, 1933–4, 1936), v, pp. 338–40; *CCR, 1237–42*, p. 42; *Rotuli litterarum clausarum*, ii, p. 69b; *Pipe Rolls, 9 John*, p. 1. Two of the knights were baronial stewards: William de Fraxino, steward of William fitz Hamo, Lord of Wolverton; and Simon de Olney of the earl of Chester (Elvey, *Luffield Priory*, ii, p. lvii; *Memoranda Rolls, 10 John*, p. 60).

[34] H. G. Richardson and G. O. Sayles (ed.), *Select Cases of Procedure without Writ under Henry III*, Selden Society, lx (1941), pp. 64–5; *CCR, 1234–37*, pp. 477, 481; *CCR, 1232–42*, pp. 44, 133, 259; *Curia Regis Rolls*, xvi, no. 1703; *Calendar of Charter Rolls*, ii, pp. 240, 323, iii, p. 489; Jenkins, *Missenden Abbey*, ii, no. 476.

[35] A. M. Leys (ed.), *The Sandford Cartulary*, Oxfordshire Records Society, xix, xxii (1938, 1941), no. 27; *Calendar of Charter Rolls*, ii, pp. 209, 339; Carpenter, 'Crisis of the knightly class', p. 246; *Rotuli hundredorum*, i, p. 43; C. Moor, *Knights of Edward I*, Harleian Society, lxxx–lxxxiv (1929–32), iii, p. 98.

[36] Carpenter, 'Crisis of the knightly class', p. 246.

of Cornwall in 1258 when he gained a respite to knighthood at her request.[37] Generally speaking, however, thirteenth-century Buckinghamshire seems to have been a county where horizontal ties with other members of the local gentry were of more importance to most knights than ties with their feudal superiors.[38]

We can now move on to examine the fates of our seventy-two families. The significance of failure in the male line as one of the main solvents of landowning society is amply borne out by the Buckinghamshire evidence.[39] Twenty-two families died out by the end of the thirteenth century; two more – the Caruns and the Beauchamps of Drayton – were extinguished in the early fourteenth century, while in a third case the inheritance passed to a daughter, whose husband assumed her family name of Tothill.[40] Another eleven families simply disappeared from the records, perhaps as a result of financial failure and selling up. Some of these too may have failed in the

[37] *CPR, 1247–58*, p. 481. The earl also played a part in the financial transactions of several knights, see below.

[38] Naughton found this to be the case in neighbouring Bedfordshire in the thirteenth and fourteenth centuries too, where again there was a paucity of great baronial landowners, K. S. Naughton, *The Gentry of Bedfordshire in the Thirteenth and Fourteenth Centuries*, Leicester University Department of English Local History Occasional Papers, 3rd series, ii (1976), pp. 10–11.

[39] King, 'Large and small landowners', pp. 48–9. Payling has called this 'the principal engine of social change narrowly defined in terms of the rise and fall of landed families. Without it, rising families would have heen entirely dependent on a sluggish land market for the estates required to increase their wealth and status.' Payling, *Political Society*, p. 49.

[40] Families extinguished in the thirteenth century: Beachampton (VCH, *Buckinghamshire*, iv, pp. 150–53; Elvey, *Luffield Priory*, ii, p. lxvii); Burton (the likely identification is with a Sir John, son of Sir Ingeram, with land in Hulcott and Aylesbury whose heir was a granddaughter Maud, according to a sixteenth century Hampden pedigree; Lipscomb, *History and Antiquities*, ii, p. 230; A. Travers, ed., *Calendar of the Feet of Fines for Buckinghamshire, 1259–1307*, Buckinghamshire Archaeological Society, xxv, 1989, ii, no. 325); Clinton (VCH, *Buckinghamshire*, ii, p. 312; *Calendar of Inquisitions Post Mortem*, i, no. 353; *Bedfordshire Eyre Roll, 1247*, no. 304); Curtfalun (VCH, *Buckinghamshire*, iv, p. 500); Doynton (PRO, Just 1/1298, m. 111v; Just 1/ 1300, m. 24v, Just 1/1309, m. 1); Dun (VCH, *Buckinghamshire*, ii, p. 304); Emberton (A. C. Chibnall, *Beyond Sherington*, London, 1979, p. 135); Otto fitz William's descendants (*Calendar of Inquisitions Post Mortem*, i, no. 483, ii, nos 56, 147, 430; W. Farrer, *Honors and Knights' Fees*, 3 vols, London and Manchester, 1923–5, iii, pp. 290–91); Houghton (VCH, *Buckinghamshire*, iv, p. 373); (Thomas) Maunsel (VCH, *Buckinghamshire*, iv, p. 446); (Ralph) Malet (ibid., ii, p. 370; PRO, Just 1/62, m. 16v); William fitz Reginald's family (Elvey, *Luffield Priory*, ii, p. lxxvii); Russell (VCH, *Buckinghamshire*, iii, p. 351); St Fey (VCH, *Oxfordshire*, vi, p. 340); Stanford (VCH, *Buckinghamshire*, iii, p. 94); Scaccario (ibid., iv, p. 71; J. G. Jenkins, *Chequers: A History of the Prime Minister's Home*, Oxford, 1967, p. 16); Stoke (VCH, *Buckinghamshire*, iii, p. 305); Valognes (ibid., iv, p. 102); Verly (see ibid., iv, p. 516, for an account of the family, although Roger de Verly's son Hugh died much later than the VCH suggests, see *Calendar of Inquisitions Post Mortem*, ii, no. 376); Visdelou (Farrer, *Honors and Knights Fees*, i, p. 59; Chibnall, *Beyond Sherington*, p. 153); Woughton (VCH, *Buckinghamshire*, iv, p. 517). For the three families dying out in the early fourteenth century see ibid., iii, p. 341, iv, p. 353; A. C. Chibnall, *Beyond Sherington* (Cambridge, 1965), p. 34.

male line.[41] This brings the number who disappeared to thirty-six. In most clear cases of failure of heirs, lands passed to husbands, sisters or daughters – although occasionally they went to one or more nephews.[42] In four cases (Dun, Russel, Stanford and Stokes) the families were extinguished on the death of the knightly juror himself, sometimes quite early on – Roger de Stanford was dead by 1235, Richard de Stokes by 1242 – but most of the extinctions occurred in the last quarter of the century.[43]

Over a twenty-five year period then, these knightly families had about an 88 per cent probability of survival in the male line. A comparison with Payling's calculations suggests that such a rate was broadly in line with fourteenth- and fifteenth-century gentry experience elsewhere, and rather better than the probabilities of survival for baronial families throughout the middle ages.[44] However, this tells us little except that the turnover rate among landowning families tended to be high generally, and that in thirteenth-century Buckinghamshire at most a third of it was attributable to financial causes. We must now turn to the economic situation of these families, which means a consideration of their changing tenurial position, since to the thirteenth-century knight, wealth still, by and large, meant land.

---

[41] The Bataille, Blackwell, Corp, fitz John, fitz Osbert, fitz Walter, Hareng, Fulbrook, (John) Maunsel, Oving and Wavendon families all disappeared. The fitz John, fitz Walter, Hareng, Fulbrook, Maunsel and Wavendon families had fallen on hard times: the fitz Johns had lost Lavendon and Stow Bidun to Paul Pever by 1251 (VCH, *Northamptonshire*, iv, p. 32; *CCR, 1254–56*, pp. 19, 36, 156; *Calendar of Inquisitions Post Mortem*, i, no. 323; *Calendar of Inquisitions Miscellaneous*, i, no. 1471); Paul also acquired Soulbury from Geoffrey Maunsel (VCH, *Buckinghamshire*, iii, pp. 415–16, 419; Travers, *Feet of Fines, Buckinghamshire*, ii, no. 43); Tickford priory acquired Inkpen (Berkshire) from Geoffrey Maunsel in 1250 (VCH, *Berkshire*, iv, p . 201); St Mary's Overy, Southwark, acquired the manor and advowson of Wexham from Geoffrey in 1262 (VCH, *Buckinghamshire*, ii, pp. 319–20); Geoffrey's son Henry Dairel Maunsel lost Lillingstone Dairel and Saunderton to John de Foxley and his wife Constance in 1287 and 1308, although Henry's son, Henry fitz Henry Dairel, bought back Lillingstone Dairel in 1309 (for Foxley, see B. F. Harvey ed., *Documents Illustrating the Role of Walter de Wenlok, Abbot of Westminster, 1283–1307*, Camden Society, 4th series, ii, 1965, p. 25 n. 1; Elvey, *Luffield Priory*, ii, no. 379); Paul Pever also acquired the manor of Richard fitz Walter at Maids Moreton and had been enfeoffed with Nicholas de Wavendon's only estate at Wavendon by 1243 (*Calendar of Inquisitions Post Mortem*, i, no. 247; VCH, *Buckinghamshire*, iv, pp. 199–200, 490; PRO, Just 1/57, m. 14d); Geoffrey de Lucy acquired Hogshaw in Fulbrook from William de Fulbrook in 1274 when the Fulbrooks ran into financial difficulties (J. M. Rigg et al., ed., *Calendar of Plea Rolls of the Exchequer of the Jews*, Jewish Historical Society, 4 vols, 1905, 1910, 1929, 1972, ii, p. 170); Simon de St Lys acquired a small manor at Hasley in Thornton from John Hareng in 1251, leaving John with a life interest (VCH, *Buckinghamshire*, iv, p. 246; H. E. Salter (ed.), *Feet of Fines for Oxfordshire, 1195–1291*, Oxfordshire Records Society, xii, 1930, p. 62); and see Table 1, p. 40.

[42] See n. 40 above.

[43] Ibid.

[44] Payling, *Political Society*, pp. 66–7, gives probabilities of survival ranging from 86.2 per cent for the Leicestershire gentry to over 90 per cent for the Derbyshire gentry. For the nobility, the survival rate was about 85 per cent between 1066 and 1327, based on figures for extinction of baronies in E. Miller and J. Hatcher, *Medieval England: Rural Society and Economic Change, 1086–1348* (London, 1978), p. 169, and then fell to about 75 per cent.

One of the most common and certainly best-documented types of land alienation was the monastic grant. Forty-three of the families are known to have made or confirmed earlier grants to monasteries in the late twelfth and thirteenth centuries.[45] Most of the major grants to monasteries were almost certainly sales (concealed or not) by financially embarrassed knights, whereas the grants genuinely made in free alms, for the sake of the grantor's soul, tended to consist of a few acres of arable or pasture land, mills or church advowsons: nothing which would damage his economic viability.[46] Monastic grants appear to be concentrated in the last decade of the twelfth and the first decades of the thirteenth century, although of course some families continued to show generosity throughout.

Equally common but less well-documented are grants made in fulfilment of family claims: marriage portions for daughters or sisters, grants to younger sons or brothers, and the provision of dower (a source of much litigation). Since in most cases these did not result in land leaving the family (at least initially) and were often temporary, they have not usually been included

[45] Barry to Goring priory, St James' abbey (Northamptonshire), St Andrew's priory (Northamptonshire), Sulby abbey, Leicester abbey, Snelshall priory and Bradwell priory. Beachampton to Snelshall, Luffield and Sandford priories. Bolbec to Missenden abbey and Rochester priory. Bracy to Oseney abbey. Broughton to Caldwell priory, Holy Trinity hospital (Northamptonshire) and St Albans abbey. Chetwood to St John's hospital (Oxford). Clinton to Missenden abbey. Corp to Oseney abbey and St Bartholomew's hospital (London). Darches to Notley abbey and Nostell priory. Doynton to St Frideswide's abbey (Oxford), St Mark's hospital (Bristol) and Glastonbury abbey. Duredent to Missenden abbey and St Bartholomew's hospital (London). Fraxino to St John's hospital (Oxford), Luffield priory and Biddlesden abbey. fitz Alan to St John's hospital (Oxford). fitz Ellis to Oseney abbey, St Frideswide's abbey and St John's hospital (Oxford). fitz Nigel to Missenden abbey, Snelshall priory, Sandford priory and Mottisfont abbey. Otto fitz William's family to the Templars. Hampdens to Missenden abbey. Haye to Biddlesden abbey and Sandford priory. Houghton to Tickford priory. Keynes to St Alban's abbey. Langport to Luffield priory, Biddlesden abbey and close connections with Oseney abbey which held land in Langport. (Ralph) Malet to Missenden abbey. (Hervey) Malet to Thame abbey, Wallingford priory and St Andrew's priory (Northamptonshire). fitz Reginald to Luffield priory and St John's hospital (Oxford). fitz Walter to Oseney abbey and Biddlesden abbey. (John) Maunsel to Luffield priory, Woburn abbey, Sandford priory, Merton priory and St Mary's Overy (Southwark). (Thomas) Maunsel to Snelshall priory and Woburn abbey. Nafford to Evesham abbey and Bordesley abbey. Noers to St John's hospital (Oxford) and Worksop priory. Olney to Lavendon abbey. Oving to Oseney abbey. Passelewe to Missenden and Woburn abbeys. Purcel to Bicester abbey. Puttenham to Woburn abbey and Canon's Ashby priory. Russell to Caldwell and Dunstable priories. Saunderton to Thame abbey. Scaccario to Missenden and Thame abbeys and Sandwell priory. Siffrewast to Goring priory. Tothill to Bushmead and Haverholme priories. Turville to Biddlesden abbey and St John's hospital (Northamptonshire), Merton and Chalcombe priories. Valognes to Notley abbey and Friars Minor (Oxford). Visdelou to Lavendon and Harrold priories. Wavendon to Woburn abbey. Wedon to Luffield priory, Missenden abbey and Sewardsley priory. Sources for the above are too numerous to be cited individually, but include VCH; Salter, *Oseney Abbey*; *Calendar of Charter Rolls*; *Book of Fees*; Leys, *Sandford Cartulary*; Lipscombe, *History and Antiquities*; and Jenkins, *Missenden Abbey*.

[46] The only entire manor which appears to have been given in free alms was Lisson Green, granted to the Templars by Otto fitz William, VCH, *Middlesex*, ix, p. 102; *Calendar of Charter Rolls*, i, p. 277; *Book of Fees*, no. 1145.

when calculating significant land losses, but their effect upon the family may nevertheless have been considerable. Only Group One and Two landowners like the Neirenuits and the Turris could afford to subinfeudate whole manors to cadets, and the Turris may have regretted it later.[47] Most younger sons must have been forced to make their own way in the world with relatively little assistance from the family and with varying degrees of success. Apparently more successful than many younger sons, Alan Darches, the cadet of a Group Three family, held just four virgates for life of the family estate of Eythrope and Cranwell, but by the time of his death in 1325 he had accumulated portions of land in Wiltshire, Hampshire, Oxfordshire and Bedfordshire held by a variety of tenures of a variety of lords.[48] Even so, the diminution in the resources available to the senior line by grants, albeit of small portions of manors and often for life only, should not be underestimated. For example, a host of younger sons and daughters, their dependants and descendants, seem to have held land of the senior line of the Barrys (a Group Two family) – an impression which is amply confirmed by a fourteenth-century inquisition post mortem which found that over ten virgates of their manor at Billing (Northamptonshire) were held for life by four different relatives, and one third of the manor was in the hands of the last holder's mother.[49]

Finally, lands were sold to other laymen, sometimes in small portions which would not have damaged the family's position greatly, but often in much larger quantities as a result of unmanageable economic pressures which led to irreversible decline. Information on the larger land losses is tabulated in Tables 1 and 2 below (p. 40).

In all, twenty families lost estates permanently between about 1230 and 1310. The losses do not necessarily indicate or presage a serious decline in family fortunes. The Dairels, for example, ended up in much the same position as they had started, having sold and then repurchased their home manor at Lillingstone Dairel and sold one other manor at Saunderton St Nicholas which they had acquired by marriage.[50]

Occasionally, land losses meant a decline that was sharp but not fatal:

[47] Geoffrey Neirenuit, the younger son, held Pitstone Neyrnuit and Fleet Marston and Kingston in Aston Rowant (Oxfordshire) from the mid thirteenth century: VCH, *Buckinghamshire*, iii, p. 408, iv, p. 741; VCH, *Oxfordshire*, viii, pp. 25–6. Both senior and cadet lines flourished in the latter part of the century. Henry de Turri, a younger son, was enfeoffed with one of the family's three manors, that at Bledlow, in the early to mid thirteenth century, but the manor then passed out of the family's hands entirely, when Henry's daughter married Alexander de Hampden: VCH, *Buckinghamshire*, ii, p. 248; Jenkins, *Missenden Abbey*, iii, no. 564; BL, Harleian Charters, 47G34; PRO, Just 1/1201, m. 20v.

[48] *Calendar of Inquisitions Post Mortem*, vi, no. 555; *Calendar of Fine Rolls*, iii, pp. 334, 353, 356.

[49] VCH, *Northamptonshire*, iv, p. 70; VCH, *Buckinghamshire*, iv, pp. 284–6, 462; *Calendar of Inquisitions Post Mortem*, vi, no. 595.

[50] Elvey, *Luffield Priory*, ii, no. 379, iii, p. 94, iv, pp. 188–91; Travers, *Feet of Fines, Buckinghamshire*, ii, no. 195; *CPR, 1301–07*, p. 122; *CCR, 1307–13*, p. 122.

Table 1
The Beneficiaries of Knightly Land Alienations

Groups	One	Two	Three	Four
Estates* acquired by curiales	1	6	2	1
Estates acquired by barons	0	3	1	0
Estates acquired by other knights	3	5	1	1
Estates acquired by monasteries	1	4	1	0
Estates acquired by ecclesiastics	0	2	0	0
Estates acquired by a number of individuals and institutions	1	0	0	0

* In this and the subsequent table anything of one hide or carucate or more has been counted as an 'estate', although the majority are much larger than this.

Table 2
Land Acquisitions and Losses *c.* 1230–1310

Groups	One	Two	Three	Four
Number of families surviving beyond 1300	6 (4)	20 (14)	10 (9)	3 (6)
Number of families suffering overall loss	1 (2)	3 (6)	2 (2)	0 (2)
Number increasing number of estates	2 (2)	8 (1)	1 (1)	1 (0)
Number maintaining number of estates	3 (0)	10 (7)	7 (6)	2 (4)

In the brackets are the families which did not survive.

the Bolbecs were in debt more than once during the century but it was in the aftermath of an inheritance dispute between Henry and Simon de Bolbec in 1304 that Henry (who had apparently won the battle but lost the war) alienated the family's larger estate at Kingsey for £200.[51] The family was left with an estate at Kimble but ceased to assume knighthood.[52]

In many cases, however, overwhelming problems led to a complete selling up. This happened to the Caruns of Sherington, to William Fitz Reginald of Morton and to Reginald de Fraxino.[53] In the case of the Caruns, it was laymen (Roger Fitz John and Lord Grey of Wilton) who benefited; in the

[51] VCH, *Buckinghamshire*, ii, pp. 305–6, iv, pp. 64–5; G. H. Fowler and M. W. Hughes (ed.), *Calendar of the Pipe Rolls of the Reign of Richard I for Buckinghamshire and Bedfordshire, 1189–99*, Bedfordshire Historical Record Society, vii (1811), pp. 193–4; *Calendar of Ancient Deeds*, ii, C2509, C2259; PRO, Just 1/59, mm. 1, 15d; *CCR, 1265–68*, p. 550; *Calendar of Inquisitions Post Mortem*, iii, no. 439; *Placitorum in domo capitulari Westmonasterii asservatorum abbreviatio Richard I–Edward II*, Record Commission (1811), p. 238; *Calendar of Fine Rolls*, i, pp. 393, 488; Travers, *Feet of Fines, Buckinghamshire*, ii, no. 571; *CPR, 1301–7*, p. 291.

[52] *FA*, i, p. 122. Henry had even alienated part of his park at Kimble.

[53] At the end of the thirteenth century Reginald de Grey of Wilton acquired two thirds of Sherington from the Caruns, while Roger fitz John acquired the other third, Chibnall, *Sherington*, pp. 19–75. For fitz Reginald, see Elvey, *Luffield Priory*, ii, pp. xlv, lvii, lix, lxii, lxiii, lxv, lxvi, lxxvii. Luffield priory and St John's hospital, Oxford, acquired much of the Fraxino estate at Thornborough from the 1240s onwards, ibid., ii, pp. lvii, lviii, lxii–lxxiii.

two latter cases it was mainly ecclesiastics (Matthew de Stratton, the archdeacon of Buckingham) and monasteries (the hospital of St John at Oxford, Luffield priory and Oseney abbey). In the first two cases their lands had been largely dissipated by the time the family was extinguished by lack of male heirs. The Fraxinos at Thornborough, having forfeited what little remained of their much eroded estate when Robert, the grandson of Reginald, was hanged for murder in 1301, none the less survived as humble freeholders by leasing back their estate from Luffield priory.

In five other cases where a drastic decline in wealth and status took place the main beneficiary was one man, Paul Pever, a curial official who had inherited a small estate in Toddington and Chalton (Bedfordshire), from his father Roger, the first traceable member of the family.[54] Paul first came into view as part of the household of William Cantilupe, whom he accompanied to Poitou in 1230. He must have attracted the attention of the king soon afterwards, for he became warden of the bishopric of Winchester in 1238, sheriff of Oxfordshire briefly in 1239, sheriff of Bedfordshire and Buckinghamshire in 1239–41, as well as becoming a trusted royal councillor, who was made royal household steward before 1244.[55] Helped by Henry III's grants of oaks for its chapel and fish for its ponds, he built a splendid house at Toddington, described by an admiring Matthew Paris as a stone-built, lead-roofed palace.[56] He died, probably still quite young, in 1251. Paul also acquired property in Buckinghamshire (his most fruitful area for expansion) and in Oxfordshire, Hertfordshire, Essex and Norfolk.[57] Calculating the extent of his estates is difficult but the fullest of the inquisitions post mortem, on Paul's grandson John in 1315, lists a total of 3¾ fees, three other manors and other rents and land, and five advowsons. Most of this had been acquired by Paul, and does not include the estates used to endow his younger sons.[58] Paul's Buckinghamshire gains included the *caput* of the small and dismembered barony of Lavendon.[59] Although not a particularly lucrative acquisition in itself, it may not be too fanciful to suggest that Lavendon's acquisition points to hankerings for baronial status on Paul's part that were to remain unfulfilled. Paul left two sons, Paul and John, the

---

[54] There is a good account of Paul's career in G. H. Fowler (ed.), *A Digest of the Charters Preserved in the Cartulary of the Priory of Dunstable*, Bedfordshire Historical Records Society, xvii (1935), pp. 316–18, on which the following is based. See too Farrer, *Honors and Knights' Fees*, i, pp. 7–8, and VCH, *Bedfordshire*, iii, pp. 439–42.

[55] Fowler, *Priory of Dunstable*, pp. 316–18; PRO, *Lists and Indexes*, ix, p. 107.

[56] Fowler, *Priory of Dunstable*, pp. 316–18.

[57] Ibid. In addition to manors at Lavendon, Wiscombe in Soulbury, Maid's Moreton, Warendon and Weston Underwood acquired from these knightly families, Paul acquired land at Tattenhoe subinfeudated by William de Cantilupe; a manor at Great Woolstone sold by La Couture abbey and land at Chilton, a Norman escheat granted by the king, VCH, *Buckinghamshire*, iii, p. 433; iv, pp. 23, 510.

[58] *Calendar of Inquisitions Post Mortem*, v, no. 597; Fowler, *Priory of Dunstable*, pp. 316–18.

[59] Farrer, *Honors and Knights' Fees*, i, pp. 7–8; Sanders, *Baronies*, p. 128.

second of whom lived to inherit and carry on a family line that flourished into the fifteenth century, although none of Paul's descendants appears to have rivalled him either as a royal official or buyer of land.[60]

The initial circumstances of the five families whose misfortunes proved so advantageous to the Pevers varied a good deal. Henry, son of John Maunsel, was apparently well placed with a home manor at Soulbury, an estate at Wexham and another at Inkpen (Berkshire).[61] The other Group Two knight, Ralph Fitz John, is a shadowy figure who acquired property in two counties through his marriage to Isabella, coheiress to the Biduns' small barony of Lavendon (Buckinghamshire) and the Clintons' lands in Stewkley.[62] Then there were the Curtfaluns, an old-established family with a manor at Weston Underwood from the early twelfth century onwards, and Richard fitz Walter and his son Walter, a cadet branch of the fitz Nigels endowed with a manor at Maids Moreton by the senior branch in the twelfth century.[63] Finally, there were the Wavendons, a Group Four family with a tiny estate (apparently only one hide in demesne) at Wavendon.[64] One negative feature these five families had in common is that none of the leading members appears to have held even local office. This applies, indeed, to all those families losing the bulk of their estates, with the exception only of John Carun who was a coroner.[65] The significance of this is difficult to assess, but it may serve to reinforce arguments for the importance of office-holding to success, which will be discussed later.

In some cases these families can be traced some way beyond the land alienation before one loses sight of them entirely. Walter fitz Richard of Moreton and his son William and Henry son of Robert de Curtfalun are found as minor tenants of the Pevers, while Henry, son of Ralph fitz John was being paid a rent of fifty-eight shillings at least until 1274.[66] How much these families resented and regretted their losses can be seen in several cases. Walter fitz Richard reoccupied Maids Moreton while John Pever II was a minor in the 1270s.[67] Others resorted to the law, with Ralph son of

---

[60] VCH, *Bedfordshire*, iii, pp. 439–42.

[61] VCH, *Buckinghamshire*, iii, pp. 319, 415–6; VCH, *Berkshire*, iv, p. 201. For family descent, see M. T. Clanchy (ed.), *The Roll and Writ File of the Berkshire Eyre of 1248*, Selden Society, xc (1972–3), no. 304.

[62] For the Bidun barony, see Sanders, *Baronies*, p. 128; VCH, *Northamptonshire*, iv, p. 32; Farrer, *Honors and Knights' Fees*, i, pp. 6, 7, 9, 98. Farrer provides a good account of the family but both he and the VCH, *Northamptonshire*, wrongly identify Ralph fitz John with Ralph of Merston (Marston Moretaine): it is clear from the 1227 Buckinghamshire eyre roll that there were two Ralphs – the man married to Isabel and Ralph fitz John of Merston who was a minor at that time (Jenkins, *Justices on Eyre*, nos 50, 550).

[63] VCH, *Buckinghamshire*, iv, pp. 484, 499–500; Elvey, *Luffield Priory*, ii, pp. lxviii, lxxvi.

[64] See above, n. 41.

[65] PRO, Just 1/60, m. 22.

[66] *Book of Fees*, no. 1404; VCH, *Buckinghamshire*, iv, pp. 199–200; *Calendar of Inquisitions Post Mortem*, ii, no. 94; CCR, *1272–79*, p. 230; *Calendar of Ancient Deeds*, v, A11072.

[67] *Calendar of Inquisitions Post Mortem*, ii, no. 94.

Nicholas de Wavendon putting forward a claim against John Pever I in the 1260s; while the Pever possession of Curtfalun lands was challenged in the courts by Henry in the 1260s and 1270s, then by Henry's heir (his niece Alice) and her husband Simon fitz John in the 1280s.[68] It was all to no avail, however, and the Pevers triumphantly held on to their gains. Most interesting of all is the case of the Wavendons. There may have been antisocial genes present here, for Nicholas Wavendon was accused of murder in the 1240s; however, when one finds his sons Ralph and John convicted of robbery in 1271/72, one does speculate whether their criminal activity was born of desperation, a consequence of their financial ruin – the hapless Ralph had not been fined for his unsuccessful claim against the Pevers in the 1260s because of his poverty.[69] None of these five families can confidently be traced into the fourteenth century, but only the Curtfaluns are known to have been extinguished by failure of male heirs.

Turning back to Table 1, it should come as no surprise to discover that here, as elsewhere in thirteenth-century England, curial and other officials were major beneficiaries of the unsuccessful struggles for survival of knightly families. In addition to the principal beneficiary Paul Pever, there was Simon de Norwich, the royal clerk who acquired land at Abinton in Lavendon from Humphrey de Visdelou in 1231. This was initially a short-term mortgage to pay off a debt, but the Norwichs kept the land.[70] There was also John de Foxley, the steward of the abbey of Westminster and later baron of the exchequer. He acquired Lillingstone Dairel and Saunderton from the Dairels in the late thirteenth and early fourteenth centuries, although he sold Lillingstone back to the family in 1309.[71] Then there were ecclesiastical officials like Matthew de Stratton, the archdeacon of Buckingham, who acquired William fitz Reginald's lands.[72]

The recruitment into the landed classes of men whose careers were rooted in administrative service to the crown has a long history. As early as the reign of Henry I chroniclers were complaining that the king was 'raising men from the dust' at the expense of his proper companions and advisers,

---

[68] See above n. 41; PRO, Just 1/58, mm. 16d and 18, Just 1/67, m. 9d.

[69] PRO, Just 1/55, m. 28; *CPR, 1232–47*, p. 257; PRO, Just 1/60, m. 33.

[70] Farrer, *Honors and Knights' Fees*, i, pp. 56, 58–9; Travers, *Feet of Fines, Buckinghamshire*, i, no. 108; *Rotuli hundredorum*, i, p. 37b.

[71] See above, n. 41. Foxley acquired other land in Buckinghamshire but he made his home at Bray (Berkshire), building up an estate by a mixture of purchase and royal grants of assarts: VCH, *Buckinghamshire*, ii, p. 264; VCH, *Berkshire*, iii, p. 102.

[72] Matthew de Stratton acquired all their manor of Maid's Moreton from William fitz Reginald and his sons John and Robert. He then granted it to Oseney abbey (Salter, *Oseney Abbey*, v, pp. 289–93, 296–7, 299–300; VCH, *Buckinghamshire*, iv, p. 200). Master Robert Fileby, presumably an ecclesiastical clerk and administrator, held a manor at Denham for life in the 1280s (for his manor, see VCH, *Buckinghamshire*, iii, pp. 256–7; for his official career, see *CCR, 1282–93*, passim and *CPR, 1281–93*, passim). In 1286 Philip Duredent quitclaimed one messuage and two carucates at Denham to him for a sore sparrowhawk, Travers, *Feet of Fines, Buckinghamshire*, ii, no. 383.

the hereditary nobility. In fact, then as later, many of these ambitious royal servants were the sons of minor knights rather than peasants, and it is debatable to what extent their rise was at the expense of the military aristocracy's wealth or political power: this clearly varied from reign to reign. However, there is no doubt that, as the Angevin administration became more complex and dependent on written records, the opportunities for literate, numerate bureaucrats increased. Such men were well placed to acquire lands by their exploitation of the financial gains of office, their inside knowledge and the patronage of the king.[73]

Economic and social advancement of this kind was not limited to the servants of the crown, however. The de la Vaches were very minor tenants of the Wolverton barony at Chalfont St Giles in the twelfth century, and little is known about them until the mid 1260s when Richard de la Vache was steward of the honour of Lewes.[74] For the next two decades at least, he seems to have been in the service of John de Warenne, the earl of Surrey (he was one of the earl's attorneys in 1285), and presumably it was the rewards of this service which allowed Richard to amass a sizeable estate in Buckinghamshire and elsewhere.[75] However, other groups identified as major beneficiaries of knightly financial embarrassments elsewhere (the nobility and the monasteries) seem to have been relatively unimportant in Buckinghamshire. There were direct monastic gains for Luffield priory, Tichford priory, the hospital of St John, Oxford, and the Hospitallers, while Oseney abbey indirectly benefited when Matthew de Stratton passed on his acquisitions to them.[76] Equally, the barons acquired a few estates, sometimes from their financially distressed tenants. For example, William de Montacute, William de Clinton's lord in the west country, acquired Clinton's manors of Aston Clinton and Carsington, and Geoffrey de Lucy acquired Hogshaw from his tenant William de Fulbrook.[77] However, one does not get the

---

[73] R. V. Turner, *Men Raised from the Dust* (Philadelphia, Pennsylvania, 1988), pp. 1–19. Laurence de Broke (from an Anglo-Saxon Buckinghamshire family), who became the king's attorney, was granted 200s. in rent in Cambridgeshire and Huntingdonshire by Robert Malet in 1242–3. Between 1237 and 1261 he spent over 650 marks on property in Oxfordshire, besides making acquisitions in Buckinghamshire, Fowler and Jenkins, *Early Buckinghamshire Charters*, p. 41; Carpenter, 'Crisis of the knightly class', pp. 747–8; and above n. 11. For another successful royal servant from relatively humble origins, see Coss, 'Sir Geoffrey Langley'.

[74] VCH, *Buckinghamshire*, iii, p. 187; A. J. Taylor (ed.), *Records of the Barony and Honour of the Rape of Lewes*, Sussex Records Society, xliv (1939), p. 34.

[75] *CPR, 1281–92*, p. 192; PRO, Just 1/59, mm. 1, 15d. For the de la Vaches generally, see VCH, *Buckinghamshire*, ii, p. 315, iii, p. 27, iv, pp. 314–15; VCH, *Cambridgeshire*, v, pp. 165–6; Moor, *Knights of Edward I*, v, pp. 82–3; Shaw, *Knights of England*, i, p. 2; *CPR, 1258–66*, pp. 461, 660; *CCR, 1268–72*, p. 132; *CCR, 1272–79*, pp. 56, 510–1; *CCR, 1279–88*, p. 110; *Calendar of Inquisitions Miscellaneous*, no. 628; Travers, *Feet of Fines, Buckinghamshire*, ii, nos 129–30, 140, 233, 266, 315, 452; PRO, Just 1/67, m. 22; Just 1/1264, m. 23d.

[76] See nn. 41, 53, 72 above.

[77] William de Montacute acquired Aston Clinton and Carsington (Oxfordshire) from William de Paris, the heir of William de Clinton (*Book of Fees*, pp. 1171, 1210–13, 1295; *Calendar of*

impression that the balance of landownership was shifting away from the gentry, perhaps in part because of the small number of great monasteries and resident magnates in Buckinghamshire.

Knights from across the whole economic spectrum alienated land, but the consequences were more likely to prove fatal for the holders of single manors. All of the six Group Three and Four families who alienated land lost everything, or almost everything; while only five out of ten Group Two families who alienated land succumbed to this fate, as did only one of the four Group One families who alienated.[78] In addition, amongst the holders of single manors, there are several unexplained disappearances which may have been due to financial failure: the Corps, for example, disappeared having earlier mortgaged lands to Jewish money-lenders because of their debts.[79] One can probably conclude therefore, with Peter Michel, that land sales forced on landowners by indebtedness were 'by no means ... unique to the lower ranks of landed families', but that families holding single manors were far more liable to disappear from the landed class entirely as a result of such sales.[80]

It would be easy in the light of this to take a rather pessimistic view of the fortunes of the thirteenth-century gentry, but of course the story is not exclusively one of downward mobility. Indeed, seventeen families made significant gains, although four of them had disappeared by the early fourteenth century.[81] The major role played by marriages to heiresses is a noticeable feature here: in eight cases, all Group One and Two families, the only significant gains were made in this way.[82] Two of these marriages were

---

Inquisitions Post Mortem, i, no. 353), although William de Clinton also made other smaller alienations at Aston Clinton before parting with the whole manor. Montacute was William's lord at Shipton Montacute (Somerset), J. Collinson and E. Rack, *The History and Antiquities of the County of Somerset* (3 vols, Bath, 1791), iii, pp. 45–7. For de Lucy, see n. 41 above.

[78] See Table 2. Families losing everything were as follows. Groups 3 and 4: Carun, Curtfalun, fitz Walter, Fraxino, Hareng, Wavendon. Group 2: Blosseville, Fulbrook, fitz John, fitz Reginald, (John) Maunsel. Group 1: Visdelou.

[79] *CCR, 1237–42*, p. 41.

[80] P. Michel, 'Sir Phillip d'Arcy and the financial plight of the military knight in thirteenth-century England', *Lincolnshire History and Archaeology*, xix (1984), p. 49.

[81] See Table 2, p. 40.

[82] William de Beauchamp acquired a third of a five hide manor at Saunderton with Emma, daughter of Roger de Stanford in *c*. 1235, VCH, *Buckinghamshire*, iii, p. 94. Robert de Chetwood acquired part of a ten hide manor at Hockcliffe (Bedfordshire) between 1283 and 1302 with Lucy Malherbe, a coheiress, and by 1351 the whole of the manor had passed into their hands, VCH, *Bedfordshire*, iii, p. 384. Henry Dairel acquired a third of the Saunderton St Nicholas manor with Joan de Stanford, VCH, *Buckinghamshire*, iii, pp. 94–5. Otto fitz William's son Thomas married Beatrice, daughter and coheiress of William II de Beauchamp, baron of Bedford, on the death of her brother John in 1265, and thereby briefly acquired a third of the barony, Sanders, *Baronies*, pp. 10–11; *Calendar of Inquisitions Post Mortem*, ii, nos 56, 147, 430, iv, no. 98; P. Morant, *History and Antiquities of the County of Essex* (London, 1768), ii, pp. 305–6. Alexander de Hampden acquired land at Bledlow and Thame (Oxfordshire) with Marina, daughter of Henry de Turri, VCH, *Buckinghamshire*, ii, pp. 247–8; PRO, Just 1/1201, m. 20d; Just 1/67, m.

spectacular ones: William de Houghton and Thomas, son of Otto fitz William, each married a coheiress to a sizeable barony, Cainhoe in Bedfordshire in William's case, and the Beauchamp honour of Bedford in Thomas's. Usually gains were more modest, involving matches at a similar tenurial level. For example, in the 1230s Henry Dairel and William de Beauchamp each acquired a third of the five hide estate at Saunderton St Nicholas held by Roger de Stanford when they married his daughters.

Most marriage alliances were made with Buckinghamshire families or at least with families from contiguous counties. Only in the case of the Scaccarios and the Valognes did marriage result in land acquisitions in more distant parts (Cornwall and Gloucestershire respectively).[83] Henry de Scaccario, sheriff and avid land purchaser, was clearly a man of more enterprising calibre and wider connections than most of his peers, and no doubt this explains the less parochial marriage he arranged for his son.[84] Lands also occasionally fell to a family by inheritance. Robert fitz Nigel, a younger brother with a small estate in Kimble, inherited the family lands in Buckinghamshire and Oxfordshire on the death of his niece in 1252.[85] The Damorys benefited from the extinction of another branch of their family at Waterperry (Oxfordshire), and the fitz Ellises acquired three estates which they claimed to be theirs by right of Emma, William fitz Ellis's mother – although in this case the lands were only secured after long and expensive lawsuits.[86]

23d; A. C. Chibnall (ed.), *Early Taxation Returns*, Buckinghamshire Archaeological Society, xiv (1966), p. 26; VCH, *Oxfordshire*, vii, pp. 175, 187. His son Reginald acquired land worth £5 a year at Ashendon and Chilton with his marriage between 1302 and 1314, VCH, *Buckinghamshire*, iv, p. 24; *Calendar of Inquisitions Post Mortem*, v, no. 597; *CCR, 1313–18*, p. 134. Simon de Houghton's son, William, married Isobel Daubigny, coheiress to the barony of Cainhoe (Bedfordshire). Their son William inherited half the barony, assessed at twenty-five fees, on his mother's death in 1262, Sanders, *Baronies*, p. 26 and n. 7; *Calendar of Inquisitions Post Mortem*, ii, no. 11. William de Noers married Isabella, daughter and coheiress of Peter de Goldington, who died *c.* 1252, holding land in four counties, VCH, *Buckinghamshire*, iv, p. 467; *Calendar of Inquisitions Post Mortem*, i, no. 274; Farrer, *Honors and Knights' Fees*, i, p. 15. The main addition to the Noers estate was apparently the moiety of a manor at Stoke Goldington; they also shared a fee at Harpole (Northamptonshire) in 1284, *FA*, iv, p . 8. William de Saunderton acquired half a five hide manor at Tythrop in Kingsey after 1261 when he married the daughter of Robert de la Rose, VCH, *Buckinghamshire*, iv, p. 66; *Rotuli hundredorum*, ii, p. 785.

[83] With his marriage Ralph, son of Henry de Scaccario, acquired land at Bodannan in St Endellion (Cornwall), worth £20 a year in 1297, J. Polsue, *Complete Parochial History of Cornwall* (4 vols, Truro and London, 1867–72), i, p. 334; J. H. Rowe et al. (ed.), *Cornwall Feet of Fines, 1195–1461*, Devon and Cornwall Records Society (1914), nos 284, 311, 416. Thomas de Valognes acquired land in Bulley (Gloucestershire) through his wife Joan de Climden, Salter, *Feet of Fines, Oxfordshire*, pp . 112, 223.

[84] PRO, *Lists and Indexes*, ix, p. 6.

[85] Robert fitz Nigel inherited the lands of his elder brother Richard at Beachampton, Mursley, Iffley and Salden (Oxfordshire) on the death of his niece Grace in 1252, Elvey, *Luffield Priory*, ii, pp. lxvii–lxviii; VCH, *Oxfordshire*, v, pp. 191–2.

[86] Carpenter, 'Crisis of the knightly class', p. 733 n. 9.

Then there were land purchases. It appears that eight knights acquired land in this way, usually in more than one village, often by a series of transactions involving several sellers.[87] In the case of Robert Malet, the extension of the home manor at Quainton was a high priority, although he also got land in Oxfordshire and Berkshire, while the Olney family spent over half a century gradually building up an estate at Hardmead, in the neighbouring parish to their original home at Clifton Reynes. On the other hand, Thomas de Valognes accumulated a considerable estate at East and Bottle Claydon, some distance from the home manor at Shabbington and partly at the expense of another of our families, the Fulbrooks. Generally speaking, it was Group One and Two knights who were best able to add to their estates by marriage or purchase. But two holders of single manors made significant additions to their lands in these ways: Thomas de Valognes, who held a fairly large ten hide estate, and the Olneys, who began as very minor knights with a one hide one virgate estate held from the time of the Conquest.[88]

A correlation between office-holding and the ability and willingness to exploit the land market may be noted here. At the humblest level, it is at least possible that it was Simon de Olney's position as a baronial steward that provided the initial impetus for the family's slow but persistent improvement of their fortunes.[89] More interestingly, two of the most active land purchasers among the knightly group were royal servants. Henry de Scaccario was a member of a family of exchequer officials and more than once sheriff of Berkshire.[90] Robert Malet was also a Buckinghamshire sheriff on one occasion, but in addition he made a very successful legal career for himself culminating in his appointment as a judge of king's bench in 1289.[91] The importance of the law as a major avenue of advancement is well documented

[87] Damory (ibid.); fitz Nigel (ibid.; Travers, *Feet of Fines, Buckinghamshire*, ii, no. 63); Hampden (ibid., ii, no. 246); (Hervey) Malet (VCH, *Buckinghamshire*, iv, p. 95); Neirenuit (cadet branch) (ibid., iii, p. 362, iv, pp. 95, 112; Travers, *Feet of Fines, Buckinghamshire*, i, nos 104, 108); Olney (Chibnall, *Beyond Sherington*, p. 142; VCH, *Buckinghamshire*, iv, p. 63 and n. 19); Scaccario (ibid., iv, p. 71; Jenkins, *Chequers*, pp. 14–16); Valognes (*Book of Fees*, nos 874, 883, 893, 895; Travers, *Feet of Fines, Buckinghamshire*, i, p. 94, ii, nos 39, 64; VCH, *Buckinghamshire*, iv, pp. 160–1; PRO, Just 1/60, m. 5d; VCH, *Berkshire*, iv, p. 63; Salter, *Oseney Abbey*, ii, p. 116; idem, *Feet of Fines, Oxfordshire*, pp. 129–31; *Curia Regis Rolls*, xviii, no. 1721H). Land purchases usually involved parcels of land rather than whole estates, no doubt mainly because the latter did not come onto the market very often, Carpenter, 'Crisis of the knightly class', p. 749; Coss, 'Sir Geoffrey Langley', p. 20.

[88] In fact another Group Three family, the fitz Nigels, also purchased lands in some quantity, but by this stage they had acquired the estates of the senior line, making them quite substantial landholders.

[89] See above, n. 33.

[90] For the Scaccario or Chekers family see VCH, Berkshire, iii, p. 321; VCH, *Buckinghamshire*, ii, pp. 335–6; N. Denholm-Young, *Collected Papers* (Cardiff, 1969), p. 201 and n. 2.

[91] PRO, *Lists and Indexes*, ix, p. l; E. Foss, *Dictionary of the Judges of England, 1066–1870* (London, 1870), p. 425; G. O. Sayles (ed.), *Select Cases in the Court of King's Bench under Edward I*, 3 vols, Selden Society (1936–39), i, pp. xlvi, xlvii, lix, cxxxi, cxxxii.

for the fourteenth and fifteenth centuries. Lawyers in this period were in a unique position to exploit the land market, using the capital amassed from salaries and fees for purchases and mortgages, and defending their gains against rival claimants with their legal expertise.[92] It appears that Robert Malet in the late thirteenth century was able to do the same.

Of course, information about significant land gains and losses does not exhaust what we know of the struggles of these families. Evidence of indebtedness is difficult to interpret but we do know that, in addition to the eight families losing land who were in debt, there were another fifteen families recorded as owing money to someone other than the king, at some stage in the century.[93] In many cases these debts (mainly but not exclusively to Jewish moneylenders) were small and presumably tolerable, for debt, after all, was a fairly normal part of landowning life. Roger de Bracy's debts of five marks and ten pounds in the 1280s, together with the fact that he was five pounds in arrears with a rent owed to Merton priory, suggest a short-term crisis but one that was presumably weathered successfully, since the family survived into the fourteenth century, lands intact.[94]

In some cases debts, far from indicating financial distress, may have been incurred in furtherance of ambitious schemes of land acquisition. This may have been the case with Robert Malet, who owed money to the abbey of Missenden and the earl of Cornwall.[95] Much more serious were the debts

---

[92] For example, M. J. Bennett, *Community, Class and Careerism in Fourteenth-Century Cheshire* (Cambridge, 1983), pp. 192–202. Payling, *Political Society*, p. 31.

[93] Families with debts who alienated land: Bolbec (n. 51 above); Carun (Chibnall, *Beyond Sherington*, pp. 51–2, 101); Doynton, (*CCR, 1242–47*, p. 372; Rigg, *Exchequer of the Jews*, i, p. 255); fitz Reginald (Salter, *Oseney Abbey*, v, pp. 289–93, 296–7, 299–300, vi, p. 202; VCH, *Buckinghamshire*, iv, p. 200; Salter, *Oseney Abbey*, vi, p. 202; n. 52 above); fitz William (Rigg, *Exchequer of the Jews*, i, pp. 61, 99); Fulbrook see n. 41 above; Nafford (*Curia Regis Rolls*, vi, pp. 308, 318, 329, 330; *CCR, 1264–68*, p. 518; *Excerpta e rotulis finium*, ii, p. 70; Rigg, *Exchequer of the Jews*, i, pp, 27, 37, 43, iii, pp. 160, 212, iv, p. 80); Visdelou (*Rotuli litterarum clausarum*, ii, 212b; *CCR, 1227–31*, p. 559; *CCR, 1231–34*, p. 6; *Calendar of Charter Rolls*, i, pp. 77, 151, ii, p. 35; *Curia Regis Rolls*, i, p. 289; L. Abrahams et al. (ed.), *Starrs and Jewish Charters in the British Museum*, Cambridge 1930, 1932, ii, p. 35, n. 107b). In all but one case (Bolbec) these were debts to Jews. Other families who got into debt were de Beauchamp (*CCR, 1259–61*, p. 217); de Bracy (PRO, Just 1/67, m. 21; *CCR, 1288–96*, p. 49); de Burton (*CCR, 1254–56*, p. 170); le Corp (*CCR, 1237–42*, p. 41); Damory (VCH, *Oxfordshire*, vi, p. 73); de Houghton (L. C. Loyd and D. M. Stenton, ed., *Sir Christopher Hatton's Book of Seals*, Northamptonshire Records Society, xv 1950, no. 136); fitz Nigel(*CCR, 1288–96*, pp. 140, 257; *CCR, 1296–1302*, p. 606); de Keynes (*Calendar of Fine Rolls*, i, p. 280; Abrahams, *Starrs and Jewish Charters*, ii, p. 79 n. 165; *CCR, 1272–79*, p. 359); Malet (*CCR, 1272–79*, pp. 228, 510, 511); Maunsel (VCH, *Cambridgeshire*, v, p. 168); de Siffrewast (*CPR, 1258–66*, p. 505; *CCR, 1268–72*, p. 563; Abrahams, *Starrs and Jewish Charters*, ii, p. 88 n. 203 (p); Rigg, *Exchequer of the Jews*, i, pp. 275–6; iv, pp. 2–3); Neirenuit (*CPR, 1266–72*, p. 180; *CPR, 1292–1301*, p. 493); de Tothill (*CCR, 1256–59*, p. 494); de Turville (*Pipe Rolls, 1 John*, p. 247; Travers, *Feet of Fines, Buckinghamshire*, i, no. 49; *CCR, 1296–1302*, pp. 484, 604; *CCR, 1302–07*, p. 339); de Verly (VCH, *Buckinghamshire*, iv, p. 516; *CCR, 1231–34*, pp. 63, 502; Rigg, *Exchequer of the Jews*, i, pp. 68–69).

[94] Travers, *Feet of Fines, Buckinghamshire*, ii, no. 374, VCH, *Buckinghamshire*, ii, pp. 307, 311.

[95] For purchasers, see, VCH, *Buckinghamshire*, iii, p. 98, iv, p. 95; VCH, *Berkshire*, iv, p. 209;

of the Keyneses, holding one manor originally by serjeanty of the crown at Milton Keynes. In 1290 the king stepped in and remitted half of the 200 marks of Jewish debt which Robert had inherited from his father John. In 1285, however, Robert had also incurred a debt of £500 to one Walter of Aylesbury, perhaps in connection with his successful attempt to hold on to an inheritance which should rightfully have gone to his half-brother Nicholas.[96] The Aylesburys finally acquired the Keynes manor when Walter's son Philip married Robert's daughter and heir Margaret, but whether the family would have survived with lands intact if there had been a male heir seems questionable, at least.[97]

None the less, what strikes one most forcefully about some of these histories is the variety of ways in which families could deal with financial pressures without seriously damaging their inheritance. On several occasions the king intervened to help. In 1245, much moved by the poverty of Thomas de Doynton (a Group One knight), Henry III ordered that lands mortgaged to Jewish moneylenders should be returned to Thomas, and reasonable terms for the repayment of his debts arranged.[98] In 1268 John Neirenuit (the cadet branch of another Group One family) was pardoned the £20 a year owed by his father Geoffrey to Jewish lenders, and in 1300 this John or his son was granted a custody to discharge a debt of 100 marks.[99] The Doyntons ended up alienating estates, despite royal assistance, but the Neirenuits, who survived and flourished, may have owed this in part at least to royal favour.[100]

If that kind of assistance was not forthcoming there were other options. Thomas Maunsel, for example, was able to lease a Cambridgeshire manor to Barnwell priory for a few years to pay off a debt without damaging his interests at Shenley, his home manor, and in much the same way Robert Damory could mortgage Bucknell (Oxfordshire), his home manor, to Oseney abbey, but later redeem it having paid his debts. Particularly interesting in this regard are the Siffrewasts: this Group One family with estates in several counties ran into difficulty when a dispute over the inheritance arose between Richard, the heir and grandson of the previous holder, and his uncle Roger,

---

PRO, Just 1/56, m. 22d; *Calendar of Inquisitions Post Mortem*, iii, no. 276. For his career, see above n. 91. It is also possible, as Saul has suggested with reference to the debts of a Sussex careerist, Sir Andrew Sackville, that Malet owed money as an agent for a third party rather than on his own behalf, Saul, *Scenes from Provincial Life*, p. 183.

[96] PRO, Just 1/67, m. 31; *Calendar of Inquisitions Post Mortem*, ii, no. 462; Travers, *Feet of Fines, Buckinghamshire*, ii, no. 255.

[97] PRO, Exchequer KR E198/3/7; VCH, *Buckinghamshire*, iv, p. 402.

[98] See n. 93 above.

[99] See n. 93 above.

[100] T. D. Fosbrooke (ed.), *Abstracts of Records and Manuscripts Respecting the County of Gloucester* (Gloucester, 1807), ii, p. 90; S. Rudder, *A New History of Gloucestershire* (Cirencester, 1779), p. 406; *Placito de Quo Warranto, Edward I-Edward III*, p. 260.

resulting in the division of the inheritance in the 1240s.[101] The senior line at one stage sold part of their Chesham estate to Reading abbey 'in their great need', and then leased Clewer (Berkshire), for a period of years.[102] This certainly did not solve the family's problems, for there were debts to Jews and others in the 1260s and 1270s, but the senior line of the Siffrewasts did survive into the fourteenth century, holding their manor at Clewer, although they were only esquires by that time.[103]

Any attempt to find monocausal explanations for the upward and downward mobility of these knightly families would be unwise. A timely warning against doing so is provided by Chibnall's detailed analysis of the decline and fall of the Caruns, which he attributes to a mixture of what have been classified here as factors internal to the county (bad decision making by individuals, family disputes, over-generous provision for family members) and external factors, such as the fact that as tenants in chief of the crown their manor fell under exchequer control during minorities, and the rising costs of knighthood for a family which continued to see active service, often overseas. However, some factors can be singled out as of particular importance. It seems clear, for example, that the vitality and resilience of knightly families in thirteenth-century Buckinghamshire depended partly upon an internal factor: their initial economic position. Families with two manors or more were less likely to suffer really damaging land losses and more likely to increase their landed wealth than holders of single manors. Presumably greater wealth meant that these families had enough of a surplus to ride out economic crises that would have destroyed smaller landowners, and they were also more likely to have the sort of political and social connections to secure royal help in meeting particularly heavy debts, or to help them make advantageous marriages.

Another internal factor which can be singled out is the malign influence of family disputes. Six families alienating land (including the Caruns), and two running into serious debt were involved in these before or around the time of the land losses. In the case of the Wavendons, inter-generational strife may have been a consequence rather than the cause of financial difficulties.[104] The nature of these disputes varied considerably. In the Bolbec and Keynes families there were tussles over inheritance between brothers, while for the Siffrewasts it was a dispute between a grandson and a son of

---

[101] *Curia Regis Rolls*, xi, nos 678, 691, xvi, no. 1369; *The Berkshire Eyre Roll, 1248*, nos 212, 392, 450, 561; M. T. Clanchy (ed.), *Civil Pleas of the Wiltshire Eyre, 1249*, Wiltshire Records Society, xxvi (1971), no. 201.

[102] B. R. Kemp (ed.), *Reading Abbey Cartularies*, Camden Society, 4th series, xxxi, xxxiii (1986–7), i, no. 245; *CPR, 1247–58*, pp. 406, 530.

[103] *Parliamentary Writs*, ii, pt i, pp. 588, 610–11; VCH, *Berkshire*, iii, pp. 72–3, and see n. 93 above.

[104] Reginald Wavendon went to court to regain the family estate which he had granted to his son Nicholas, on the grounds that Nicholas had failed to support him according to their agreement, PRO, Just 1/57, m. 14d.

the previous holder.[105] In the case of Ralph fitz John the problems involved in partitioning a small barony led to lawsuits.[106] Humphrey de Visdelou got enmeshed in a legal battle with his stepmother Hawise and her second husband over the fate of his father's lands.[107] Finally, Henry de Nafford (a man of violent temper who on one occasion tore a charter out of a monk's hands in the royal court) had bitter quarrels with his mother Denise, Bordesley abbey and others.[108] Whatever the circumstances, however, litigation entailed expenditure and might disrupt land exploitation, regardless of the ultimate verdict of the court.[109]

A third factor which can be tentatively identified as contributing to knightly decline is simply personal inadequacy. Elvey roundly condemns William fitz Reginald of Moreton as an economic weakling, and since he managed to destroy the family fortunes in one generation for no discernible reason, one is certainly inclined to suspect gross incompetence.[110] Likewise, Reginald de Fraxino's long series of land sales may be explicable only in terms of his personal shortcomings; certainly no alternative explanation emerges from the records.[111] Finally, the fact that Henry Dairel's son Henry was able to repurchase the home manor, having failed to prevent its sale twenty years earlier, does perhaps suggest that the sale was due to bad decision-making in response to a short-term crisis, rather than necessity.[112]

However, we must not underestimate the role played by the external factors of relations with the crown and, especially, office-holding, which provided money for land purchases and the less tangible but equally important benefits of royal patronage, a network of useful connections, and various kinds of legal and administrative expertise. The fact that two of the knights who exploited the land market most assiduously were sheriffs and one of them a judge is significant, and the importance of *curiales* as acquirers of estates from knights who ran into difficulties has been examined at some length.

Another aspect of the interplay between court and county – the reverse side of the coin – was royal displeasure. Several declining families seem to have incurred disfavour for political reasons or because of criminal activities. Humphrey de Visdelou was probably involved in rebellion in the 1220s and

---

[105] Above, p. 40 n. 51; p. 49 n. 96; p. 50 n. 101.

[106] Above, p. 42 n. 62.

[107] Chibnall, *Beyond Sherington*, pp. 152–3.

[108] *Curia Regis Rolls*, xv, no. 1128, xvi, no. 265; D. M. Stenton (ed.), *Rolls of the Justices of Eyre, Being the Rolls of Pleas and Assizes for Gloucestershire, Warwickshire and Shropshire, 1221–22*, Selden Society, lix (1940), pp. xxxviii and xxxix, xl, nos 419, 427, 446, 605, 820–21, 1461; *CCR, 1237–42*, pp. 32, 72–3, 134.

[109] For the role of litigation in knightly affairs, see Carpenter, 'Crisis of the knightly class', pp. 745–46; King, 'Large and small landowners', pp. 46–7.

[110] Elvey, *Luffield Priory*, ii, p. lxii.

[111] See also n. 40, p. 36, and n. 53.

[112] See above, n. 41.

forfeited lands to Fawkes de Breauté on this account; the Bolbecs, the cadet branch of the Neirenuits (who had debt problems, although they made no alienations), and the Turris were all involved in the Barons' Wars, while Nicholas de Wavendon had to buy a royal pardon for his misdeeds at a cost of fifty marks – the final blow which probably allowed the Pevers to acquire this land.[113] However, in general the links between economic status and political involvement are inconclusive. Ten other families opposed the king in the Barons' Wars, without any perceptible long-term consequences, and so did Richard de la Vache who did so well thereafter.[114] What, however, of their social status?

Table 3
Maintenance of Knighthood *c.* 1220–1320

Groups	One	Two	Three	Four
Number of families surviving beyond 1300	5 (4)	21 (14)	9 (9)	3 (6)
Number suffering overall loss, 1200–1300s	1 (2)	3 (6)	2 (2)	0 (2)
Number increasing number of estates	2 (2)	8 (1)	1 (1)	1 (0)
Number maintaining number of estates	3 (0)	10 (7)	7 (6)	2 (4)

In the brackets are the families which did not survive.

As Table 3 above shows, sixteen families were still represented by knights in the early fourteenth century, and eight were represented by esquires or men at arms. In general, the take-up of knighthood tallies fairly closely with either initial or achieved economic status, in that it was largely the holders of single manors who had dropped out.[115] This change does not necessarily

[113] For the Visdelous see Chibnall, *Beyond Sherington*, pp. 152–3. For the Bolbecs and Neirenuits see PRO, Just 1/59, mm. 1, 15d. For the Turris see PRO, Just 1/59, mm. 16. For the Wavendons, see *CCR, 1242–47*, p. 152, and n. 42 above.

[114] Other knights apparently involved in the Barons' Wars against the king were: Richard Darches (PRO, Just 1/59, mm. 5d, 18d); Robert fitz Nigel (VCH, *Oxfordshire*, v, p. 192); Eustace de Grenville (PRO, Just l/59, m. 9; *CPR, 1258–66*, p. 323); Stephen de la Haye (PRO, Just 1/59, m. 3; *CCR, 1268–72*, p. 260); Thomas Maunsel (VCH, *Buckinghamshire*, iv, p. 446); John Passelewe (*Calendar of Inquisitions Miscellaneous*, i, no. 633); Fulk de Rycote (VCH, *Buckinghamshire*, iv, p. 325); Robert de Tothill (PRO, Just 1/59, m. 7); William de Turville (*CPR, 1258–66*, p. 528); John and Ralph de Wedon (*Supplementary Close Rolls, 1244–66*, nos 395, 465, 498). Eustace de Grenville and Thomas Maunsel were both captured at Northampton. John Passelewe was captured and Robert fitz Nigel died at the battle of Evesham, C. H. Knowles, '"The Disinherited", 1265–80' (unpublished University of Wales Ph.D. thesis, 1959), appendix 1, pp. 56–7. For Vache, see PRO, Just 1/59, mm. l, 9, 15d. The relatively easy reabsorption of most rebels into the social and political community was noted by Knowles. He suggested that the deaths of Montfort and other leaders, depriving the rebels of a focus of opposition, plus the humane terms of the Dictum of Kenilworth and the large numbers of men involved, all help to account for this, 'The Disinherited', pt iii, pp. 116–17.

[115] Assessing whether a family continued to take up knighthood in the fourteenth century has proved difficult without extensive research into family histories after the 1320s. This category therefore comprises those families known to have provided knights in the 1320s, mainly using

reflect any real decline in the status of the families without military title, merely a change in the character of knighthood as it became more exclusive.[116] To some extent the possession of a coat of arms was a function of family longevity as much as status (since the evidence for them is often sixteenth or even seventeenth century), but it is worth noting that twenty-two of these families bore arms in the middle ages or later.[117] Three of them were only producing esquires and six had no military title in the early fourteenth century. They presumably acquired arms later, when qualifications for doing so were relaxed to include esquires and later simple gentlemen.[118] Fourteenth- and fifteenth-century architectural remains and epitaphs provide further evidence of maintained status and prosperity, even among families who had encountered setbacks in the thirteenth century.[119]

Administrative or political involvement at various levels provides another

parliamentary writs. Knightly families extinguished by failure of heirs at the beginning of the century and those whose military status is doubtful are not included in the figures.

[116] The only Group Four family taking up knighthood in the fourteenth century were the Olneys, but John Olney married Maud de Haversham, an heiress with several manors in and outside the county, which must have increased his resources and improved his standing considerably. For Olney's marriage see VCH, *Buckinghamshire*, iv, p. 368; *Calendar of Ancient Deeds*, v, A9003–5; *Calendar of Inquisitions Post Mortem*, vi, no. 694; G. F. Farnham, 'Claybrooke: notes on the descent of the manor', *Transactions of the Leicestershire Archaeological Society*, xii (1921–2), p. 207.

[117] Carpenter, 'Crisis of the knightly class', p. 738; Coss, *Lordship, Knighthood and Locality*, pp. 15–16, and chapter 7.

[118] **Knights:** Chetwood (W. H. Rylands ed., *Visitation of Buckingham, 1634*, Harleian Society, lviii 1909, p. 151); Damory; fitz Ellis; fitz Nigel (Carpenter, 'Crisis of the knightly class', p. 737 n. 4); Hampden; Malet (Rylands, *Visitation of Buckinghamshire*, pp. 69, 94); Neirenuit (Lipscomb, *History and Antiquities* i, p. 326; and VCH, *Buckinghamshire*, iii, p. 232, for senior line; F. A. Blaydes, ed., *Visitation of Bedfordshire, 1566, 1582 and 1634*, Harleian Society, xix 1884, p. 36, for cadet line); Noers (R. H. Ellis, *Catalogue of Seals in the Public Record Office: Personal Seals*, London, 1978, i, p. 580); Puttenham (Rylands, *Visitation of Buckinghamshire*, p. 200); Siffrewast (Ellis, *Personal Seals*, i, p. 722, for senior line; VCH, *Buckinghamshire*, iii, p. 210, for cadet line); Turville (W. de G. Birch, *Catalogue of Seals in the British Museum*, 6 vols London, 1887–1900, ii, no. 6489, iii, nos 14017, 14019); Wedon (Rylands, *Visitation of Buckinghamshire*, p. 220).

Esquires: Duredent (VCH, *Buckinghamshire*, iii, p. 259; Royal Commission on Historical Monuments, *An Inventory of the Historical Monuments in Buckinghamshire*, London 1912–13, i, p. 115); Passelewe (Lipscomb, *History and Antiquities*, iii, p. 340; VCH, *Buckinghamshire*, iii, p. 345); Rycote (Carpenter, 'Crisis of the knightly class', p. 737 n. 4).

Others: Darches (Royal Commission on Historical Monuments, *Inventory of Historical Monuments, Buckinghamshire*, ii, p. 92); Broughton, (Blaydes, *Visitation of Bedfordshire*, p. 12); Carun; Dairel; Grenville (Rylands, *Visitation of Buckinghamshire*, pp. 44, 36, 66); Haye; Keynes (VCH, *Buckinghamshire*, iv, pp. 171, 402).

[119] The Broughtons, for example, a family with small estates at Broughton and Crawley, apparently relinquished knighthood after the 1270s, but they became armigerous and produced sheriffs and MPs in the later middle ages, *Return of Members of Parliament* (London, 1878), i, pp. 212, 241; PRO, *Lists and Indexes*, ix, p. 2; Chibnall, *Beyond Sherington*, p. 99. In the fifteenth century the Broughtons acquired the Pever estates when John de Broughton married Mary, daughter and heiress to Thomas Pever (d. 1429), VCH, *Bedfordshire*, iii, p. 440.

gauge of social mobility. In a grand assize list dated 1285/86, three of the four knights electing the twelve jurors and seven of the twelve jurors elected were members of families who furnished grand assize jurors in the 1220s – something which bears witness to a continuity among the knightly families of the county.[120] Of course, a number of families never held public office, and rarely acted even as ad hoc commissioners or justices. This includes such families as the Bolbecs, fitz Nigels and Grenvilles, who were active knights for much of the century, something which they may have seen as an alternative form of public service.[121] However, eighteen (just over half) of the surviving families acted in one administrative capacity or another, often in several, in the decades around the turn of the century, with twelve acting as MPs, and sixteen as sheriffs, conservators of the peace, coroners or verderers, for either Buckinghamshire or other counties.[122] While it was no longer necessary for landowners to be knights in order to be eligible for such offices, the correlation was in fact high, although there were families of esquires like Robert Barry and William de Saunderton who were extremely active in the administrative and public sphere.[123]

[120] For example, parts of a fourteenth-century house, probably built by Thomas Duredent, were incorporated into a later Duredent home, Savoy Denham, and there is a fifteenth-century brass to a particularly prolific Duredent in Denham church, VCH, *Buckinghamshire*, iii, p. 256; Royal Commission on Historical Monuments, *Inventory of Historical Monuments, Buckinghamshire*, i, p. 115. Similarly, the Grenvilles ceased to assume military title but built a chapel at Wotton Underwood in 1343, according to a modern plaque in the church, while the Dairels, in eclipse at the turn of the century, clearly managed to fight back successfully: they were esquires in the ffifteenth century and have left a monument in the church at Lillingstone Dairel (ibid., i, p. 326; ii, p. 169,).

[121] PRO, Just 1/67, m. 10. They were: Robert de Chetwood, William de Saunderton, Gilbert de Bolbec, Philip Duredent, Walter de Upton, John Neirenuit, William de Turville, Alexander de Hampden, Robert Barry, William de Noers.

[122] For Bolbec military service, see, *CPR, 1247–58*, p. 232; PRO, C 47/1/5/1; *Calendar of Chancery Rolls*, i, p. 368; *Parliamentary Writs*, i, pp. 203, 234, 237. For fitz Nigel, see, *CPR, 1247–58*, p. 595; *CPR, 1281–92*, p. 271; *CCR, 1296–1302*, pp. 885, 381; *Calendar of Chancery Rolls*, i, pp. 84, 91, 94, 370; *Parliamentary Writs*, i, p. 353; ii, pt i, pp. 428, 587 (although Robert fitz Nigel did take a part in the organisation of the array in the early fourteenth century, ibid., i, pp. 330, 342; ii, pt i, p. 738). For the Grenvilles, see, *CCR, 1231–34*, p. 547; *CPR, 1247–53*, p. 597; *CPR, 1272–81*, p. 220. Naughton implies that knights active in administration were unlikely to be active militarily as well, *The Gentry of Bedfordshire*, p. 15.

[123] **MPs**: Robert Barry (Buckinghamshire and Northamptonshire); William de Beauchamp; John de Chetwood (Buckinghamshire and Surrey); Robert Malet; Miles and John Neirenuit; Amory de Noers; John de Olney (Buckinghamshire and Leicestershire); William de Saunderton; John de Siffrewast (Buckinghamshire and Dorset); Robert de Tothill; William and Nicholas de Turville; Ralph de Wedon (*Return of Members of Parliament*, passim). Three other families providing Buckinghamshire MPs later in the century were Dairel, Duredent and Puttenham (ibid.).

Sheriffs: Robert Damory (Oxfordshire); Robert Malet; Amory de Noers (Northamptonshire); John de Olney (Warwickshire/Leicestershire); Otvel Purcel (Oxfordshire); William and Nicholas de Turville; Ralph de Wedon (PRO, *Lists and Indexes*, ix, passim).

Conservators of the Peace: Robert Barry (*Parliamentary Writs*, i, p. 390; *Calendar of Inquisitions Miscellaneous*, i, no. 1447; *CPR, 1281–92*, p. 265); John Neirenuit (*Parliamentary Writs*, ii, pt ii,

Among the gentry who were relatively inactive in the county administration, some were found to be unqualified for office. John de Cowley (from a Group Four family) was replaced as coroner for Oxfordshire in 1313 when he was said to have no land in the county. Ralph de Langport failed to meet the criterion for verderers (the possession of land within the forest).[124] For the middling knights (Group Two), involvement in administration may have been partly a matter of personal choice, but there is a clear correlation with levels of wealth. Holders of single manors were not usually active in county government by the early fourteenth century, and the most active were often the wealthiest Group One knights like the Neirenuits and the Noers.[125] It is also noticeable that active knights usually came from families with a tradition of office-holding. The Hampdens, for example, were sheriffs and keepers of the county in the mid thirteenth century, coroners in the 1280s, and coroners and justices in the early fourteenth century.[126] The only real exception is John de Olney, the first prominent member of his family.[127]

To conclude, we can say that there was considerable mobility amongst Buckinghamshire knightly families in the thirteenth century. There were a number of complete economic failures and these were more common among the minor knights with one manor who were less able to weather financial crises than their wealthier neighbours. It has to be stressed, however, that

p. 12; *CPR, 1317–21*, p. 461); Ralph de Wedon (*Parliamentary Writs*, ii, pt ii, p. 282; *CPR, 1317–21*, p. 92; *CPR, 1321–24*, p. 249; *CPR, 1324–27*, p. 286).

Coroners: Robert and John de Chetwood (PRO, Just 1/60, m. 22; *CCR, 1279–88*, p. 35; *CCR, 1302–7*, p. 415); Alexander and Reginald de Hampden (PRO, Just 1/66 mm. 1 and 12d; Just 1/70, m. 5; *Parliamentary Writs*, ii, pt i, p. 587); Stephen de la Haye (PRO, Just 1/66, m. 1); John de Keynes (ibid.), William de Saunderton (ibid.; *CCR, 1307–1313*, p. 16; *Calendar of Inquisitions Miscellaneous*, i, no. 2271).

Verderers etc: John Chetwood (*CCR, 1302–7*, p. 415); Richard de Turri (*CCR, 1288–96*, pp. 106, 161); Walter de Upton (Salter, *Boarstall Cartulary*, p. 182).

[124] In addition to activities mentioned above in n. 123, Robert Barry was active from the 1280s to the 1370s as a tax assessor and collector, and as a justice suppressing illegal meetings (*CPR, 1292–1301*, p. 104; *Parliamentary Writs*, i, pp. 27, 64; ii, pt i, pp. 39, 535; pt ii, p. 119); and William de Saunderton was a commissioner in 1295 (*CPR, 1292–1301*, p. 165).

[125] The Cowleys held a small estate at Preston Bisset in Buckinghamshire, near the Oxfordshire border. For Cowley see *CCR, 1313–18*, p. 32; VCH, *Buckinghamshire*, iv, p. 217. For Langport see ibid., iv, pp. 235–6; *Rotuli hundredorum*, i, pp. 32–33; Salter, *Oseney Abbey*, v, pp. 275–6; *CCR, 1309–13*, p. 304.

[126] In addition to the activities mentioned above (n. 123), Miles Neirenuit was constable of Wallingford in the early fourteenth century and a commissioner of array, *Calendar of Fine Rolls*, iii, p. 428; *CCR, 1323–27*, p. 624; *Parliamentary Writs*, i, pp. 409–10. John Neirenuit was a tax collector and justice of gaol delivery, e.g., *Calendar of Fine Rolls*, ii, pp. 217, 219, 222; *CPR, 1317–21*, pp. 20, 354, 428. For Amory de Noers, see n. 22 above.

[127] For the Hampdens' administrative activities, see n. 123 above, and PRO, Just 1/58, m. 20, Just 1/60, m. 22, Just 1/66, m. 12d; *CCR, 1254–56*, pp. 103, 105, 115, 225, *CCR, 1256–59*, p. 89, *CCR, 1259–61*, p. 305, *CCR, 1261–64*, p. 82; *CPR, 1258–66*, pp. 164, 327; *Calendar of Liberate Rolls, 1245–51*, pp. 244, 291, 326, *Calendar of Liberate Rolls, 1251–60*, p. 68, *Calendar of Liberate Rolls, 1260–62*, pp. 2, 34, 96, 128.

the most common cause of family disappearance was the failure of male heirs rather than economic decline.

Almost as many families bettered their position, and the failure of male heirs, this time within other families, was often crucial to their success. This group of rising families cannot be described as economically dynamic, in that only a few of them were active land buyers (given the limited nature of the land market in the thirteenth century it could hardly be otherwise), but a number of them made useful marriages to heiresses. This was clearly the main route to tenurial advancement, in Buckinghamshire as elsewhere in late medieval England.[128]

A considerable number of families (thirty-nine in all, twenty-two surviving ones) simply held on to what they had, and the other measures of status available, such as take-up of knighthood and administrative involvement, also tend to suggest that continuity and stability within the gentry class were at least as marked a feature of their collective thirteenth-century experience as mobility. Admittedly only one third of the surviving families still took up knighthood by the end of the period, and only about half were MPs or administrators, but the changing status of knighthood accounts for the former; in the case of the latter, activity as anything more than ad hoc commissioners and justices or grand assize jurors had always been the province of a fairly limited proportion of the knightly class. Many of the families which survived the century therefore, appear to have maintained their economic and social status relative to the rest of their social group largely unaltered over the period.

What is more, although the combination of failure of male heirs and economic decline led to considerable changes in the composition of the gentry class, there is little to suggest that the social structure of landowning society altered greatly in Buckinghamshire. The marriage market largely served to move land around a group of families of similar status, the main beneficiaries of land sales being curial or baronial officials like the Pevers and de la Vaches, who were recruited and assimilated into the gentry community, and who often began as minor landed gentry anyway. In short, the Buckinghamshire evidence does not clearly point to any *general* economic crisis of the knightly class. It would be unwise to generalise too fully from the evidence of one county, but it is worth noting that the figures presented by Carpenter and Coss for decline and failure amongst sample groups of knightly jurors' families in Oxfordshire and Warwickshire are broadly comparable with those for Buckinghamshire.[129]

A wide range of circumstances precipitated changes in status. Internal factors, such as initial economic standing and family disputes, and factors

---

[128] In addition to activities in n. 123 above, John was very active in the 1320s raising troops and pursuing rebels, e.g., *Parliamentary Writs*, ii, pt i, pp . 684–5, 704, 717, 725; ii, pt ii, pp. 182, 184.

[129] Given-Wilson, *English Nobility*, p. 10.

external to the county, such as office-holding and court connections, have been stressed here. The factors could be interrelated of course. For example, it seems likely that the unfavourable economic position of most knights holding only one manor not only made them particularly vulnerable to financial problems in an age of inflation and rising costs of knighthood, it also meant that they had few opportunities to make advantageous marriages, and they were less likely to hold office and attract royal patronage.

Office-holding and favour at court did not depend solely on wealth, however, and indeed for men of ambition and ability service to the crown represented one of the best ways of achieving wealth from relatively humble beginnings. In Buckinghamshire vertical relationships with the crown clearly mattered a great deal. This was particularly the case for those seeking to claw their way into the gentry class, but it also held true for established families who were trying to maintain their position in the face of indebtedness, or who hoped to increase their wealth and status by land acquisitions. Along with the failure of male heirs, which made land available both to established families and to newcomers, links with central government seem to have provided one of the most dynamic forces for change and development at the county level at this period. Without it most gentry families could look forward to at best stagnation and at worst decline.[130]

---

[130] Carpenter, 'Crisis of the knightly class', pp. 750–1; Coss, *Lordship, Knighthood, and Locality*, pp. 294–98.

4

Mid Thirteenth-Century Reformers and the Localities: The Sheriffs of the Baronial Regime, 1258–1261

H. W. Ridgeway

The 'Baronial Movement', which for three momentous years between 1258 and 1261 took power from the hands of Henry III, enacted a remarkable series of reforms intended to improve the conduct of sheriffs throughout England. These celebrated measures have been frequently and enthusiastically described. They were part of what was arguably the first political programme in English medieval history and certainly the first to link the reform of central with that of local government.

For the past sixty years the standard analysis of this achievement has been that of R. F. Treharne.[1] In his view the barons responded generously to the widespread demand for reform by offering the localities enlightened aristocratic government. In so doing the regime acknowledged the growing importance of the knights and gentry in politics and local administration. The reforms in their turn kindled enthusiasm by placing the knights and the support they could offer on the political map where they were to be so effectively deployed by Simon de Montfort in 1261–65 and, after that, by Edward I. Whereas Henry III was set on collision with the knights and gentry, the barons generated harmony. Recent work on thirteenth-century politics and society necessitates a reexamination of Treharne's conclusions.[2] There is no question that reform was required in 1258 or even that some relief was provided. But it is more questionable that, given the complexities of contemporary society, 'baronial government' could go very far in the reform of local administration. This is revealed by a survey of the origins of sheriffs appointed and their conduct in office. The relationship between the mid thirteenth-century reformers and the localities proves to be far less harmonious than was previously thought.

---

[1] R. F. Treharne, *The Baronial Plan of Reform, 1258–1263* (Manchester, 1932), pp. 97, 121–5; and see W. A. Morris, *The Medieval English Sheriff to 1300* (Manchester, 1927), pp. 169–75. My thanks to Drs D. A. Carpenter, C. H. Knowles, J. R. Maddicott, J. A. Quick, J. R. Studd and Professor D. Crouch for their kind help with this essay.

[2] See D. Crouch et al., 'Debate: bastard feudalism revised', *Past and Present*, cxxxi (1991), pp. 165–203.

There is now a clearer appreciation than was available in Treharne's day of the political emergency which precipitated the reforms of 1258. Discontent in the provinces does not seem to have caused the crisis. Rather, it began with a factional power struggle at the centre which was swiftly resolved by the exile of the king's detested Lusignan favourites. The new 'baronial' regime was composed of the king's old councillors and their allies, mainly a handful of the great earls, feeding speculation that the reforms of 1258 may well have begun as an attempt to win broader support for a courtier coup.[3] However, such a view ignores the need for reform in the localities which had endured twenty years of Henry III's personal rule and hand to mouth policies. Paradoxically, the baronage had contributed to these burdens by denying the king access to supplies in parliament, so that he had been encouraged to shift the burden onto the localities and other weaker groups, such as the Jews. In addition, the oppressions of the great mens' estate officials passed unchecked.[4]

The misconduct of sheriffs, however, was in the reformers' minds and an immediate and thoroughgoing overhaul of the office was perceived as central to any redress for the localities. Despite the creation of additional layers of officialdom, the sheriffs were still the linchpin of local government and the king's principal agents in the shires. Only later, during the Barons' Wars, was their political role undermined, to some extent, by the powers of the keepers of the peace.[5] The developments affecting sheriffs before 1258 have been analysed by David Carpenter.[6] After 1236 the king gradually adopted the policy of replacing 'curial sheriffs', powerful regional governors, with officials who were more amenable to tight exchequer supervision. As the pressures imposed by the exchequer diminished the attractiveness of the office for courtiers, it fell into the hands of lesser knights who were more susceptible to demands from the centre. In many counties by the late 1250s the exchequer had succeeded in imposing extortionate increments above

[3] D. A. Carpenter, 'What happened in 1258 ?', in J. Gillingham and J. C. Holt (eds), *War and Government in the Middle Ages: Essays in Honour of J. O. Prestwich* (Woodbridge, 1984), pp. 106–19; H. W. Ridgeway, 'The Lord Edward and the Provisions of Oxford: a study in faction', in P. R. Coss and S. D. Lloyd (ed.), *Thirteenth-Century England*, i, *Proceedings of the Newcastle upon Tyne Conference, 1985* (Woodbridge, 1986), pp. 89–99; idem, 'Foreign favourites and Henry III's problems of patronage, 1247–1258', *EHR*, civ (1989), pp. 590–610.

[4] D. A. Carpenter, 'King, magnates and society: the personal rule of King Henry III, 1234–1258', *Speculum*, lx (1985), pp. 39–70; J. R. Maddicott, 'Magna Carta and the local community, 1215–1259', *Past and Present*, cii (1984), pp. 25–65; S. L. Waugh, 'Reluctant knights and jurors: respites, exemptions and public obligations in the reign of Henry III', *Speculum*, lviii (1983), pp. 937–86; R. C. Stacey, '1240–60: a watershed in Anglo-Jewish relations?', *BIHR*, lxi (1988), pp. 135–51; F. M. Powicke, *King Henry III and the Lord Edward*, 2 vols (Oxford, 1947), i, pp. 307–22.

[5] Morris, *English Sheriff*, chapters 7–10, passim; A. Harding, 'The origins and early history of the keeper of the peace' *TRHS*, 5th series, x (1960), pp. 85–109.

[6] D. A. Carpenter, 'The decline of the curial sheriff in England, 1194–1258', *EHR*, xci (1976), pp. 1–32.

the traditional shrieval farm, in some cases multiplying fourfold the levels recorded in 1230. The conduct of many sheriffs deteriorated as they struggled to make a living against this background. As Carpenter puts it, the system of heavy increments 'aggravated the corruption endemic in medieval local government'.[7]

To make matters worse, the 1250s also saw the king begin to sell exemptions from county offices, including the shrievalty, on an unprecedented scale. Over the decade more than five hundred were bought up in what J. R. Maddicott describes as a mass 'retreat from office-holding'.[8] To make up the shortage, the exchequer began in some places to recruit men of little or no local standing, to the outrage of the community, even occasionally importing from outside the shire professional administrators (often the hated seigneurial type) who were moved from county to county. As this was often the juncture at which increments were increased, it became the standard jibe of his opponents that Henry III, in addition to all his other tyrannies in the shires, had packed the office of sheriff with ignoble men 'coming from far away and utter strangers in the counties'.[9] By the mid 1250s there were calls for reform even in some quarters of the king's government and investigations by royal councillors brought a few tyrannical sheriffs to book. An ambiguous clause in the councillors' oath of 1257 may suggest a plan for a more general review.[10]

In addition it is too easily forgotten that by 1258 there were important regional variations in the approach to shire administration. In some areas the shrievalty could be attractive for the wrong reasons. Looking back in 1264 the Montfortians could accuse the king of auctioning the office between unscrupulous men, to the ruin of the counties which had to provide the funds to justify outlandish bids made to the exchequer.[11] But some shires were treated with comparative generosity. Hampshire, for which the king had great personal affection, had few non-local sheriffs and such as there were escaped very high increments.[12] Some sheriffs had favourable reputations.[13] The appointment of non-local sheriffs during the period was less common than might be assumed. Over half the shires escaped the

---

[7] Ibid., p. 28.

[8] Maddicott, 'Magna Carta and the local community', p. 45. See also, R. C. Stacey, *Politics, Policy and Finance under Henry III, 1216–1245* (Oxford, 1987), pp. 53–66, who concludes that it was in the 1250s, and not earlier, that Henry III's regime in the localities became really burdensome.

[9] Carpenter, 'Decline of the curial sheriff', p. 29 and n. 2.

[10] H. R. Luard (ed.), *Annales monastici*, Rolls Series (1864–69), i, p. 396, iii, p. 199; PRO, E 159/30, mm. 5d, 9d, and schedule.

[11] R. F. Treharne and I. J. Sanders (ed.), *Documents of the Baronial Movement of Reform and Rebellion, 1258–1267* (Oxford, 1973), p. 275.

[12] T. E. Maciver, 'Aspects of the gentry of thirteenth-century Hampshire' (unpublished University of Oxford M. Litt. thesis, 1984), pp. 127–142, 193 nos v–vi.

[13] For example Robert le Savage, sheriff of Bedfordshire-Buckinghamshire in 1255–56, and not a local (Carpenter, 'Decline of the curial sheriff', p. 29 n. 2), was remarkably described by the normally caustic Dunstable Annalist as 'vir prudens et discretus', *Annales Monastici*, iii, p. 196.

phenomenon altogether and those which suffered usually did so briefly. For in many, perhaps up to one-third of cases, frequent changes of sheriff after as little as one or two years was becoming the rule.[14] There was much diversity and contradiction (not uncommon qualities in Henry's government) built into the system. In Herefordshire and Lincolnshire, for example, there was a quick turnover of local men, whereas Norfolk-Suffolk had long stretches of strangers and Kent was administered between 1249 and 1257 by a locally based professional, Sir Reginald de Cobham.[15] Some remote counties, such as Westmoreland, retained magnate sheriffs.[16] One can even observe, for as many as a third of the shires, a drift towards a system anticipating the 1258 reforms, that is local knights as sheriff with frequent changes.[17] But if some sheriffs were better than others, it can only have fuelled the sense of injustice of the majority of localities evidently burdened by the harsh financial terms imposed by the exchequer upon the localities in the 1250s.

It was this harsh and unequal system which the barons sought to remedy. Among the first acts of the council of magnates which took office in June 1258 was an order for the empanelling of four knights from every shire to collect and report grievances against sheriffs and bailiffs. As a result, many bailiffs and a handful of sheriffs were punished in the following year in proceedings before the justiciar. It was a mere fraction of the mountain of complaints received, for there were too many to deal with.[18]

---

[14] Cambridge-Huntingdonshire, Hampshire, Herefordshire, Kent, Lancashire, Lincolnshire, Northumberland, Nottingham-Derbyshire, Oxford-Berkshire, Shropshire-Staffordshire, Somerset-Dorset, Warwick-Leicestershire, Wiltshire had only local landholders as sheriffs between 1250–58. This point is based mainly upon comparison of the *List of Sheriffs for England and Wales*, PRO, Lists and Indexes, ix (1898), with *The Book of Fees*, 3 vols (London, 1921–31). Cf. G. Templeman, *The Sheriffs of Warwickshire in the Thirteenth Century*, Dugdale Society Occasional Papers, vii (1948), pp. 38–41; J. C. Wedgwood, 'The sheriffs of Staffordshire', *Collections for a History of Staffordshire by the William Salt Archaeological Society* (1912), pp. 276–7; H. M. Cam, 'Cambridgeshire sheriffs in the thirteenth century', in her *Liberties and Communities in Medieval England* (2nd edn, London, 1963), pp. 36–41, and her conclusions on p. 48. See also D. C. Cox, 'Early medieval local government in Shopshire', VCH, *Shropshire*, iii (1979), pp. 15–17. He appears to be mistaken about Robert de Grendon (sheriff of Shropshire-Staffordshire 1250–55), a landowner with interests at least in Staffordshire reappointed by de Montfort in 1265. D. A. Carpenter ('Decline of the curial sheriff', pp. 28–9) observes that 'there were probably as many local knights controlling shires in the 1240s and 1250s ... as there had been before 1236'.

[15] See previous note; Carpenter, 'Decline of the curial sheriff', p. 29 n. 2; J. A. Quick, 'Government and society in Kent, 1232–80' (unpublished University of Oxford D. Phil. thesis, 1986), pp. 190–201.

[16] Morris, *English Sheriff*, pp. 179–181; below, p. 64.

[17] During the 1250s this was true, with only brief exceptions, for Cambridge-Huntingdonshire, Devonshire, Gloucestershire, Herefordshire, Lincolnshire and Surrey-Sussex. If we include Elias de Rabayn, who acquired local landholdings, it is also true of Somerset-Dorset. The same tendency can also be traced in Essex-Hertfordshire and Northamptonshire: see above, n. 14.

[18] E. F. Jacob, *Studies in the Period of Baronial Reform and Rebellion, 1258–1267* (Oxford, 1925), chapter 2; Treharne and Sanders, *Documents of the Baronial Movement*, pp. 98–9; 112–15.

Organic reform was attempted under the Provisions of Oxford of June 1258. It was ordained that sheriffs should be sound landowners of the shire drawn from the richer knights, vavasours, who would hold office for one year only and (perhaps to prevent extortion) as 'custodians', that is, accounting for all the returns of the shire with a fixed allowance, rather than responding to a farm. This was not a new idea, a similar experiment having been undertaken by the exchequer between 1236 and 1241.[19] But now detailed guide-lines were laid down to regulate the conduct of sheriffs and their subordinates and to eliminate bribery and other abuses. They were proclaimed to the localities in the Ordinance of Sheriffs of October 1258, a copy of which was sent in Latin, French and English to every shire to be read out frequently henceforth by the sheriff in the county court.[20] Couched in the phraseology of royal proclamation, the ordinance's ringing denunciations of years of shrieval misdeeds must have left many audiences bemused, even though these were some of the best-publicised of the 1258 reforms.

In the same month most of the incumbent sheriffs were dismissed in favour of new men. These held office for only a year and were then replaced by a further series who remained two years in office before Henry III dismissed them as part of his attempt to recover personal power. Thus, between 1258 and 1261 thirty-nine individuals were appointed by the baronial regime to take charge of twenty-two shires, or pairs of shires. As a well-defined group of officials, through whom we can see how the reforms operated in practice, these men merit more detailed consideration than the cursory and occasionally inaccurate remarks ventured by Jacob and Treharne. By tracing their careers during the Barons' Wars, more light can be shed on the political allegiances and attitudes of that vital class of administrative gentry on whose work not only the baronial reformers but medieval government in general was coming to depend.

Let us look at the sheriffs appointed in October 1258 and the months immediately following. Jacob and Treharne were impressed that the baronial regime effected an almost complete clean-out of the old order and the appointment of a new set of sheriffs, very few of whom had held office before and who fulfilled the strict new conditions of appointment laid down by the Provisions of Oxford. Furthermore, while accepting that ultimate power of appointment remained with the officials of central government, the justiciar, treasurer and the barons of the exchequer under conciliar supervision, they toyed with the idea of placating the political aspirations of knights in the localities by permitting the indirect nomination, or election, of new sheriffs in the form of knightly delegates sent to Westminster from the county courts.[21]

---

[19] Ibid., pp. 108–9, cap. 17; Morris, *English Sheriff*, p. 170; Carpenter, 'Decline of the curial sheriff', pp. 17–21.

[20] Treharne and Sanders, *Documents of the Baronial Movement*, pp. 118–23.

[21] Treharne, *Baronial Plan of Reform*, pp. 121–5, 204–9; Jacob, *Studies in the Period of Baronial Reform*, pp. 49–52.

No doubt the regime wanted to create the impression of sweeping improvement. But in practice not all the shires were immediately given new sheriffs. In about a third (nine out of twenty-six shrievalties) the existing sheriff was retained, and in other areas change was not so drastic as Treharne thought. By considering these regional variations we may come closer to discovering the new regime's real intentions and understanding its difficulties.

First, it must have been difficult to recruit new sheriffs at all. The reforms of the Ordinance of Sheriffs, however laudable, actually made the sheriff's task much more demanding. Moreover, as previously shown, by 1258 many suitable knights held charters of exemption from holding local office. Of the sheriffs eventually appointed in 1258 and 1259 almost one-third had purchased them. The regime's drastic solution, at least in 1258, was to attempt to quash these documents.[22] When the original panels of four knights to enquire into abuses were summoned from every shire under the Provisions of Oxford, it was specifically forbidden that anyone should plead a charter of exemption to avoid this call 'made for the common good of the whole realm'. When these panels reported their findings to the parliament at Westminster on 6 October 1258, their individual members suddenly found that they had been made candidates for the office of sheriff, which cannot have pleased some of them. The case of Robert de Meisy shows that it was especially hard to persuade the potential sheriffs of the more distant provinces to rely on the promises of the new regime rather than exemptions purchased from the old. Meisy appeared before the justiciar, the treasurer and the barons of the exchequer in November, produced his royal exemption and requested release from the shrievalty of Gloucester to which he had just been appointed. He was referred to the council where his objections seem to have been overridden. He took up office in December, presumably to the ultimate satisfaction of both sides, for in the next year he was chosen as sheriff of Herefordshire, a post he held for over two years, followed by other county appointments.[23]

Then there was the knotty problem of the handful of shrievalties which had been held for many years in fee: the king's brother, Richard, earl of Cornwall, had held Cornwall since 1225 and Rutland since 1227. On an even more ancient basis, the Vipontes held Westmoreland and the Beauchamps held Worcestershire. Henry III's heir, the Lord Edward, had held the county palatine of Chester since 1254.[24] These counties might have

[22] Treharne and Sanders, *Documents of the Baronial Movement*, pp. 98–9. The baronial regime soon softened its tough and presumably unpopular policy towards exemptions from inquisitions and assizes. This explains the significant absence of legislation on exemptions from the shrievalty: Waugh, 'Reluctant knights and jurors', pp. 984–5.

[23] Treharne, *Baronial Plan of Reform*, p. 124. See also, PRO, *List of Sheriffs*, p. 59; *CPR, 1247–58*, pp. 490, 522; *CPR, 1258–66*, p. 481; *CCR, 1259–61*, pp. 189, 198. For Meisy, see Waugh, 'Reluctant knights and jurors', pp. 965–6.

[24] Morris, *English Sheriff*, pp. 179–182; E. Mason (ed.), *Beauchamp Cartulary Charters, 1100–1268*, Pipe Roll Society, new series, xliii (London, 1980), pp. xlix-li.

welcomed change. Chester apart, each duly produced its panel of four knights in 1258.[25] In the hundred rolls enquiries of 1274–5 the knights of Cornwall were to express a long-standing grievance that Richard of Cornwall had deprived them of the right of electing their own sheriff.[26] In Cheshire there were rumbles against the Lord Edward, whose officials were a byword for harshness. By August 1259 Edward was publicly promising better standards from his administration whereby he might recover 'the favour of both God and man'.[27] The problem was that the baronial regime could not impose drastic changes in these shires without offending the great men who possessed the shrievalties. In 1258 they needed to avoid alienating the likes of Richard of Cornwall, now king of Germany. In the matter of great men's property the new council, itself full of great men, was thoroughly conservative, as shown by its refusal to confiscate even the estates of the king's exiled favourites.[28] Furthermore, some of the hereditary sheriffs had friends in high places: William Beauchamp of Salwarpe, for instance, attended parliament in 1258 in the entourage of the earl of Gloucester, a member of the council.[29] Thus in the counties where the shrievalty was held in fee, the baronial regime was unable to impose changes of sheriff between 1258 and 1261. The Lord Edward, like his father the king, was placed under the tutelage of council, but there were no noticeable changes of official in Cheshire.[30]

The dictates of security may have prevented changes in some other places. Instability in Anglo-Scottish and Anglo-Welsh relations had played their part in bringing about the 1258 crisis.[31] Thus, for the time being, in the northern border counties important men were required as sheriffs against an emergency. In Cumberland the earl of Aumale, a member of the new ruling council who had been sheriff since 1255 and who had a castle at Cockermouth, remained in office, accounting through an undersheriff, until his death in early 1260. In Yorkshire, likewise, William le Latymer, sheriff since

[25] *CPR, 1247–58*, pp. 645–9.

[26] Maddicott, 'Magna Carta and the local community', pp. 29, 41.

[27] D. A. Carpenter, 'The Lord Edward's oath to aid and counsel Simon de Montfort, 15 October 1259', *BIHR*, lviii (1985), p. 235. Dr Robin Studd has kindly drawn my attention to a protracted conference between the Lord Edward and the knights of Cheshire, 5–6 September 1260, where the liberties of the men of the Palatinate appear to have been discussed: J. R. Studd, 'A catalogue of the acts of the Lord Edward' (unpublished University of Leeds Ph.D. thesis, 1971), pp. 609–10, documents 843–4.

[28] H. W. Ridgeway, 'King Henry III and the "aliens", 1236–1272', in P. R. Coss and S. D. Lloyd (ed.), *Thirteenth-Century England*, ii (Woodbridge, 1988), pp. 91–2.

[29] *CCR, 1256–59*, p. 316.

[30] For example, J. Tait (ed.), *The Cartulary of Chester Abbey*, Chetham Society, new series, lxxix, p. v. Mr Martin Page, who is completing an Oxford doctorate on thirteenth-century Cornwall, has kindly drawn my attention to errors in the PRO, *List of Sheriffs*. However, his discovery of changes of sheriff in Cornwall *c.* 1256–60 appears to support my point by showing that all the appointees made during this period had connections with Richard of Cornwall.

[31] F. M. Powicke, *The Thirteenth Century* (2nd edn, Oxford, 1962), pp. 137–8, 592.

1254 and a man with court connections, carried on until early 1260. A simpler explanation for these appointments, however, may be the continuing tradition of appointing local magnates in the north, as suggested earlier; at any rate, these men were important local landowners. Interestingly enough, they were replaced in 1260 by much lesser figures.[32] In the Welsh marches too there were, initially at least, special measures in response to the threat presented by Prince Llywelyn of Wales since 1256. Gilbert Talbot, a retainer of the Lord Edward and custodian of border castles, who had served as justiciar of Chester, was appointed to Herefordshire. In fact, he never took office, perhaps because the worst of the crisis seemed to be past, and the existing sheriff, Henry de Pembridge, a local, continued for six months before being replaced by another local knight.[33] In Shropshire and Stafford-shire Peter de Montfort, a councillor appointed to meet the emergency in 1257, actually gave way in 1258–9 to William Bagot, a Staffordshire knight, who none the less had and later showed his ability to hold the fort.[34]

A stronger case for the demands of security as a limitation upon change may be made in Hampshire and the joint shrievalty of Essex and Hertford-shire. In Hampshire the regime appointed Ralph Harengod, a wealthy knight with local connections whose interests lay however primarily in Sussex, but he refused office, ostensibly on the grounds of 'ill-health'.[35] In February 1259 four Hampshire knights elected John St Valery, a man with few local interests but with connections at court and the patronage of Richard of Cornwall. But either he too refused office or the council preferred to leave matters as they were, for James le Sauvage, the incumbent

[32] PRO, *List of Sheriffs*, pp. 26, 161; B. English, *The Feudal Lords of Holderness* (Hull, 1979), pp. 51–2; G. E. Cokayne, *The Complete Peerage of England*, 12 vols in 13 (London, 1910–59), vii, pp. 460–1. Aumale's undersheriff was his Yorkshire retainer, Remy de Pocklington, later used by the Aumales as sheriff of Holderness, *c*. 1261–4: English, *Feudal Lords of Holderness*, pp. 71, 227–34. Further to the point of security, the new sheriff of Northumberland, a local knight, was not given the custody in 1258 of the castles of Bamburgh or Newcastle-upon-Tyne: Treharne and Sanders, *Documents of the Baronial Movement*, pp. 112–13; *CPR, 1247–58*, p. 655. Both Aumale and Latymer were replaced in 1260 by local knights: Robert de Mulcaster, Cumberland (C. Moor, *Knights of Edward I*, 5 vols, Harleian Society Publications, lxxx-lxxxiv, London, 1929–32), iii, p. 232); John de Octon, Yorkshire (ibid., iii, p. 284).

[33] Treharne, *Baronial Plan of Reform*, p. 122; *CCR, 1254–56*, pp. 134, 264–5; Studd, 'Acts of the Lord Edward', pp. 186, 195, documents 4, 25–6. Pembridge used a local man as undersheriff (PRO, *List of Sheriffs*, p. 49).

[34] Wedgwood, 'Sheriffs of Staffordshire', p. 276; G. Wrottesley, 'A history of the Bagod family', *William Salt Archaeological Society*, new series, i (1908), pp. 128–37; Bagod also had holdings in Warwickshire. Significantly, Peter de Montfort retained the castles of Bridgnorth and Shrewsbury until 1260: VCH, *Shropshire*, iii, pp. 15–16.

[35] Maciver, 'Gentry of thirteenth-century Hampshire', pp. 139–40; *Sussex Archaeological Collections*, lviii (1916), pp. 466, 523. Although there is little trace of Harengod's landed interests in Hampshire, he served as forest commissioner in the county in the 1250s: *CPR, 1247–58*, p. 433; *CCR, 1251–53*, p. 200. A branch of the family held land in the shire in the thirteenth century, VCH, *Hampshire*, iv, p. 450.

since 1256, continued for another year.[36] It may be significant that at this point the sheriff of Hampshire had the task of keeping order against recalcitrant officials who remained loyal to the exiled bishop of Winchester, Aymer de Lusignan.[37] Perhaps it was also for fear of the Lusignans (William de Valence, Aymer's brother, was lord of Hertford) that the council maintained the status quo in Essex-Hertfordshire, where Hubert de Munchensi, appointed in 1257 and certainly not a local knight, continued until October 1259.[38] Occasionally, the continuation of an existing sheriff even defies informed speculation, as in Berkshire where Nicholas de Hendred, who had held the shire in conjunction with Oxfordshire since 1250, remained in office until October 1259.[39]

Interesting as these exceptions are, the key point remains the degree to which changes implemented in the remaining eighteen shires took into account the desires and aspirations of the localities for a better regime. This is hard to judge because we still do not know for certain how the new sheriffs were chosen, although on balance the evidence suggests that central appointment continued much as before. Jacob and Treharne discovered two counties, Hampshire, mentioned above, and Lancashire, where in February 1259 the chosen panel of four knights arrived at the exchequer and duly, on oath, elected a sheriff; in the case of Lancashire one of the four, who was admitted by the justiciar and treasurer as sheriff. Treharne speculated that this was the method generally adopted in the autumn of 1258. Jacob, more cautiously, merely noted that in seventeen out of eighteen cases the sheriff chosen at the exchequer was one of the four knights empanelled in August 1258. Since these knights must have been elected in the county court, what later took place was an indirect election of sheriffs.

There are serious difficulties with both these theories. It has already been shown that the circumstances under which serving sheriffs remained in office militate against any notion that sheriffs were generally elected by their shires. Indeed the Hampshire election was overruled by the council, while the memoranda rolls specifically record that Robert de Meisy of Gloucestershire

---

[36] Treharne, *Baronial Plan of Reform*, p. 206; Maciver, 'Gentry of thirteenth-century Hampshire', pp. 133, 139; N. Denholm-Young, *Richard of Cornwall* (Oxford, 1947), p. 91; Moor, *Knights of Edward I*, iv, p. 197 (there is some slight evidence of John de St Valery's holdings in Hampshire: VCH, *Hampshire*, iii, p. 457; iv, p. 407n.). He was appointed Montfortian sheriff of Oxford-Berkshire in 1264–5, and then by the king to the shrievalty of Somerset-Dorset in 1271–4. Although appointed keeper of the peace in Hampshire by Montfort in July 1263, an appointment extended by the king in December 1263, though now held in conjunction with associates (*CPR, 1258–66*, pp. 271, 327, 358, 475, 587), but his landholdings appear to have been in Oxfordshire: *Calendar of Inquisitions Miscellaneous*, i, no. 854; *CCR, 1268–72*, p. 554.

[37] H. W. Ridgeway, 'The politics of the English royal court, 1247–1265' (unpublished University of Oxford D. Phil. thesis, 1983), pp. 320–25.

[38] For Munchensi: *Calendar of Inquisitions Post Mortem, Henry III*, no. 883. Another delicate task for the sheriff of Essex in 1258 was the deposition of the proscribed Poitevin, Guy de Rochford, from his life-custody of Colchester castle, PRO, E 159/32, m. 5d.

[39] PRO, *List of Sheriffs*, p. 107.

was appointed by the council.[40] Nor is there evidence that the panels of four knights were elected in the county courts. Nowhere, even in the Ordinance of Sheriffs, are the knights deemed to have been 'elected'. When in August the outgoing sheriff of Devon, Roger le Poitevin, and two of the empanelled knights wrote to the justiciar and chancellor informing them that the other two knights of Devon were ill, and asked for instructions on how to proceed, it was the sheriff who was ordered to find substitutes. Similarly, it would appear that Peter de Montfort in Shropshire swiftly removed three of the knights 'because they are not fit' and substituted three others.[41] Sheriffs with plenty of business to transact which required small juries of knights no doubt kept lists of potential appointees up their sleeves. Perhaps, given all the excitement aroused in the localities by the promises of reform, even the outgoing sheriffs took local wishes into account when compiling their lists. The justiciar, treasurer and council, when making their choice from the panel of four knights, may well have done the same: that is all one can say.

All the knights thus chosen were natives of their shires, 'vavasours' drawn from the wealthier knights holding one or two manors and sometimes even with holdings in adjacent shires.[42] They therefore represented the cream of the office-holding knightly class which generation after generation provided the crown with its local officials, escheators, coroners, justices of gaol delivery, tax assessors and the like. Two of them, the new sheriffs of Warwickshire-Leicestershire, Anketil de Martival, and Wiltshire, Godfrey de Escudamore, already had experience as sheriffs, the former as sheriff of adjacent Rutland

[40] Treharne, *Baronial Plan of Reform*, pp. 205–7; Jacob, *Studies in the Period of Baronial Reform*, pp. 22–3, 50–1. For Meisy, see PRO, E 159/32, m. 5d.

[41] PRO, SC 1/6/179; *CPR, 1247–58*, pp. 647–8. See also, J. C. Holt, 'The prehistory of parliament', in R. G. Davies and J. H. Denton (ed.), *The English Parliament in the Middle Ages: A Tribute to J. S. Roskell* (Manchester, 1981) p. 17. The men of Devon, significantly, were ignorant of new titles, addressing 'the king's justiciar and chancellor'.

[42] It lies beyond the scope of this essay to supply a full list, but richer sheriffs of the 1258–9 period who held more than one manor include: Richard de Bagingden of Hereford, *The Book of Fees* (3 vols, London, 1921–31), i, p. 440; ii, pp. 803, 819; William le Botyller of Lancashire (see below, p. 70); William de Courtenay of Devon, *Excerpta e rotulis finium*, ii, p. 36, and O. J. Reichel, *The Hundreds of Devon*, Devonshire Association, extra vols i–x, in 1 (1928–38), pp. 179, 343, 516; Godfrey de Escudamore of Wiltshire, *Book of Fees*, ii, pp. 712, 717, 725, 733–4, 746, 1178, 1226; Hamo Hautein of Norfolk-Suffolk, ibid., i, p. 182, ii, pp. 1033, 1051, and F. Blomefield, *An Essay Towards a Topographical History of the County of Norfolk* (11 vols, London, 1805–10), vi, p. 477, x, pp. 426–7, xi, p. 222; David de Jarpenvill of Surrey-Sussex, *Book of Fees*, ii, p. 684, *Calendar of Charter Rolls, 1257–1300*, p. 134, and Moor, *Knights of Edward I*, ii, pp. 271–2; Robert de Meisy of Gloucestershire, W. Farrer, *Honors and Knights' Fees* (3 vols Manchester, 1923–5), iii, p. 91, *CCR, 1253–54*, p. 130, *CCR, 1261–64*, p. 286, and VCH, *Hampshire*, iii, p. 415; iv, pp. 361–2; Simon de Pateshull of Buckingham-Bedfordshire, *Calendar of Inquisitions Post Mortem, Edward I*, iii, p. 232; Fulk Peyforer of Kent, Quick, 'Government and society in Kent', pp. 218, 225; Eustace de Watford of Northamptonshire, Moor, *Knights of Edward I*, v, p. 170, *Book of Fees*, i, p. 603; John du Plessis of Northumberland, J. Hodgson, *A History of Northumberland* (3 vols in 7, Newcastle, 1820–68), pt ii, vol ii, pp. 293–76.

since 1257, the latter in Dorset-Somerset in 1249.[43] Peter de Foliot, the new sheriff of Oxfordshire, had been the escheator in his shire since 1253 and Simon de Hedon (Nottinghamshire-Derbyshire) had served as coroner in Nottinghamshire. He continued as undersheriff there between 1261 and 1264.[44] Five other new 1258 appointees had held other lesser local offices in the 1250s. These were Fulk Peyforer (new sheriff of Kent), Richard de Bagingden (Herefordshire), William Everard (Somerset-Dorset), Eustace de Watford (Northamptonshire) and John du Plessis (Northumberland).[45] Of the remainder, two came from important county families with a record of office-holding: William le Moine (Cambridge-Huntingdonshire), was a kinsman of John le Moine, sheriff there in 1253–5. More exceptionally, Simon de Patteshull (Bedfordshire-Buckinghamshire) came from a family which had produced high judicial and financial officials for John and Henry III. William Bagot may have been related by marriage to Robert de Grendon, an earlier sheriff of Shropshire-Staffordshire.[46]

Moreover, several of the appointees of 1258 had strong links with powerful magnates who had interests in the locality. The all-powerful Richard de Clare, earl of Gloucester, figures prominently as usual.[47] William Everard (Somerset-Dorset) is likely to have been the earl's man in 1258, since he was in his service by early 1260. Hamo Hautein (Norfolk-Suffolk) and Simon de Patteshull, both prominent Clare tenants, may have been linked with Richard, since we know that later on in the Barons' Wars they were bachelors in the household of his son, Gilbert de Clare.[48] William le Moine, a former

---

[43] PRO, *List of Sheriffs*, pp. 112, 122. Escudamore was also assessor of tallage for Wiltshire in 1252, *CCR, 1251–53*, pp. 213.

[44] Ibid., p. 422; *CCR, 1256–59*, pp. 271, 276.

[45] Peyforer, justice of gaol delivery, Kent, 1256 (*CPR, 1247–58*, p. 471); Bagingden, to view state of Hereford castle, 1254, forest inquisition, Gloucestershire, 1255 (*CPR, 1247–58*, pp. 432–43; *Calendar of Inquisitions Miscellaneous*, i, no. 205); Everard, to survey Exeter castle, 1251, forest commission, Somerset, 1255 (*CPR, 1247–58*, pp. 127, 433); Watford, to survey Northampton castle, 1252, to assess tallage in Northamptonshire, 1252 (*CCR, 1251–53*, pp. 79, 212); Plessis, to survey Bamburgh castle, 1253 (*CPR, 1247–58*, p. 234). It is probable that a survey of judicial records would show that these men were active in other county business.

[46] Cam, 'Cambridgeshire sheriffs', p. 40; *DNB*, xv, pp. 474–5; VCH, *Shropshire*, iii, pp. 15–16. Additionally, the Foliots (Oxfordshire and Berkshire), the Martivals (Leicestershire) and the Peyforers (Kent) were local administrative families, *CPR, 1247–58*, pp. 50, 399, 598, 647; G. F. Farnham and A. H. Thompson, 'The Manor of Noseley', *Leicestershire Archaeological Society Transactions*, xii (1921–22), p. 219; Quick, 'Government and society in Kent', pp. 218–26.

[47] The following list should not be considered exhaustive. S. L. Waugh, 'Reluctant knights and jurors', p. 966 n. 98, suggests that Robert de Meisy was a client of the earl of Gloucester, who twisted his arm to accept office in 1258 (however, Meisy and his son may have been in the retinue of the prominent Marcher, Roger de Clifford, during the Barons' Wars: *CPR, 1266–72*, p. 382). For Gloucester's connections with 1258–61 sheriffs, and his alleged abuse of them to strengthen his position in the localities, see below, p. 77.

[48] *CCR, 1256–59*, p. 41; *CPR, 1266–72*, pp. 143, 145, 147, 268; *Calendar of Inquisitions Miscellaneous*, nos 632, 828–9; Blomefield, *History of the County of Norfolk*, ii, p. 380, vi, p. 477, x, pp. 426–7, xi, p. 222; Farrer, *Honors and Knights' Fees*, iii, pp. 154, 388; M. Altschul, *A Baronial*

yeoman of the chancellor, Henry de Wengham, came from a family which, like Wengham, had connections with the queen. William Bagod was linked with John de Plessis, earl of Warwick, also acting as his undersheriff in 1261–2. Anketil de Martival, besides serving Richard of Cornwall in Rutland, was by 1263, if not before, steward of Simon de Montfort, a natural connection in view of his long association with the Segraves, who were Montfort clients.[49] Godfrey de Escudamore was the brother-in-law of the important local magnate, John de Giffard, and his son (at least) was in Giffard's service during the Barons' Wars.[50] William de Courtenay, the new sheriff of Devon, was a kinsman, possibly brother, of John de Courtenay, one of the largest landowners in the shire.[51] Significantly, in February 1259 the knights of Lancashire 'elected' as sheriff William le Botyller, one of the wealthiest barons of the region, a man, for good measure, connected with the earl of Derby.[52] Clearly, there was a widely held view that the sheriffs of 1258 had excellent credentials.[53]

After they had completed their year in office they were changed. Treharne was more certain than ever that the new sheriffs were elected this time by the elected panel of four knights from each county, under oath and at the exchequer.[54] But here again the evidence is contradictory: the 'Administrative'

Family in Medieval England: The Clares, 1217–1314 (Baltimore, 1965), p. 105; Jacob, *Studies in the Period of Baronial Reform*, p. 129; I. J. Sanders, *English Baronies: A Study of their Origin and Descent* (Oxford, 1963), pp. 11, 46.

[49] For Moine, see *CPR, 1247–58*, pp. 232, 343, 376, 387, 587; Ridgeway, 'Politics of the English royal court', pp. 66, 412, 418. Note however that the name le Moine is common. John le Moine, an earlier sheriff of Cambridge-Huntingdonshire, was certainly linked with Peter of Savoy, the queen's uncle (ibid., p. 418), and both the queen and Peter had significant links with men of those shires. For William le Moine's lands, see VCH, *Huntingdonshire*, ii, p. 199; iii, pp. 51, 61, 204. For Bagod, see Mason, *Beauchamp Cartulary Charters*, pp. 174–75. For Martival, see Farnham and Thompson, 'The manor of Noseley', pp. 219–22 (which discusses Martival's long association with the Segraves); HMC, *Report on the MSS of Reginald Hastings Esq.* (1928), i, p. 42; PRO, KB 26/173, m. 19d. I owe these references to Professor Crouch, who believes that Martival can be associated with Montfort at Kenilworth in 1253.

[50] *CPR, 1266–72*, pp. 222, 378; Moor, *Knights of Edward I*, iv, p. 232; Cam, 'Pedigrees of villeins and freemen in the thirteenth century', in her *Liberties and Communities*, p. 130.

[51] *CPR, 1247–58*, p. 31; *Excerpta e rotulis finium*, i, p. 388, ii, p. 36; Reichel, *Hundreds of Devon*, pp. 179, 343.

[52] *Calendar of Charter Rolls, 1226–57*, p. 385; ibid., *1257–1300*, p. 135; Moor, *Knights of Edward I*, i, p. 121; Cokayne, *Complete Peerage*, ii, pp. 230–1; below, p. 79.

[53] Some sheriffs kept on their predecessors' clerks and undersheriffs, e.g. William de Engleby and William Everard, PRO, *List of Sheriffs*, pp. 78, 122.

[54] Treharne, *Baronial Plan of Reform*, p. 207. Although Treharne makes much of the orders on the memoranda roll to all 'removable' sheriffs to attend the exchequer in various batches, on appointed dates from November 1259 to January 1260, along with four knights of their shires, to hear orders from the justiciar, this does not prove that sheriffs were now elected by knights of the shire. The memoranda roll makes no reference to the 'election' of sheriffs: PRO, E 159/33, mm. 4, 4d, 5, 6, 6d. Nor does it give any evidence of how the knights to accompany the sheriffs were to be chosen. Although these summonses were undoubtedly linked with shrieval

Provisions of Westminster of October 1259 state that sheriffs were to be chosen in that year by the justiciar, treasurer and barons of the exchequer, and Thomas fitz Michael was indeed appointed sheriff of Northumberland in this way.[55] But in their reply, given in April 1261 to the king's charges of misconduct, the baronial party professed (perhaps disingenuously) that sheriffs were not chosen by the council but by the four knights of each shire, a point repeated in the baronial case laid before Louis IX at Amiens in 1264.[56] The latter method had, indeed, been promised under the Administrative Provisions for the next series of sheriffs, which was never chosen. However, it must be significant that in January 1262 the baronial representatives in negotiations with the king merely proposed that, for ten years, properly qualified sheriffs should be selected by the king's council from the landholders of the shire.[57] As will become clear, it is more than likely, for all the barons' blustering in 1261 and the two above-mentioned examples of 'elections' found by Treharne, that the sheriffs of 1259 were centrally chosen (perhaps with some thought for local feelings), and that the baronial regime carried on, in this respect, much as before.

The sheriffs of 1259 were a broadly similar group to those of 1258, drawn from the administrative gentry. They certainly needed to be as carefully chosen as their predecessors because in fourteen cases the exchequer, in a surprising retreat from the custodial system laid down in the Provisions of Oxford, returned to the old method of putting the shire out to farm, even with increments.[58]

appointments (see the oaths recorded on m. 4d), it is worth noting that the sheriff of Essex-Hertfordshire had been appointed before the meeting (m. 2), and that there was a summons to the continuing sheriff of Cumberland, the earl of Aumale (d. mid 1260). Treharne, *Baronial Plan of Reform*, p. 208 n. 4, also notes that the nominee for the shrievalty of Norfolk-Suffolk, William of Stalham, did not take office, and that Hervey de Stanho was 'appointed' in his place. Both were knightly delegates, and it may be that Stalham refused the shrievalty. If so, this also suggests that the decision on whom to nominate as sheriff was not fixed beforehand in the localities. Dr Carpenter has suggested to me that the four knightly delegates were none other than the knights appointed under cap. 20 of the 'Administrative' Provisions of Westminster of 1259 to report on shrieval misconduct (Treharne and Sanders, *Documents of the Baronial Movement*, pp. 152–4). This is possible, but there is no evidence that they were 'elected'.

[55] PRO, E 159/36, m. 3d; Treharne and Sanders, *Documents of the Baronial Movement*, pp. 154–5, cap. 22.

[56] Ibid., pp. 220–3, cap. 3; pp. 262–3, cap. 10.

[57] Ibid., p. 155, cap. 22 (and see Treharne, *Baronial Plan of Reform*, p. 182–3); T. Rymer (ed.), *Foedera, conventiones, litterae*, Records Commission (3 vols in 6, London, 1816–30), i, pt i, p. 415. Dr Maddicott, however, has suggested to me that by 1262 the baronial representatives, facing defeat, may have been prepared to concede this point; and that their proposals for the shrievalty might not necessarily refer to the 'reformed' practice of earlier years.

[58] Those known to have been farmers (mainly from pipe roll evidence) are: Simon of Aslocton, Nottinghamshire-Derbyshire (*CCR, 1264–68*, p. 270; PRO, E 372/104, m. 17); Geoffrey of Cheetham, Lancashire (PRO, E 372/104, m. 13); John de Cobham, Kent (ibid., m. 6); William de Caverswall, Shropshire-Staffordshire (ibid., m. 5); Hervey de Stanho, Norfolk-Suffolk (ibid., m. 9); Richard de Tany, Essex-Hertfordshire (ibid., m. 11); Godfrey de Escudamore, Wiltshire (ibid., m. 13d); Walter de la Ryvere, Oxfordshire-Berkshire (ibid., m. 14); John de Walton, Surrey-Sussex (ibid., m. 15; PRO, E 159/33, m. 4d); Robert de Mulcaster, Cumberland appointed

Presumably, a system of custodial sheriffs was not so effective at raising revenue as the tried and tested method of farming.[59] Furthermore, the baronial regime allowed the 1259 sheriffs to remain in office for nearly two years, again in breach of the original Provisions. It is hardly surprising, therefore, that the new sheriffs were an elaborate mix of elements and that a few more old hands at the game were spirited back. Overall, changes were made at this time in twenty-two shires. Seven of the new sheriffs had experience in the office. Four were appointees from 1258, now moved on to adjacent shires (William Bagot to Warwick-Leicestershire; Hamo Hautein to Lincolnshire; Robert de Meisy to Hereford-shire; and Simon de Patteshull to Northamptonshire). Three sheriffs of the period before 1258 returned to the office: Alexander de Hamden to Bedford-Buckinghamshire, where he had been sheriff between 1249 and 1252; John de Vernun to Wiltshire, which he had administered as recently as 1255–58; and John de Scalariis to Cambridge-Huntingdonshire, which he held briefly in 1249. Furthermore, John de Cobham of Kent was the nephew of the previous sheriff, Reginald de Cobham (1249–57).[60] Philip de Cerne of Somerset-Dorset (the son of a previous undersheriff of Devon) had been escheator in Wiltshire in 1255, whereas Ralph de Doddiscombe of Devon had been escheator in his shire in 1257 and William de Wintreshull of Hampshire was a former forest official.[61] This means that in eleven appointments, half the number made in 1259, the exchequer opted for tried and tested men. All but two were suitably qualified as local landholders. It is not certain that Robert de Meisy held land in Herefordshire and Philip de Cerne's main lands and activities, despite his name, were in Wiltshire not Dorset.[62] In these last two instances, particularly, we can be fairly sure that there was no 'election' by the knights of the shire. In addition,

---

mid 1260 (PRO, C 60/57, m. 8); Alexander de Hamden, Buckinghamshire-Bedfordshire (PRO, E 159/34, m. 2d.; *The 31st Annual Report of the Deputy Keeper of the Public Records*, London, 1870, pp. 267, 357, 364–5; John de Oketon, Yorkshire (ibid.); John de Vernun, Wiltshire (ibid.), William de Wintreshull (Maciver, 'Aspects of the gentry of thirteenth-century Hampshire', p. 193, nos v–vi).

[59] Morris, *English Sheriff*, pp. 171–2; and see Carpenter, 'Decline of the curial sheriff', p. 3 n. 2, which points out that the custodial system was simply more troublesome to run, entailing more detailed accounting.

[60] PRO, *List of Sheriffs*, passim. For Cobham, see Quick, 'Government and society in Kent', pp. 192–3, 196, 226.

[61] For Cerne, see J. Hutchins, *The History and Antiquities of Dorset* (4 vols, 3rd edn, London, 1861–74), iv, p. 385; *CCR, 1254–56*, p. 92. Phillip was escheator in Wiltshire for barely a year, purchasing exemption from local office in February 1256 (ibid., p. 277; *CPR, 1247–58*, p. 462). Perhaps he was related to a certain Rannulf de Cerne, a Yorkshire sheriff's clerk in the 1240s, PRO, *List of Sheriffs*, p. 161. For Doddiscombe, *CCR, 1256–59*, p. 44. He was escheator again by 1263, *CPR, 1258–62*, p. 291. For Wintershull, *Calendar of Liberate Rolls, 1251–60*, p. 161.

[62] Philip de Cerne: *Book of Fees*, ii, pp. 743, 1178; of Draycot Cerne (Wiltshire), valued at £20 p. a. in 1250 (ibid., p. 1225). There are two references to his witnessing charters connected with Wiltshire landholders: *CCR, 1251–53*, p. 261; *Catalogue of Ancient Deeds* (6 vols, London, 1890–1915), iii, no. D 217. He was also escheator in Wiltshire. Hutchins, *Antiquities of Dorset*, iv, p. 385, does not link him with Dorset.

it is hard to think of the men of Bedfordshire and Buckinghamshire willingly electing Alexander de Hamden again to hold office over them at farm. There is good evidence that he was everywhere remembered as a harsh administrator who, in the vivid words of the hundred rolls enquiry, had introduced 'unjustly an injury called *beauplaider*' from which he raised enormous fines.[63] Nor is it likely that the men of Wiltshire elected John de Vernun, so recently ousted as sheriff in 1258. Experienced local official though he was, he may well have been unpopular. Such a suggestion is necessarily speculative, but six months after he had originally taken office, one of his sons had been murdered.[64] Rather, in the return to old methods and some old faces we have our first glimpse of a slackening in the baronial movement's reforming impetus and the reassertion of conservative elements.

These tendencies may well have been masked, if they needed to be, by the appointments made to the other eleven shires. Here there was a more definite continuation of the policies laid down in 1258. All the sheriffs were prosperous gentry and local landowners, and in four instances drawn from the ranks of the four knightly commissioners appointed in the shires in 1258.[65] If this group appears to include a greater number of apparently minor figures with little previous office-holding experience or connections, the impression is a misleading one created by the fact that eight individuals had avoided office during the 1250s by purchasing exemption. Most of them continued to hold local office after 1261, as we shall see.[66] A few, additionally,

---

[63] *Rotuli hundredorum*, 2 vols, Records Commission (London, 1812–18), i, pp. 4, 5, 7, 27, 38. Hamden was a local landholder of some substance: (*Book of Fees*, i, pp. 464–5), sheriff of Buckinghamshire-Bedfordshire, 1249–52 and 1259–64, dying in office; he was a bailiff of the Lord Edward, acting mainly in East Anglia, *c.* 1255, where he was remembered for his harshness (*CPR, 1247–58*, pp. 420, 423, 433; *Rotuli hundredorum*, i, pp. 486–7). He could be taken to epitomise the 'professional administrator' in local office.

[64] *CCR, 1254–56*, pp. 252, 263–4 (December 1255). Vernun, a local knight (*Book of Fees*, ii, pp. 710, 723), was sheriff of Wiltshire, April 1255 to June 1258, 1259–60, dying in office, late in 1260 (*Calendar of Liberate Rolls, 1260–7*, p. 110, *CCR, 1259–61*, pp. 71, 111; *CPR, 1258–66*, p. 163). He was coroner in Wiltshire until 1250, then escheator, 1250–5 (*CCR, 1247–51*, pp. 278, 384; ibid., *1254–56*, p. 92).

[65] Simon de Aslocton (Nottinghamshire-Derbyshire), John le Brun (Gloucestershire), Geoffrey de Cheetham (Lancashire), and Walter de la Ryvere (Oxfordshire-Berkshire) were knightly commissioners in 1258, *CPR, 1247–58*, pp. 645–49.

[66] Exemptions: William de Caverswall (1251), Philip de Cerne (1256), Thomas fitz Michael (1256), John de Oketon (1253), Hervey de Stanho (1257), Richard de Tany (1253), John de Walton (1253), William de Wintreshull (1257): *CPR, 1247–58*, pp. 93, 175, 192, 233, 462, 494, 537, 578. This is virtually all that is presently known about these knights before 1258, except that Wintreshull and Walton went on campaign with the king to Gascony in 1253: ibid., p. 233. As Waugh argues, such exemptions were generally obtained by those who could afford to buy them, or who had connections at court ('Reluctant knights and jurors', pp. 971–80). So we are certainly not dealing with nonentities here. By comparison, seven of the 1258 sheriffs had purchased various exemptions: William Everard and John du Plessis (1252), William de Engleby (1253), William le Moine and Eustace de Watford (1254), Robert de Meisy (1256), Anketil de Martival (1257): *CPR, 1247–58*, pp. 127, 163, 176, 387, 349, 536. Of these, le Moine and Watford went to Gascony in 1253–4.

were well-connected: John de Walton of Surrey-Sussex was in the earl of Gloucester's retinue in 1255 and was a Clare tenant in Surrey; Ralph de Doddiscombe of Devon was, like his predecessor, possibly a client of the Courtenays; William de Caverswall of Shropshire-Staffordshire was connected to the retinue of the earl of Derby; John de Oketon of Yorkshire was an executor of the king's secretary John Mansel in 1265.[67] Others were important in the shire in their own right, such as Richard de Tany in Essex-Hertfordshire.[68] In all, the appointee in 1259 differed little from that of 1258.

Since the letter of the Provisions of Oxford was considerably modified in practice, it might be asked whether the sheriffs of the baronial movement really offered a better regime for their localities than the men they replaced. On the financial front, it certainly seems that the terms offered to the localities by the custodial sheriffs reintroduced in 1258 were the most generous that they had experienced for many years. In Northumberland, for instance, John du Plessis accounted for a profit of a mere £26, nearly a third of the annual figure of £64 imposed upon his predecessors since 1247.[69] However, there are signs that in 1259 the exchequer desired to apply more pressure, with the reintroduction of farms and increments. Nevertheless, the sums demanded stopped well short of the extortion of recent years and so, from the sheriffs point of view at least, offered some margin for extracting profit from the office. In many cases, increments were reduced by a quarter, or even a third, against rates set in the 1250s, creating conditions reminiscent of those which prevailed in the late 1240s. Thomas Fitz Michael, the new sheriff of Northumberland, accounted for an annual increment of £40, a figure not increased again until 1269.[70] In Norfolk-Suffolk the increment

[67] *CCR, 1254–56*, p. 131; *CPR, 1258–66*, pp. 502, 633. Walton was one of the wealthiest of the 1259 sheriffs: for his lands, extending over several counties, see *Book of Fees*, ii, pp. 685, 692; *Calendar of Charter Rolls, 1257–1300*, pp. 88, 330, 403, 455. He succeeded in 1244, married the daughter of a former sheriff of Gloucester in 1255 and died *c*. 1305, having been sheriff again 1275–78: *CCR, 1242–7*, pp. 172, 191; ibid., *1254–6*, p. 131; Moor, *Knights of Edward I*, v, pp. 149–150. For Doddiscombe, see *CPR, 1247–58*, p. 31, where Doddiscombe is shown to have served in Gascony in 1248, apparently in the Courtenay retinue. For Doddiscombe's not inconsiderable estates, see *Book of Fees*, ii, pp. 759–60, 767, 790, 793; *Calendar of Inquisitions Post Mortem, Henry III*, p. 176. He was escheator in Devon *c*. 1257 and *c*. 1263–4, and from February 1262 to late 1264 (when he died), he held the wardenship of the Stannary in Devon *CPR, 1258–66*, pp. 200, 393; *CCR, 1261–64*, pp. 340, 381. For Caverswall: Staffordshire County Record Office, Acc. 938/487; 938/488 (both undated); I owe these references to the kindness of Professor Crouch.

[68] For an indication of Tany's wealth and importance, see *Calendar of Inquisitions Post Mortem, Henry III*, nos 764, 818, 888; *Calendar of Inquisitions Miscellaneous*, nos 189, 706. In the 1250s he invested heavily in charters of free warren and market rights, and even a double marriage deal with the courtier, Phillip Basset, activity on a scale altogether greater than the vast majority of knights under discussion here, *Calendar of Charter Rolls, 1226–57*, pp. 418, 429, 440.

[69] Hodgson, *History of Northumberland*, pt iii, vol. iii, pp. 212, 244–5.

[70] Ibid., pp. 253, 276–7. Dr Carpenter has pointed out to me that the 1259 increments could have been set at a level where they matched the allowances of 1258 but that, unfortunately, there

was 300 marks in 1259, compared with 400 marks a year charged in the mid 1250s. In Yorkshire the increment was 350 marks compared with 470 marks, in Hampshire, £66 compared with £80, and in Devonshire 100 marks compared with 130 marks. In Cambridge-Huntingdonshire an increment of sixty marks compared with one of eighty-five marks charged in the mid 1250s was reduced to fifty marks in 1261.[71] It is interesting to note that increments continued to be charged at these levels, more or less without alteration, for the remainder of Henry III's reign.[72]

Even so, in several shires the exchequer seems to have driven as hard a bargain as was possible under the political circumstances of 1259, and some sheriffs complained. It was noted against the £200 increment demanded from Hamo Hautein for Lincolnshire that, should he not be able to meet it, it could be reduced by £20.[73] Geoffrey of Cheetham, appointed to Lancashire, demanded, suggestively, a 'memorandum of what the sheriff was expected to perform for nothing'.[74] In Salop-Staffordshire, the 1259 increment was 150 marks p.a. (compared with 190 marks in 1257), but it must have been thought too high, for in 1261 it was reduced to 100 marks.[75] Thomas fitz Michael of Northumberland was deprived of the wards traditionally pertaining to the custody of the castle of Newcastle-upon-Tyne; and John le Brun of Gloucestershire was denied his predecessors' lucrative perquisite of the custody of Winchcombe manor and hundreds.[76] Some of the other 1259 sheriffs, for instance Simon de Patteshull of Northamptonshire, at first evaded taking charge of royal castles which would have had to be maintained at their private expense.[77] On the other hand, it is interesting to note the degree of diversity in the terms offered to the localities in 1259, though this quality is rather less marked than it had been before 1258. John de Cobham, for instance, was appointed to Kent in 1259 to render 500 marks' increment on the annual farm, barely different from the

is at present no means of knowing whether this was so, because there is little record (and nothing on the pipe rolls) as to the amounts of the 1258–9 allowances, or whether they were even received.

[71] Originalia rolls 44 and 45 Henry III (PRO, E 371/24, m. 1 schedule; E 371/25, m. 3 schedule) compared with earlier figures in Carpenter, 'Decline of the curial sheriff', pp. 22, 26, 29 n. 2; Maciver, 'Gentry of thirteenth-century Hampshire', p. 193, nos v–vi.

[72] Figures for the late 1260s are given in J. R. Maddicott, 'Edward I and the lessons of baronial reform: local government, 1258–80', in Coss and Lloyd, *Thirteenth-Century England*, i, pp. 5–6.

[73] PRO, E 371/24, m. 1 schedule; and see Treharne, *Baronial Plan of Reform*, p. 372.

[74] PRO, E 371/24, m. 1 schedule: 'memorandum etiam quod est gratis facienda'; it is a guess that Cheetham himself demanded this, although it must be significant that these questions were raised in 1259.

[75] PRO, E 371/25, m. 3 schedule; Carpenter, 'Decline of the curial sheriff', p. 22.

[76] PRO, E 159/36, m. 3d; E 371/24, m. 1 schedule (Winchcombe was restored to his successor in 1261).

[77] PRO, E 371/24, m. 1 schedule; the sheriffs of Hampshire, Herefordshire, Nottinghamshire-Derbyshire, Surrey-Sussex and Wiltshire are not charged, in contrast to their 1261 successors, with the custody of royal castles – although some may have taken custody later on in 1260.

arrangements terminated in 1258, whereas in Northamptonshire the 1259 increment of 100 marks was scarcely more than half the 180 marks demanded in 1257.[78] Similarly, in Cumberland Robert de Mulcaster, who replaced the earl of Aumale in May 1260, contracted to farm the shire at a mere £40 per annum.[79] Simon de Aslocton's contract for Nottingham-Derbyshire in 1259 was thought so generous by the king that in 1261 his successor, the courtier John de Balliol, was granted the shire on the same terms as a favour.[80] The general conclusion is that between 1258 and 1261 the baronial regime reduced the fiscal pressures placed upon most sheriffs during the 1250s, though it did so in varying degrees. Nor were these reforms reversed by Henry III, for the terms negotiated with the sheriffs of 1261 (most of whom took charge of castles) were often even more generous.[81] What is less certain is whether these advantageous terms were always reflected in the manner in which the sheriffs executed their responsibilities in the shires.

For in considering the actual conduct of the 1258–61 sheriffs we reach a very difficult matter. Unlike their well-documented predecessors, they were not subjected to any general enquiry on the scale of the *querelae* proceedings of 1258–9, or at least any which survive. Henry III, in a manifesto addressed generally to the localities in August 1261, justified his overthrow of the Provisions of Oxford and the replacement of the 1259 sheriffs with hand-picked knights of his own household by claiming that the sheriffs of the baronial regime were lesser men, lacking in authority, who could not stand up to the magnates who had put them in their positions. They could not defend ordinary folk against the oppressions of the magnates and, moreover, 'as we hear *on oath from some of you*, many magnates have occupied those things belonging to us and have compelled you to perform undue suits and other intolerable services'.[82] This argument, indeed, was first put forward by the king in his grievances against the council of March 1261.[83] Setting aside the strong suspicion that Henry was whistling in the dark about sworn depositions, there may well have been some damaging material on file, perhaps the annual reports on the sheriffs drawn up by the four knights of the shire and sent on to the justiciar, as laid down in cap. 20 of the

---

[78] Quick, 'Government and society in Kent', p. 230; PRO, E 372/104, m. 6; E 371/24, m. 1 schedule; Carpenter, 'Decline of the curial sheriffs', p. 22.

[79] PRO, C 60/57, m. 8.

[80] *CCR, 1264–68*, p. 270.

[81] This deduction is based on a comparison between PRO, E 371/24 and E 371/25 (originalia rolls, 1259–60, 1261). A good example of a reduction in the county farm is that of Alexander de Hamden, from 220 marks in 1259 to 200 marks in 1261. In five cases the 1261 terms are identical to those of 1259.

[82] Rymer, *Foedera*, i, pt i, pp. 408–9; cf. Treharne, *Baronial Plan of Reform*, pp. 362–4.

[83] Treharne and Sanders, *Documents of the Baronial Movement*, pp. 212–19, caps 5, 10; pp. 219–39, caps 3, 13, 14, 29. It is interesting that the king stressed this theme so heavily in these documents.

Administrative Provisions of Westminster of 1259.[84] But nowhere in his 1261 manifestos does the king allude to oppressions committed by the actual sheriffs themselves. For here is the rub: they were lesser men too shackled by legislation and the scrutiny of their peers in the localities for misconduct.

A few scraps of evidence can be gleaned from the hundred rolls enquiries of 1274–5. It may be significant that only one of our sheriffs was remembered in a completely positive fashion: John du Plessis of Northumberland (1258 to January 1260), who, along with the 'Montfortian' incumbent, Robert de Insula (1264–5), had not taken bribes or practised extortion.[85] Otherwise, apart from trivial complaints, more sins of omission than commission, there seems to be some grumbling, much of it of a circumstantial nature, that the 1258–61 sheriffs were too prone to carry on as before. Thus, Godfrey de Escudamore (Wiltshire 1258–9) 'oppressed the men of Old Sarum as his predecessors did before'.[86] This too was the complaint against Richard de Bagingden in Herefordshire, that he had farmed out the Hundred of Culvere to oppressive bailiffs as everyone had done before.[87] Such was the drift of the complaints remembered against William Bagot from his time as sheriff of Shropshire and Staffordshire in 1258–9, whereas from another time and another guise, as coroner, he was accused of receiving bribes from various vills of Staffordshire.[88] Hamo Hautein in Lincolnshire (1259–61) was accused, like his predecessors, of appointing evil and extortionate bailiffs in some wapentakes and even of defrauding a simpleton.[89] More serious, in the light of King Henry's 1261 manifestos, might be the evidence that in some counties the earl of Gloucester exploited his power on the council and his connections with various sheriffs to make hay in the localities while the sun shone. In Somerset and Dorset, for instance, both William Everard and his successor, Phillip de Cerne, were unable to prevent the earl from withholding from his estates suits due to the shire, such as sheriff's tourn or sheriff's aid, or from usurping liberties, such as plea of withernam or return of writ. The sheriffs of Essex-Hertfordshire also suffered at the earl's hands.[90] No doubt,

---

[84] Ibid., pp. 152–5.

[85] Hodgson, *History of Northumberland*, pt ii, vol ii, p. 293; *Rotuli hundredorum*, ii, p. 24.

[86] Ibid., ii, p. 268.

[87] Ibid., i, p. 187.

[88] Ibid., ii, pp. 67, 107, 109, 117, 225.

[89] Ibid., i, pp. 245, 247, 264, 450, 514. There is far more evidence of this type: for complaints against the sheriffs of Kent, ibid., i, pp. 202, 209, 224; Northumberland, ibid., ii, p. 24; Shropshire-Staffordshire, ibid., ii, pp. 109–11; Yorkshire, ibid., ii, pp. 113, 115–17, 120, 128, 130, 132; Cambridgeshire-Huntingdonshire, ibid., i, 407, 452, 481.

[90] Ibid., i, pp. 100, 191; ii, p. 132. I am grateful to Dr Maddicott for drawing my attention to this material. It is worth noting that at the height of his political ascendancy in the baronial council, in early 1260, Gloucester obtained a grant of the franchise of return of writ in his honour of Clare: *CPR, 1258–66*, p. 99; Ridgeway, 'Politics of the English royal court', pp. 361–3; M. T. Clanchy, 'The franchise of return of writs', *TRHS*, 5th series, xvii (1967), pp. 64–8. See also, Treharne, *Baronial Plan of Reform*, pp. 364–5.

other great magnates behaved in like fashion when they could. Indeed, satisfaction with the incumbent sheriffs' compliance may well explain why the magnates and the earl of Gloucester in particular did not see fit to change them at Michaelmas 1260.[91] However, before we take Henry III's complaints too seriously, we should recall Dr Carpenter's recent findings that, during his personal rule before 1258, Henry himself had been most lax and indulgent in allowing magnates to usurp liberties under the noses of the sheriffs.[92] It seems that there was little scope for the baronial reformers to do any worse.

There is, therefore, no very clear-cut or extensive evidence in the hundred rolls. Some sheriffs still behaved better than others. Perhaps the safest conclusion is that the relative scarcity of complaints, added to the known improvement in financial terms, makes it likely that the 1258–61 sheriffs marked at least some general improvement. Had this not been so, there would probably not have been uproar after Henry III overthrew the new system in 1261, when some shires were administered in 1261–2 by rebel sheriffs in defiance of the king's appointees.[93] However, this demonstration, much though Treharne made of it, does not necessarily prove that there was a widespread or spontaneous wave of nostalgia in the localities at the passing of the baronial regime. In the majority of shires the king was able to effect appointments which placed them under local landowners who were also either loyal magnates or knights of the royal households. These sheriffs, as previously shown, were under no heavier financial pressure from the exchequer than those of 1259. Where rebel sheriffs prevailed, not one of the 1258–61 sheriffs was reappointed. Indeed, there was a tendency for the rebel magnates in 1261 to impose their men on the shires, rather than permit local election of sheriffs, much as happened before. Ten rebels took charge of twelve pairs of shires, just under half the total, but at least half these areas were placed under two retainers of Simon de Montfort and two associates of Peter de Montfort and the earl of Gloucester.[94] Nevertheless,

---

[91] This is a further point I owe to Dr Maddicott. For Gloucester's political position by Michaelmas 1260, see Ridgeway, 'Politics of the English royal court', pp. 363–80, and the further considerations in Ridgeway, 'King Henry III's grievances against the council in 1261', *BIHR*, lxi (1988), pp. 231–32.

[92] Carpenter, 'King, magnates and society', pp. 49–52, 66–69.

[93] Treharne, *Baronial Plan of Reform*, pp. 267–72.

[94] Ralph Basset of Sapcote, Thomas de Estleye (both retainers of Simon de Montfort), John de la Haye (connected with Peter de Montfort, himself one of Simon de Montfort's closest retainers), and John de Eyville (connected with the earl of Gloucester) between them controlled five pairs of shires: Treharne, *Baronial Plan of Reform*, pp. 267–8; *CPR, 1247–58*, p. 31; Bodleian Library, MS Dugdale 13, f. 256; MS Dugdale 17, f. 33; HMC, *Report on the MSS of Lord Middleton* (London, 1911), pp. 67–9; M. W. Labarge, *A Baronial Household of the Thirteenth Century* (London, 1965), p. 139. For Ralph Basset's appointment as rebel sheriff of Leicestershire 'by letters of the barons which he received' (rather than local election), see PRO, E 368/36, m. 11d. Treharne, *Baronial Plan of Reform*, pp. 268–69, states that a further sheriff, John de Walton (sheriff of Surrey-Sussex 1259–61) was a rebel sheriff in those counties in 1261. I can find no corroborative

it is clearly important that when Simon de Montfort cast around for allies to buttress his personal rule in 1264–65, he thought it worthwhile for the time being to reintroduce the 1258 reforms in their entirety into the localities and, in a handful of cases, even to restore the 1258 sheriffs, though balancing these with his own hand-picked 'keepers of the peace'.[95]

My final line of enquiry is to investigate a little further the careers of the forty knights who participated as sheriffs in the first phase of the reform movement. What happened to them during the civil war between Henry III and Simon de Montfort, beginning in 1263, and the various struggles which followed? Apart from six who died in the meantime and six about whom little or no evidence can be found, these men are comparatively well documented.[96] The most striking observation is that so few of them took an active part during the Barons' Wars. Only four (or at most five) can be considered Montfortian rebels, while a further six actively supported the king's cause. The rest were lukewarm: thirteen trimmers to varying degrees and three apparently loyalist.[97]

The Montfortians were certainly some of the wealthiest and best-connected of the group, more barons than knights. William le Botyller's part in the war is obscure, but it is possible that he fought alongside Robert de Ferrers, earl of Derby, at the battle of Chesterfield. At any rate he submitted shortly afterwards, in July 1266, redeeming under the Dictum of Kenilworth his lands which had been given by the king to Prince Dafydd ap Gruffudd as

evidence for this, although it may reflect his earlier connection with the earl of Gloucester, now in opposition (above, p. 78). However, it must be noted that in July to October 1261 the king himself reappointed Walton to the shrievalty because his successor, William de la Zouche, was ill (*CPR, 1258–66*, pp. 163, 168, 177). In 1264 Walton was a Montfortian keeper of the peace: see below, p. 82.

95 Morris, *English Sheriff*, pp. 173–4, and below, p. 82.

96 Those who died were: earl of Aumale (1260), Peter de Foliot (1261), John de Vernun (*c.* 1260), Simon de Aslocton (*c.* mid 1260s), Ralph de Doddiscombe (1264), Alexander de Hamden (1264). Those for whom no sure evidence of political activity has been found are: John le Brun (Gloucestershire 1259–61, d. 1266, but see *CCR, 1264–68*, p. 127, which might suggest he was a Montfortian), William de Courtenay, Geoffrey de Cheetham, Thomas fitz Michael (Northumberland, 1260–1, d. 1267), Walter de la Ryvere (Oxfordshire-Berkshire 1259–61, but see *CCR, 1261–64*, p. 380, which might suggest he was a royalist), Philip de Cerne (but see *CCR, 1261–64*, p. 380, which suggests that Cerne was a royalist in 1264).

97 This seems to square with the conclusions reached by Jacob, *Studies in the Period of Baronial Reform*, pp. 276–329 (esp. p. 298), and D. A. Carpenter, 'Was there a crisis of the knightly class in the thirteenth century: the Oxfordshire evidence', *EHR*, xcv (1980), pp. 721–52 (esp. pp. 751–2). There was an important pioneering attempt to list individuals' loyalties in W. H. Blaauw, *The Barons' War* (London, 1871), pp. 363–80. While there is nothing in my analysis of individuals which directly conflicts with it, Blaauw's list clearly exaggerates the proportion of 'gentry' which favoured Montfort, since he worked from lists of forfeitures of rebel estates. In what follows, a fairly narrow interpretation of what constituted royalist or Montfortian sympathies has been employed. It also indicates, however, how misleading some of the evidence can be. The best discussion that can be found on the matter is in Jeremy Quick's important but unpublished thesis, Quick, 'Government and society in Kent', pp. 242–61. His conclusions broadly mirror mine, although he suggests a slightly greater proportion of Montfortians.

a grant worth £200 annually.[98] Simon de Patteshull's fate was similar: he redeemed his estates under the Dictum for a massive £900. He had fought at Northampton and Kenilworth, was a knight bachelor in the military household of the rebel Gilbert de Clare, and had been reappointed sheriff of Bedford-Buckinghamshire by de Montfort.[99] He is the only sheriff considered here who supported the posthumous miracle-cult of Simon de Montfort, claiming to have received healing in 1273 through the merits of the martyred earl.[100] Hamo Hautein had been appointed justice of the Jews briefly in 1265, perhaps through de Clare's influence, and he also joined the latter's revolt as a knight bachelor.[101] John de Cobham, another important figure, was accused by the king of having joined the rebels' forces in the siege of Rochester castle in 1264. But if he was deemed a rebel, he was quickly reconciled with the king, holding judicial office again by 1268, if not before.[102]

Richard de Tany submitted as a rebel in 1266. His name can be found on the list of baronial partisans in their case laid before the king of France at the Mise of Amiens in January 1264. He was returned to power in Essex by de Montfort in 1264, this time as keeper of the peace.[103] Tany had a good war. While he spent much of it systematically plundering the manors of Robert de Tattershall senior, a prominent loyalist in Essex, his son, Richard de Tany junior, conveniently placed himself in the royalist camp, in the entourage of that arch-careerist Sir Roger de Leyburn. The Tanys are thus a telling example of a prominent local family ensuring its success by hedging its bets in time of civil war. In February 1266, with Henry III now holding the upper hand, Richard de Tany junior was appointed as the new keeper of the peace in Essex.[104] Not surprisingly, his father made his peace with the king and was quickly pardoned. The family benefited from a licence to construct a park granted by de Montfort to Tany senior and Tany junior's money fee of £20 a year from the king. For a while, at least until his chicanery was exposed, Tany junior also held the choice plum of

---

[98] *CPR, 1266–72*, pp. 19, 22, 199; *CCR Supplementary, 1244–66*, no. 459; *CCR, 1264–68*, pp. 71–2; *Calendar of Charter Rolls, 1257–1300*, p. 135.

[99] *DNB*, xv, pp. 474–5; *CPR, 1258–66*, pp. 327, 528; *CPR, 1266–72*, pp. 145, 205, 326, *CCR, 1264–68*, p. 520.

[100] J. O. Halliwell (ed.), *The Chronicle of William de Rishanger and the Miracles of Simon de Montfort*, Camden Society, old series, xv (London, 1840), p. 106.

[101] C. A. F. Meekings, *Studies in Thirteenth-Century Justice and Administration* (London, 1981), chapter 4, p. 186; *CPR, 1266–72*, pp. 143, 147, 268.

[102] *CPR, 1258–66*, p. 316; *CPR, 1266–72*, pp. 255, 278, 320, 434, 475; *CCR, 1264–68*, p. 248; *CCR, 1268–72*, pp. 36–7; *Calendar of Liberate Rolls, 1267–72*, nos 1098, 2105; Moor, *Knights of Edward I*, i, p. 217.

[103] *CPR, 1258–66*, p. 575; Treharne and Sanders, *Documents of the Baronial Movement*, pp. 284–5; Rymer, *Foedera*, i, pt i, p. 422.

[104] Jacob, *Studies in the Period of Baronial Reform*, pp. 177, 194–5, 229–30; *CPR, 1258–66*, pp. 635, 655, 657; *Calendar of Charter Rolls, 1257–1300*, p. 175. For other examples of families with a foot in both camps, see Harding, 'Origins of the keeper of the peace', p. 95.

Theydon manor (Essex) which he had seized through a forged royal charter from Robert de Sutton, on the spurious grounds that the latter was a Montfortian rebel.[105]

The fervent royalists were figures such as William Bagot, who held the difficult portfolio as the king's sheriff from 1262–4 and 1265–71 in the Montfortian heartland of Warwick-Leicestershire. He profited from rebels' lands in the area and by 1268 had joined (and soon became seneschal of) the household of Henry III's younger son, Edmund, who granted Bagot the manor of Ashby St Ledgers in Leicestershire. So Bagot too had a good war, although he deserved to do so more than Richard de Tany.[106] Others held shires for the king against Montfortian insurgents. The veteran royalist Alexander de Hamden held Bedford-Buckinghamshire until his death in 1264. The position of Simon de Hedon in Nottingham-Derbyshire was similar. William le Moine was keeper of the peace in Cambridge-Hunting-donshire.[107] John de Oketon held out in Scarborough castle against de Montfort and the king reappointed him sheriff of Yorkshire in 1266, before Oketon gravitated to the household of Prince Edmund.[108] William le Latymer, who had risen from the Yorkshire shrievalty to a place in the world of high diplomacy, helped present Henry III's case at the Mise of Amiens in 1264.[109]

There was also a handful of knights who, while less striking in their loyalty to the king, none the less did him some good service. William Everard served on inquisitions in 1263, was summoned by the king to his forces in mid 1264 and in 1265 was a royal commissioner confiscating rebels' lands in Somerset after the battle of Evesham. Thereafter, he was periodically active in local affairs until his death in 1279.[110] William de Caverswall continued in office in Shropshire-Staffordshire after 1261 as the undersheriff of his successor, the powerful local magnate, James de Audley. He was presumably loyal during the war, although this was a strongly Montfortian area, and was appointed sheriff again in 1268–70 as well as serving on later county

---

[105] *CPR, 1258–66*, pp. 394, 548; *Calendar of Charter Rolls, 1257–1300*, pp. 57, 165 (which indicates Tany junior's continued nervousness about the consequences of civil war in 1271); Jacob, *Studies in the Period of Baronial Reform*, pp. 199–201. Tany senior died in 1270 (*Calendar of Inquisitions Post Mortem, Henry III*, no. 764).

[106] Wrottesley, 'History of the Bagot family', pp. 130–7.

[107] *CPR, 1258–66*, pp. 315, 327, 360, 592–3, 610–11, 634, 646. Simon de Hedon was again sheriff of Nottinghamshire-Derbyshire, 1267–69, and William le Moine sheriff of Cambridgeshire-Huntingdonshire, 1275–8.

[108] *CPR, 1258–66*, pp. 333, 346, 390–1, 491, 501, 590; *CPR, 1266–72*, p. 172; *Calendar of Charter Rolls, 1257–1300*, pp. 135, 161–2; *CCR, 1268–72*, p. 265. Oketon was also an executor of the king's secretary, John Mansel, in 1266 (*CPR, 1258–66*, pp. 502, 633). For his later career as royal justice in the north, see Moor, *Knights of Edward I*, iii, p. 284.

[109] *Complete Peerage*, vii, pp. 460–1; *CPR, 1258–66*, p. 294. Latymer was again sheriff of Yorkshire, 1266–67 (d. 1268).

[110] *CCR, 1261–64*, pp. 205, 381; *CPR, 1258–66*, p. 490; *Calendar of Liberate Rolls, 1267–72*, no. 2073; Moor, *Knights of Edward I*, i, p. 316.

commissions.[111] The pattern of Robert de Mulcaster's career was very similar. All we can tell of his allegiances is that he was appointed to confiscate rebels' lands for the king in 1265, serving for the next two decades on local commissions in Cumberland.[112]

The conduct of these men may be easier to understand, however, when considered alongside that of the large and interesting group of trimmers. Between 1264 and 1265 Simon de Montfort reappointed as sheriffs Richard de Bagingden in Herefordshire, Fulk Peyforer in Kent, Eustace de Watford in Northamptonshire, John de Scalariis in Cambridge-Huntingdonshire and Harvey de Stanho in Norfolk-Suffolk. In the same period, three of those who had served as sheriff between 1258 and 1261 were appointed as keepers of the peace: John de Walton in Surrey and Sussex, Godfrey de Escudamore in Wiltshire and John du Plessis in Northumberland.[113] The surprising point about these knights is that none was punished by the king after 1265 for serving under the rebel regime. Nor is there any mention of them under the elaborate definition of 'rebellion' in the Dictum of Kenilworth. Indeed by 1265 three, Fulk Peyforer, John de Walton and Richard de Bagingden, were eagerly seizing rebels' lands on the king's behalf.[114] These men went on to occupy local offices with hardly a break: Fulk Peyforer was sheriff of Kent again in 1267–8.[115] Hervey de Stanho performed a local inquiry in 1266 and when, in 1270, a review was taken of his tenure of office in 1264–5 he was not termed a 'rebel' sheriff at all, but pardoned outstanding debts on account of the difficulties he encountered in carrying out his duties.[116] Eustace de Watford was pardoned by the king in 1268 for 'any trespasses charged against him in the time of the recent disturbances', but this was in return for his 'long services'.[117] John de Walton and John du Plessis were used by the king in local administration between 1266 and 1272, and were rewarded with grants and favours.[118] Even Anketil de Martival, de Montfort's steward and emissary, was immediately reconciled with the king.[119]

---

[111] *CCR, 1261–64*, p. 192; *Calendar of Liberate Rolls, 1267–72*, no. 1857; Moor, *Knights of Edward I*, i, p. 187. He received a grant from the king in 1262: *CPR, 1258–66*, p. 197; VCH, *Staffordshire*, i, pp. 227–8; VCH, *Shropshire*, iii, pp. 16–17.

[112] *CPR, 1258–66* p. 491; *Calendar of Liberate Rolls, 1267–72*, no. 2131; Moor, *Knights of Edward I*, iii, p. 232.

[113] *CPR, 1258–66*, pp. 327, 347; Rymer, *Foedera*, vol. i, pt i, p. 442; PRO, *List of Sheriffs*, passim.

[114] *CPR, 1258–66*, pp. 491, 651.

[115] *CPR, 1266–72*, pp. 124, 173, 230, 236, 269, 693.

[116] *CPR, 1258–66*, p. 671; *CCR, 1268–72*, p. 207. For his later career in royal service, see *CPR, 1266–72*, pp. 678–9; Moor, *Knights of Edward I*, iv, p. 276.

[117] *CPR, 1266–72*, pp. 248, 621. He was a justice of gaol delivery in 1266 and still active in local office in 1272, *CPR, 1258–66*, p. 631; *Calendar of Liberate Rolls, 1267–72*, no. 1305.

[118] *CCR, 1264–68*, pp. 160, 268; *CCR, 1268–72*, p. 588; *Calendar of Charter Rolls, 1257–1300*, p. 88; *Calendar of Inquisitions Miscellaneous*, nos 677, 1185, 2234; *CPR, 1266–72*, pp. 400, 465, 605. Walton was sheriff of Surrey-Sussex again in 1275–78.

[119] Farnham and Thompson, 'The manor of Noseley', pp. 219–23. Martival remained sheriff of Rutland for Richard of Cornwall until 1272.

It is now well known that Henry III showed great clemency towards Montfortian rebels, wisely aiming to pacify his realm as quickly as possible after the recent civil war.[120] Additionally, as we have seen, several Montfortians had been drawn into the conflict merely as followers of greater men. Others by 1265 enjoyed the patronage of important magnates whose support the king now needed to cultivate. Godfrey de Escudamore may well have belonged to this category. His swift reconciliation with the king probably stemmed from the protection of his powerful kinsman, the arch-turncoat Sir John de Giffard, who in turn came within the orbit of the Clares. Godfrey's son, Peter, joined the earl of Gloucester's rebellion in 1267 in Giffard's retinue. Yet he too was swiftly reconciled to the king and can later be found, like his father, in local office in Wiltshire.[121]

It is difficult to provide such a clear interpretation of the conduct of most of the knights under discussion. More typical was the convoluted experience of Richard de Bagingden. Between 1262 and 1263 the king restored him to the shrievalty of Herefordshire, to which he had originally been appointed in 1259. Then, in June 1264, he duly received a writ from the Montfortians ordering himself and two other knights of the shire to 'elect' a sheriff.[122] The lot fell, once again, to Bagingden, who was kept busy by the new regime on a round of commissions and arbitrations, and even the defence of Hereford castle against insurgent royalists.[123] However, in May 1265 the Montfortian council, for an unknown reason, overturned the election and replaced Bagingden with someone else. By September 1265 Bagingden was in the royalist camp, impounding rebel lands.[124] The king appointed him sheriff once again, in 1267 (after, as it would appear, the courtier Gilbert Talbot had again refused the job), and he died in office a year or so later. His son, Richard junior, who had served as undersheriff, acted as sheriff until Michaelmas 1269.[125] In the exotic world of marcher politics it was difficult to choose whether to be rebel or loyalist: Richard junior was momentarily caught out and denounced as a rebel in 1265.[126] The obvious point is that in a civil war reliable and willing men who could administer the localities were in short supply. In Herefordshire, for both Simon de Montfort and Henry III, only Richard de Bagingden could fit the bill. In other words, this was not the behaviour of partisans of the reformers but the twists and turns of gentry with family traditions of administrative service to the

[120] C. H. Knowles, 'The resettlement of England after the Barons' War, 1264–67', *TRHS*, 5th series, xxxii (1982), pp. 25–43.

[121] *CPR, 1266–72*, pp. 21, 35, 86, 222, 378; *CCR, 1264–68*, pp. 187, 215; *Calendar of Charter Rolls, 1257–1300*, p. 73; Moor, *Knights of Edward I*, iv, 232–3. Escudamore senior died in 1266.

[122] *CPR, 1258–66*, pp. 198, 265, 328.

[123] Ibid., pp. 397, 481; *Calendar of Inquisitions Miscellaneous*, no. 291.

[124] *CPR, 1258–66*, pp. 426, 491.

[125] PRO, *List of Sheriffs*, p. 59; *CPR, 1266–72*, p. 161.

[126] *Calendar of Inquisitions Miscellaneous*, no. 936.

government of the day, caught with varying degrees of suffering and inconvenience in the cross-fire of civil war.

Such a view seems consistent with the main observations of this essay about the interaction between central government and the localities in the mid thirteenth century. In the first place, the analysis of Jacob and Treharne, that in 1258 the barons entered into an alliance on equal terms with the gentry of the localities, responding to pressure from below and permitting them to elect their own representatives and sheriffs, cannot be sustained. In the first flush of emergency, declarations of openness and reform may have been made, but a closer look at the baronial council shows it to have been as authoritarian in its dealings with the localities as any of its predecessors. Apart from its rather patchy distribution of financial relief, the advantage for the localities of the baronial reforms was not so clear cut as was once believed.

Once the emergency had passed, some of the less practical aspects of the Provisions of Oxford and the Ordinance of Sheriffs were quietly laid aside, regardless of the wish of the localities. Yet while old ways were restored, the regime continued to show the pragmatic edge essential to effective government by taking care to avoid a repetition of the confrontation which had built up in the 1250s. Whether Henry III, when his power was restored in 1261, was so foolish as to undo all the gains made since 1258 is a point which requires a study of its own. However, it has been shown that the king certainly did not restore the unacceptable financial pressures of the 1250s. In that respect, at least, the remainder of the reign saw no attempt to turn back the clock.

As for the response of the localities themselves, if the forty knights under discussion are in any way typical, they reveal political attitudes in the 'Period of Baronial Reform' which were more ambiguous than past commentators have allowed. To describe them as tepid might not be unjust. That is not to deny that many were caught up in the conflict between the king and his opponents; or were even, once the two parties had crystallised, inspired by the respective 'royalist' and 'baronial' ideologies.[127] What we should discard is the assumption that, while Montfort and the reformers had lost magnate support by 1263, they retained that of the gentry. On the contrary the ambivalent attitudes of the knightly class must have played their part in precipitating the downfall of Simon de Montfort in 1265.[128]

In their efforts to remedy the abuses of the shrieval office, the reformers faced three primary obstacles. First, as a result of Henry III's divisive rule before 1258, the diversity of conditions and traditions between localities, as well as the variable quality of candidates for office, meant that the rigid

---

[127] Ridgeway, 'Politics of the English royal court', chapter 9, passim.
[128] I am very grateful to Dr Maddicott for this point.

enforcement across the shires of a unitary pattern of management, however well intended, was impractical, even undesirable. Furthermore, there existed a profound gulf between the politics of the centre, which sometimes tended towards idealism, and the realities at work at local level, where magnate affinities were often the principal determinants of political life. Thus in Shropshire-Staffordshire control of the shrievalty was clearly one of the key objectives in the protracted feuding between the great families of Audley, Strange and Corbet, as they struggled to dominate those counties in the 1250s and 1260s. While the south-western shires were particularly active in campaigning for their liberties during the 1240s and 1250s, their sheriffs under the baronial regime of 1258–61 were some of those most demonstrably under the influence of the great magnates.[129] Further research will undoubtedly reveal many more knights and gentry who were subject to the pressures of 'bastard feudalism'.[130]

The final obstacle to reform was the antipathy of many knights towards holding office as sheriff. The tendency towards professionalisation of the office under Henry III, which allowed the shrievalty to be monopolised by networks of administrative families in certain areas, narrowed the government's choice of potential agents in the execution of any intended change or reform. S. L. Waugh has shown that, once the crisis of 1258 had passed, the ensuing period of reform went only part of the way towards tackling the difficulties posed for effective local government by the practice of selling exemptions from office. As indicated above, the 1258 Ordinance of Sheriffs did not necessarily increase the attractiveness of the office to many. It was impossible to raise a full set of new sheriffs even in 1259.[131]

Some changes were begun in 1258, some reform was achieved, but three years were hardly enough. The difficulties were many and the localities full of challenging complexities. It is doubtful whether Montfort and the reformers, trammelled by their haste and by the precarious status characteristic of a rebel opposition, really did (or could have done) more than offer temporary financial relief and identify some other issues which required redress. It may be doubted whether they really consulted the political will of local society. As S. L. Waugh and J. R. Maddicott have demonstrated, it was the crown, in the person of Edward I with his authoritative and thorough approach, which later on provided effective solutions. Under Edward reform of a sort became a reality, consolidating that peculiarly English and

---

[129] VCH, *Shropshire*, iii, pp. 14–17; above, pp. 69, 70, 74, 77; Maddicott, 'Magna Carta and the local community', p. 41.

[130] Crouch et al., 'Debate: Bastard Feudalism revised', pp. 165–203. This issue is explored at length in S. Walker, *The Lancastrian Affinity, 1361–1399* (Oxford, 1990). See also, A. J. Gross, 'The king's lordship in the county of Stafford, 1312–22', *Midland History*, xvi (1991).

[131] See above, pp. 72–3; Waugh, 'Reluctant knights and jurors', pp. 984–5. I owe the point about the 'professionalisation' of sheriffs to Dr Studd.

constitutionally momentous legacy from the middle ages: local administration performed by unpaid local knights and gentlemen.[132]

---

[132] Waugh, 'Reluctant knights and jurors', p. 985; Maddicott, 'Edward I and the lessons of baronial reform', pp. 1–30. See also, J. Gillingham, 'Crisis or continuity? The structure of royal authority in England, 1369–1422', in R. Schneider (ed.), *Das spätmittelalterliche Königtum im europäischen Vergleich* (Sigmaringen, 1987), pp. 71–2, 76–80. Since the completion of this essay, Dr C. H. Knowles has very kindly drawn my attention to his unpublished thesis, '"The Disinherited", 1265–80' (unpublished university of Wales Ph.D. thesis, Aberystwyth, 1959), pt ii, pp. 67–81, where some aspects of the political outlook of knights, 1258–67 are discussed. I am glad that, working independently, I have reached broadly similar conclusions. Also in agreement is P. R. Coss, *Lordship, Knighthood and Locality: A Study of English Society, c. 1180–1280* (Cambridge, 1991), pp. 273–6, 305–326.

5

The Commons and the Early Justices of the Peace under Edward III

Anthony Verduyn

Edward III's reign has long been recognised as a period of profound develop-ment in the history of parliament, and particularly of the house of commons. In this assembly representatives of the shire communities were brought into direct contact with the king and his government: parliament was an interface between the centre and the localities. The mid fourteenth century was also a period of change in the administration of the shires, particularly in the judicial system. Peace commissions were rising in importance in the dispens-ation of justice. This period saw the development of opinions by the commons in parliament on these changes, and this illustrates the complexities inherent in the relationship of central authority and local opinion.

The keepers of the peace had a history stretching back to the twelfth and thirteenth centuries. They were largely drawn from the gentry of the shires, but they were usually selected by the king and council. Until 1308 the use of keepers was usually confined to being crisis measures against acute disorder. The keepers often had a military function, although their work was usually the taking of indictments preparatory to gaol delivery sessions. They had no power to hold trials themselves but their work became increas-ingly important as the amount of trespass litigation rose.

Under Edward II the keepers of the peace effectively became a permanent part of the local judicial establishment.[1] Then, under Edward III, they were occasionally given powers to conduct trials and they became justices. Until the 1350s the appointment of these justices of the peace was irregular and their power was often circumscribed by the appointment of magnate overseers. The king and council several times preferred to appoint leading magnates and lawyers on general commissions of oyer and terminer, com-monly called trailbastons. However, after 1350, the justices of the peace

---

[1] A. Harding, 'The origins and early history of the Keepers of the Peace', *TRHS*, 5th series, x (1960), pp. 85–109; VCH, *Wiltshire*, 13 vols. (1957), v, p. 31; M. Gollancz (ed.), *Rolls of Northamptonshire Sessions of the Peace*, Northamptonshire Record Society, xi (1938), pp. ix–xx; B. H. Putnam (ed.), *Kent Keepers of the Peace, 1316–1317*, Kent Archaeological Society, xiii (1933), pp. xv–xxi.

became more established and the gentry became an increasingly important element in the dispensation of justice in the shires. This apparent rise in gentry authority at the expense of the king and his magnate and lawyer counsellors has been thoroughly examined by B. H. Putnam and her followers.

In her seminal article of 1929, 'The transformation of the keepers of the peace into the justices of the peace, 1327–1380', B. H. Putnam outlined what was to become the orthodox interpretation of the development of the justices of the peace under Edward III.[2] In her view there were two schools of thought on the operation of justice in the shires. Many leading royal counsellors, headed by Geoffrey le Scrope, chief justice of the king's bench, believed powerful commissions composed of leading judges and magnates should periodically tour the country under general commissions, such as trailbastons or the general eyre. However, from 1327 the commons in parliament and their supporters favoured the conversion of keepers of the peace into justices. This would increase the power of the local gentry who typically served as both keepers of the peace and knights of the shires in parliament. Throughout Edward III's reign, and particularly in the period before the Black Death, there was constant vying between the two schools of thought: in 1327 keepers of the peace were appointed throughout England, but the minority government soon appointed magnate overseers to supervise their work; in 1328 trailbaston commissions were issued; in 1329 justices of the peace were appointed for the first time, but they were rapidly overshadowed by a revived general eyre, and in 1331 they were formally demoted to keepers again and a new trailbaston began; in 1332 justices of the peace were appointed for the second time, they were almost immediately overshadowed by new special commissions dominated by magnates, but similar in composition and powers to justices of the peace, and called 'keepers of the counties'; in 1335 new keepers of the peace were appointed with special powers of arrest, but in 1336 they were replaced by another trailbaston; in 1338 justices of the peace were appointed for the third time although, once again, magnates were appointed to oversee their work; in the early 1340s peace keeping was dominated by major trailbaston commissions, but justices of the peace still operated; and in 1344 both justices of the peace and trailbaston commissions were withdrawn, and keepers of the peace reinstituted. Only after the Black Death were justices of the peace regularly appointed, and even then there were several changes in power before 1377, including the loss of authority to try felons between 1364 and 1368.[3] The rise of the justices of the peace was anything but smooth.

---

[2] B. H. Putnam, 'The transformation of the keepers of the peace into the justices of the peace, 1327–1380', *TRHS*, 4th series, xii (1929), pp. 19–48; also see introduction to B. H. Putnam (ed.), *Proceedings before the Justices of the Peace in the Fourteenth and Fifteenth Centuries: Edward III to Richard III* (London, 1938).

[3] A similar reduction of powers occured in the 1380s: E. Powell, 'The administration of

Frequent changes in the administration of justice, particularly in the late 1320s and 1330s, apparently support B. H. Putnam's thesis that there were two vying schools of thought. Furthermore, crediting the commons with the eventual establishment of the justices of the peace fits neatly with general interpretations of Edward III's political relations with the gentry at large. Edward III used parliament to secure taxation for his French wars, and historians have often contended that the price for concessions was the levelling off or reduction in 'royal activism' in the country at large.[4] This relaxation is apparent in the rise of the justices of the peace. The justices' first appointments were short-lived, but once war with France became the norm the king conceded the maintenance of law and order to them as the commons requested. This concession was a key development for peaceful domestic politics. However, such conventional political interpretations of Edward III's reign have recently been challenged. W. M. Ormrod has convincingly demonstrated that the French wars did not precipitate a decline in royal government. Indeed, after the political crisis of the early 1340s, the king rapidly consolidated his authority and governed with great success for the following thirty years. The middle years of his reign were marked by careful political management and capable administration at home as well as much military success abroad.[5] In such circumstances the king was unlikely to have been forced into making substantial concessions and he typically acted according to his own perceived interest. So why did the king allow justices of the peace to become established? To answer this question properly the situation from 1327 onwards has to be reassessed.

The argument that there were two competing schools of thought in judicial policy is difficult to sustain. The evidence that the commons supported the creation of the justices of the peace is nowhere near as unequivocal as B. H. Putnam suggested. The key commons petition for her argument was submitted in the first parliament of Edward III's reign in 1327.[6] It stated that good and loyal men should be appointed to keep the peace in the counties and that they should have the power to punish offenders according to the law. However, this petition has to be understood in context. Keepers of the peace had been well established in Edward II's reign and some of them had exercised power as justices. For instance, a few keepers had been appointed to deliver gaols, and thus tried people who had been originally

criminal justice in late medieval England: peace sessions and assizes', in R. Eales and D. Sullivan (ed.), *The Political Context of Law: Proceedings of the Seventh British Legal History Conference, Canterbury, 1985* (London, 1987), p. 55.

[4] R. W. Kaeuper, *War, Justice and Public Order: England and France in the Later Middle Ages* (Oxford, 1988), pp. 290–2.

[5] W. M. Ormrod, 'Edward III and the recovery of royal authority in England, 1340–1360', *History*, lxxii (1987), pp. 4–19; W. M. Ormrod, *The Reign of Edward III: Crown and Political Society in England, 1327–77* (London, 1990).

[6] *RP*, ii, 11 (40), response 12 (40).

indicted before them.[7] Furthermore, as recently as 1326 keepers had been given power to amerce people who refused to assist them in their sessions.[8] Such power actually led some people to describe the keepers as justices under Edward II.[9] It may have been that in 1327 the commons thought they were doing little more than propose an extended form of current practice. The request was certainly not a major element in commons demands at the parliament. For instance, it was notably absent from the first draft of the commons' petitions.[10] The request was apparently accepted by the king and council, but powers to hold trials were neither mentioned in the statute that resulted from parliament nor in the subsequent nationwide commissions.[11] As in 1326, the keepers had power to amerce people in certain circumstances.

After 1327 there were no more commons' petitions in favour of the creation of justices of the peace before their appointment in 1338.[12] Indeed, the situation is quite the opposite. If one was to assume that the commons were dogmatic, it would be considerably easier to suggest that they favoured trailbaston commissions to peace commissions. The ordinance of trailbaston was promulgated in parliament in 1305, and an examination of trailbaston commissions issued between 1318 and 1339 shows that they were all the result of parliaments with the commons in attendance. The trailbaston of 1318 was the result of a petition in the name of the prelates, earls, barons and 'all the commonalty of the realm'. The trailbaston of 1320 was also the result of such a petition. Furthermore, a petition of around this date, only in the name of the commonalty of the realm, requested the extension of the powers of the trailbaston justices.[13] No similar petitions in favour of justices of the peace under Edward II exist. The trailbastons of 1328 and

[7] Putnam, *Kent Keepers*, pp. xx–xxi.

[8] Gollancz, *Northamptonshire Sessions*, p. xviii; E. L. G. Stones, 'Sir Geoffrey le Scrope, chief justice of the king's bench, 1324–1338' (unpublished university of Glasgow Ph.D. thesis, 1950), p. 130. Granting powers of amercement could have been the result of a letter from some keepers complaining that they needed powers to constrain people to come before them: PRO, SC 1/36/172. Powers to amerce uncooperative people were continued under Edward III: Putnam, 'Transformation', p. 26.

[9] *RP*, i, 379 (72). Somerset keepers of the peace in April 1327 called themselves 'justices': PRO, KB 145/2/2/8, m 2.

[10] H. G. Richardson and G. O. Sayles (ed.), *Rotuli parliamentorum Anglie hactenus inediti, MCCLXXIX–MCCCLXXIII*, Camden Society, 3rd series, li, (1935), pp. 116–26.

[11] *Statutes of the Realm*, i, 257 cap. 14; *CPR, 1327–30*, pp. 88–90.

[12] However, most surviving commons petitions are concentrated in 1333, 1334 and 1337: Richardson and Sayles, *Rotuli parliamentorum*, pp. 224–239, 267–272. The petitions for 1337 are often misdated to 1339, see E. B. Fryde, 'Parliament and the French war, 1336–1340', in T. A. Sandquist and M. R. Powicke (ed.), *Essays in Medieval History Presented to Bertie Wilkinson* (Toronto, 1969), p. 256 n. 34.

[13] M. C. Prestwich, *Edward I* (London, 1988), p. 285; H. Cole (ed.), *Documents Illustrative of English History in the Thirteenth and Fourteenth Centuries*, Record Commission (1844), pp. 6–7; F. Palgrave (ed.), *Parliamentary Writs* (2 vols, 1830), ii, appendix 135, 154–5; *CPR, 1317–21*, pp. 298–300, 548–9; PRO, SC 8/80/3960.

1331 were direct results of discussions in parliament, although the extent of commons involvement is unknown.[14] The trailbaston of 1336 was the indirect result of parliament. In an ordinance made after a parliament in March the king had promised to appoint justices to make summary arrests and hold trials throughout the realm, but he failed to honour this. In a great council at Nottingham in September the commons pressed him on his promise and the king gave way.[15] The resulting trailbaston maintained marked support from the commons and in the parliament of March 1337 they stated that it had 'begun well' and that it should be continued. The king and council were not so satisfied. They stated that complaints were being received that the trailbaston was doing more harm to magnates and good people than it was to the criminals.[16]

Here is a perfect example of B. H. Putnam's thesis turned on its head: the king, council and magnates opposed to a trailbaston and the commons supporting it. The commons petition was successful and the trailbaston continued, although the justices were warned to carry out their duties properly. This success was short-lived. Three months after the parliament, the trailbaston justices were ordered to wind up proceedings. The government said the operation of the courts was hindering the array of men for war. This may have been true. However, the decision was probably taken at the council of Stamford in late May. It may have been that in this, the first council since the last parliament, the magnates had complained about their interests continuing to be damaged by the commissions. The king may have forsaken the trailbaston for the goodwill of the magnates in the coming war.[17] The purpose of outlining these examples is not to suggest that all trailbastons were appointed at the behest of the commons. The important point is that the commons did not concentrate their support on peace commissions. Indeed, a good deal of the time, commons attitudes seem to have *responded* to recent policy rather than directed it: they favoured the advancement of keepers of the peace in 1327 after keepers had been extensively used since 1308; they favoured keepers of the counties in 1333 and 1334 following their appointment in 1332; and they favoured the maintenance of the 1336 trailbaston in 1337. Furthermore, the commons in 1339 thought the justices of the peace appointed in the preceding year had been successful and should continue in their work.[18] Essentially the commons were conservative in their outlook. They tended to accept innovations from the king and council, or complain at the lack of action, rather

---

[14] *Statutes of the Realm*, i, pp. 257, 259 cap. 7; *CPR, 1327–30*, p. 297, *1330–34*, pp. 133–4.

[15] *Statutes of the Realm*, i, p. 277; Richardson and Sayles, *Rotuli parliamentorum*, pp. 268 (2), 271 (2); *CPR, 1334–38*, pp. 367–71.

[16] Richardson and Sayles, *Rotuli parliamentorum*, pp. 268 (2), 271 (2).

[17] *CCR, 1337–39*, p. 134.

[18] *RP*, ii, 11 (40), 104 (10); Richardson and Sayles, *Rotuli parliamentorum*, pp. 225 (7), 232–3 (2), 268 (2).

than propose new initiatives. The most consistent element in their petitions seems to have been their general support for gentry involvement in judicial commissions. The support for the keepers of the peace was most probably based on the fact that the gentry who composed the commons in parliament usually held that office. The gentry were significant amongst the keepers of the counties appointed in 1332. However, in 1334 the commons did not pursue the appointment of members of the gentry as justices to complete the business of keepers of the counties.[19] Commons support for the trail-baston of 1336–37 was also based upon the large numbers of the gentry who were appointed as justices alongside lawyers: magnates had been poorly represented on these commissions and that probably explains their dislike of them.[20]

This analysis leads to a difficult question. If it was not the commons who favoured the creation of justices of the peace, then why were they appointed in 1329, 1332 and 1338? Furthermore, how can the frequent changes of judicial policy in the first decade of Edward III's reign be fully explained?

The appointment of justices of the peace in 1329 can best be understood in the context of the politics of the minority regime of Isabella and Mortimer (1327–30). In the late 1320s peace-keeping was an important political issue. Edward II had singularly failed to maintain order during much of his reign and there was turmoil when he was overthrown.[21] In his coronation oath Edward III promised to do justice equally and properly to his subjects, but this could not be achieved until there was peace in the country.[22] Immediately after the coronation was not a good time for action on peace keeping because of the more pressing demands of achieving a political settlement. Reliance was placed on new keepers of the peace and the issuing of special commissions of oyer and terminer (authoritative panels of justices appointed to deal with serious crimes). Later in March magnates were appointed as supervisors of the keepers of the peace in the most disturbed counties and where the unstable government felt most threatened.[23]

In April 1328 parliament met at Northampton. For contemporaries the most important work of the parliament concerned the ratifying of an un-satisfactory peace with Scotland. Historians have been more struck by the

[19] Ibid., pp. 232–3 (2).

[20] Ibid., p. 268 (2); *CPR, 1334–38*, pp. 367–71.

[21] For a detailed study of the politics of the minority see P. C. Doherty, 'Isabella, queen of England, 1296–1330' (unpublished University of Oxford D.Phil thesis, 1978). For examples of disorder in the cities and towns see J. A. Tuck, *Crown and Nobility, 1272–1461* (London, 1985), p. 90; VCH, *Northamptonshire* (4 vols, 1930), iii, p. 8; G. Lambrick, 'Abingdon and the riots of 1327', *Oxoniensia*, xxix–xxx (1964–5), pp. 129–41; M. D. Lobelt, 'A detailed account of the 1327 rising at Bury St Edmunds and the subsequent trial', *Proceedings of the Suffolk Institute of Archaeology and Natural History*, xxi (1933), pp. 215–31.

[22] *CCR, 1327–30*, p. 100.

[23] *CPR, 1327–30*, pp. 88–90, 152, 154, and passim; *CCR, 1327–30*, p. 204.

issuing of a statute concerning law and order and leading to the appointment of the first trailbaston commissions of the new reign. Apparently the commons pressed for action, but the council probably decided on the form this should take.[24] Although identified as crucial to peace-keeping efforts in subsequent years, the initial achievements of the parliament and Statute of Northampton were hardly impressive. A broad swathe of English counties was omitted from the trailbaston and the operation of these courts rapidly ground to a halt as tensions between Isabella and Mortimer and the recalcitrant Henry, earl of Lancaster, led towards civil war. As the crisis deepened the earl of Lancaster used the failure to maintain law and order as a weapon against Isabella, Mortimer and the young king. Similarly Isabella and Mortimer used the provisions of the Statute of Northampton concerning the prohibition of riding armed against the earl, and oaths taken by magnates to help reduce disorder, as propaganda.[25] In January 1329 the minority government successfully outfaced Lancaster. Relations with France then came to dominate affairs. The young king was dispatched to France in May to do homage for his French lands. Eight days before his departure justices of the peace were appointed throughout England for the first time.[26]

In the context of recent political events the creation of justices of the peace can be seen as the government reemphasising its concern for peace-keeping after damaging civil disobedience. However, there was more to it than that. Traditionally, when kings left the realm special precautions were made to keep the peace in their absence. For instance, when Edward II went to do homage for his French lands in 1307 keepers of the peace were specially appointed, a precaution repeated during his absence in 1320. In 1314 keepers of the peace were appointed when Edward II went to Scotland.[27] For Edward III the appointment of keepers of the peace upon his departure to France would not have had the same symbolic value that it had had for his father. This was because keepers had already effectively become a permanent feature of the local judicial system. Furthermore, their permanence had been acknowledged in a statute of 1327.[28] The government's answer to this problem was to issue especially powerful peace commissions: they created the first true justices of the peace. B. H. Putnam offered an alternative interpretation of events in 1329. She believed that the commissions represented a triumph for the party that favoured justices of the

---

[24] *Statutes of the Realm*, i, pp. 257–61; *CPR, 1327–30*, p. 297; H. M. Cam, 'The general eyre, 1329–30', *EHR*, xxxix (1924), pp. 241–52.

[25] A. H. Thomas (ed.), *Calendar of Plea and Memoranda Rolls: 1323–64* (6 vols, Cambridge, 1926), pp. 78, 81; *CCR, 1327–30*, pp. 413, 418, 420–1; *CPR, 1327–30*, p. 355. For the course of the rebellion and further references to the statute of Northampton see G. Holmes, 'The rebellion of the earl of Lancaster, 1328–29', *BIHR*, xxviii (1955), pp. 84–9.

[26] *CPR, 1327–30*, pp. 429–31.

[27] Putnam, *Kent Keepers*, pp. xvii–xx; Gollancz, *Northamptonshire Sessions*, pp. ix–xx.

[28] *Statutes of the Realm*, i, 257, cap. 16. A similar statute was promulgated in 1330: ibid., i, 261–2, cap. 2.

peace, notably the commons in parliament.[29] However, this cannot easily be sustained in the circumstances of 1329. The most recent parliament had ended three months earlier and there is no evidence of any commons' petitions having been submitted at it. Furthermore, only one knight from the parliament was appointed as a justice of the peace in May, far fewer than was usual if a commission was associated with a parliament.[30]

On the young king's return from France the problems of law and order were debated again. At the council of Windsor it was decided to revive the long moribund general eyre.[31] This did not supplant the justices of the peace, who continued to operate in many counties.[32] In autumn 1330 a palace coup established the personal rule of Edward III. In the parliament of November 1330 he replaced the eyre with trailbaston commissions, which allowed the swift prosecution of corrupt officials whose action had been tolerated by Mortimer and Isabella. In the same parliament justices of the peace were formally demoted to keepers. In fact, in some counties justices of the peace had already been behaving like keepers by allowing men indicted before them to be tried by justices of gaol delivery.[33] It would seem that the intention was to simplify matters and to avoid a surfeit of justices in the counties. The trailbaston continued until late 1331, but by that time the king had tired of seeking to punish the officials of his father's and mother's regimes. The minority was viewed as an embarrassment best forgotten. The king thus reestablished good relations with his mother and dropped the trailbaston.[34]

November 1331 saw the effective end of the trailbaston, but not the end of law and order problems. In February 1332 justices of the peace were to be appointed again, but in very different circumstance to those of 1329. On 14 January 1332 the infamous Folville gang robbed, abducted and ransomed Richard Willoughby, a puisne justice of the king's bench. A great council had been summoned to meet on 20 January 1332, and the abduction was probably known then.[35] Parliament was summoned for 16 March, but in the

---

[29] Putnam, 'Transformation', p. 27.

[30] *Return of the Names of Every Member Returned to Serve in Each Parliament, 1213–1874*, 2 vols, Parliamentary Papers (1878), ii, pp. 87–8, compared with commissions in *CPR, 1327–30*, pp. 429–31. Similar comparisons have been made for later parliaments and commissions.

[31] Cam, 'General Eyre', pp. 241–52; D. Crook, 'The later eyres', *EHR*, xcvii (1982), pp. 261–2; D. W. Sutherland (ed.), *The Eyre of Northamptonshire 3–4 Edward III, 1329–30*, 2 vols, Selden Society, xcvii–xcviii (1983), i, pp. xxvi–xxxii.

[32] For references see Putnam, 'Transformation', p. 27 n. 9.

[33] *Statutes of the Realm*, i, 261–2, cap. 2; Putnam, 'Transformation', p. 27.

[34] Doherty, 'Isabella', p. 320. Isabella's pension was converted from cash to land in the autumn parliament of 1331 and later that year Edward III named his eldest daughter after her: *RP*, ii, pp. 61–2 (8); E. M. Thompson (ed.), *Chronicon Angliae, 1328–1388*, Rolls Series (1874), p. 4. The birth was erroneously recorded under 1334.

[35] E. L. G. Stones, 'The Folvilles of Ashby-Folville, Leicestershire, and their associates in crime, 1326–1347', *TRHS*, 5th series, vii (1957), p. 122. Richard Willoughby had been summoned to the great council: *Report Brought from the Lords on the Dignity of a Peer* (4 vols, London, 1826), iii, pp. 406–7.

meantime justices of the peace were appointed on 12 February. B. H. Putnam characterised the appointment of justices of the peace in 1332 as evidence of a persistent conflict of opinions in peace-keeping.[36] However, given the circumstances, it seems more likely that the appointment of justices of the peace was a response to the crisis in law and order.

The parliament that met in March 1332 further discussed the crisis in peace-keeping. Geoffrey le Scrope outlined the problem posed by gangs like the Folvilles. The lords alone were asked for their advice and on their behalf Henry de Beaumont proposed that magnates should be appointed as justices in each county, with justices of the peace, sheriffs and other officials 'attendant' upon them. The magnates should array local people to resist and capture gangs, even assisting in their pursuit if necessary. Beaumont also suggested that the king should personally tour the country to check on the work of these noble 'keepers of the counties' and, if necessary, reinforce them with his own men.[37] The advantage of this course of action for the magnates was obvious. It would give them considerable extra power with minimal supervision. However, they may not have been totally cynical. Many magnates already had considerable personal influence in the localities and judicial authority as justices of the peace. Furthermore, their plan was clearly related to a recent magnate undertaking to obey the law and assist in its enforcement.[38] The magnates' proposal was approved by king, prelates and commons and rapidly put into effect. However, the commissions issued included some changes of plan with powers of array exchanged for special powers of arrest. Furthermore, the commissions were issued not just to magnates but also to lawyers and members of the gentry.[39]

B. H. Putnam saw the appointment of keepers of the counties as very distinctive. No mention was made in their commissions of the statute of Winchester, which she believed was needed to create keepers or justices of the peace, or of the statute of Northampton, an important part of recent legislation.[40] In fact, the differences between the keepers of the counties and the justices of the peace that preceded them are somewhat exaggerated: the keepers of the counties were little more than justices of the peace with a few additional powers, and the personnel of the commissions was largely identical. Similarities in powers and personnel probably extended to similarities in the execution of their duties. Despite the wording of their commissions the keepers of the counties conducted the trials of trespasses and felonies as if they had authority to enforce the statutes of Winchester

[36] *CPR, 1330–34*, pp. 285–8; Putnam, 'Transformation', p. 28.

[37] *RP*, ii, pp. 64–5 (5).

[38] *CCR, 1330–33*, p. 422.

[39] *RP*, ii, p. 65 (11); B. H. Putnam, 'Shire officials: keepers of the peace and justices of the peace, 1327–1380', in J. F. Willard, W. A. Morris and W. H. Dunham (ed.), *The English Government at Work, 1327–1336* (3 vols, Cambridge, Massachusetts, 1940–50), iii, pp. 192–3; *CPR, 1330–34*, pp. 292–7, 348–9.

[40] Putnam, 'Transformation', pp 23–4, 29.

and Northampton.[41] In effect, the keepers of the counties acted like especially powerful justices of the peace.

In the September parliament of 1332 Scottish affairs dominated discussions, but there was some attention given to peace-keeping. It was felt that the crisis had passed and there began the replacement of keepers of the counties and, by extension, justices of the peace with keepers of the peace.[42] No doubt the king wished to free magnates and senior councillors from judicial work, so that they could concentrate on the coming war with Scotland. It was the rapid removal of the keepers of the counties that inspired complaints from the commons and calls for commissions properly to finish their work in 1333 and 1334.[43] However the years 1333 to 1335 saw little judicial innovation. The king was apparently too concerned about the war with Scotland to do much more than issue proclamations to keep the peace and authorise the appointment of a few special commissions to maintain order in particularly troubled areas.[44] It was only in 1335 that the king apparently started taking notice of law and order problems, and appointed keepers of the peace; and only in 1336, when he finally conceded another trailbaston, that action started to be effective. Even then the trailbaston was removed as the king began preparations in 1337 for a new war with France.[45]

The events surrounding the appointment of justices of the peace in 1338 are complex and can only be summarised here. Despite the king and council sacrificing the trailbaston of 1336–37, there can be little doubt that they recognised the risk of disorder once the king had left the country on campaign. The situation looked all the more dangerous by April 1338 when rumours of threatened French invasion began to spread.[46] The king and council responded with a unique consultation process. They met with knights who had been personally summoned from each of the counties of England. These knights composed lists of men suitable to be appointed to defend the coast, array men and keep the peace.[47] Interestingly, these lists included many magnates and some bishops, as well as members of the gentry. The bishops were no doubt principally chosen to help with defence rather than judicial matters.[48] From these lists it is apparent that the king and council

---

[41] *CPR, 1330–34*, pp. 285–8, 292–7, 348–9; Putnam, 'Shire officials', pp. 192, 200–1.

[42] *CCR, 1330–33*, p. 610.

[43] Richardson and Sayles, *Rotuli parliamentorum*, pp. 225 (7), 232–3 (2).

[44] *CPR, 1330–34*, pp. 445, 495–6, 573–4, 584; *1334–38*, pp. 70, 136; *CCR, 1333–37*, p. 120; Putnam, 'Shire officials', p. 194; Putnam, 'Transformation', p. 31.

[45] *CPR, 1334–38*, pp. 208–10; see above, nn. 15–17.

[46] H. J. Hewitt, *The Organization of War under Edward III, 1338–62* (Manchester, 1966), p. 3. I hope to publish a detailed analysis of the events of 1338 shortly.

[47] T. Rymer (ed.), *Foedera, conventiones, literea et cujuscunque generis acta publica*, Record Commission edn (3 vols, London, 1816–30), ii, 1013–14; PRO, C 267/9, mm. 1–18; SC 8/35/1714; SC 8/107/5327; SC 8/115/5741; SC 8/142/7077; SC 8/264/13186.

[48] The text of some of the nominations hints at the defence obligations of the clergy: PRO,

had sought the nomination of keepers of the peace rather than justices of the peace. The knights of Cornwall and Devon suggested in their nominations that the men should be appointed as justices, but there is no other evidence to suggest that most knights, or the shire communities, tried to influence the form of commission the king would issue upon his departure. As it was, the king and council did not seem to be too impressed with the men the knights nominated. Just under 40 per cent of the people appointed in July had been nominated, the rest were either knights summoned to the April meetings or other men chosen by the king and council.

On 6 July 1338 the king and council appointed justices of the peace throughout England. The next day eighteen noblemen were appointed as overseers.[49] These commissions were clearly timed to coincide with the king's departure for the Low Countries on 16 July. Authority to hold trials was only given for offences committed after the date upon which the commission had been issued, underlining the link with anticipated disorder. The justices and overseers also had powers to array men for defence. A great council met at Northampton on 26 July and the commissions to the overseers were changed: the number of commissions rose from seven to ten and the number of magnates on each commission was increased. Senior judges were also added. Overseers were now given summary powers of arrest.[50] The justices of the peace were the leading officials maintaining order throughout the country between 1338 and 1340: the overseers seem to have largely been inactive in judicial matters.[51]

The creation of the justices of the peace in 1329, 1332 and 1338 was unconnected with parliament or pressure from the commons. Indeed it is ironic that, although none of these commissions was issued as a result of parliament, they were all to be withdrawn in parliaments.[52] It would seem that each time the justices of the peace were appointed it was in response to specific circumstances: the absence of the king abroad in 1329 and 1338, and a particularly serious crime wave in 1332. The search to identify a school of thought in the council or the country at large that favoured the use of

SC 8/35/1714; SC 8/264/13186. For the role of bishops and others in defence in general, see A. K. McHardy, 'The English clergy and the Hundred Years War', in W. J. Sheils (ed.), *The Church and War*, Studies in Church History, xx (1983), pp. 173–4; B. McNab, 'Obligations of the church in English society: military arrays of the clergy, 1369–1418', in W. C. Jordan, B. McNab and T. R. Ruiz (ed.), *Order and Innovation in the Middle Ages: Essays in Honor of Joseph R. Strayer* (Princeton, 1976), p. 298 and passim; D. Hughes, *A Study of Social and Constitutional Tendencies in the Early Years of Edward III* (London, 1915), p. 20; Hewitt, *Organization of War*, pp. 11–13.

[49] *CPR, 1338–40*, pp. 134–40.

[50] Ibid., pp. 141–2.

[51] Overseers did act against disorder in Cumberland and Sussex, but apparently not elsewhere: M. S. Arnold (ed.), *Select Cases of Trespass from the King's Court, 1307–1399*, Selden Society, c (1984), pp. 44–5; N. Saul, *Scenes from Provincial Life: Knightly Families in Sussex, 1280–1400* (Oxford, 1986), pp. 73–4; PRO, KB 145/2/13; C 81/251/11513; *CCR, 1339–41*, p. 94.

[52] In November 1330, September 1332 and June 1344 respectively: see above, nn. 33 and 42, and below, n. 66.

peace commissions is a vain one. Similarly, it seems unlikely that there was any group wholly opposed to peace commissions and supportive of trailbastons or eyres. B. H. Putnam was never able to present any clear evidence that Geoffrey le Scrope objected to peace commissions, while E. L. G. Stones in his biographical thesis is notably cagey about ascribing these views to him. After all, under this long-lasting chief justice of the king's bench, justices of the peace were appointed nationwide on two, or probably three, occasions. As E. L. G. Stones commented: 'One may suspect that Scrope's part in this, as in politics, may prove to have been dictated substantially by considerations of immediate advantage to the government of the day'.[53] It might be added that the government's action on peace-keeping was not above criticism. It is clear that there were frequent and radical changes in policy over much of the period 1327 to 1338. In broad terms this was the result of governmental weakness. These years were marked by frequent changes in the incumbents of important offices of state, and faltering policies can be identified not only in peace-keeping, but also in strategy towards the wool staple and the organisation of escheators.[54] Government in this period found it difficult to maintain any medium- or long-term policies and the constant changes in commissions, although often explicable in their various circumstances, are really a reflection of this.

The 1340s form a contrast to the preceding years of Edward III's reign. There were less frequent changes of policy by the government, and the commons began to give lasting support for the justices of the peace. The decade began with a major political crisis. The king in the Low Countries had been demanding vast sums of money to maintain his ineffective war effort. The home council was incapable of maintaining supply and on the night of 30 November 1340 the king suddenly returned to take his revenge on them. There followed a rapid series of arrests as the king rounded up key councillors. He then embarked upon a very public campaign to collect information against them and all other royal officials who had failed him.[55] On 10 December trailbaston commissions were issued; justices were to hear and determine all manner of offences committed by officials from the keeper

[53] Stones, 'Geoffrey le Scrope', passim; quotation from E. L. G. Stones, 'Sir Geoffrey le Scrope (*c.* 1280 to 1340), chief justice of the king's bench', *EHR*, lxix (1954), p. 12.

[54] Ormrod, *Reign of Edward III*, pp. 83–4.

[55] Many works discuss the arrests of 1340: for a vivid near contemporary account see G. J. Aungier (ed.), *Croniques de London*, Camden Society, xxviii (1844), pp. 83–86. Other works on the political crisis and the judicial commissions include: G. L. Harriss, *King, Parliament and Public Finance in Medieval England to 1369* (Oxford, 1975), chapter 13; Ormrod, *Reign of Edward III*, pp. 14–18 and passim; Hughes, *Constitutional Tendencies*, pp. 100–211; N. M. Fryde, 'Edward III's removal of his ministers and judges, 1340–41', *BIHR*, xlviii (1975), pp. 149–61 (see especially 149 n. 4); W. R. Jones, '*Rex et ministri:* English local government and the crisis of 1341', *Journal of British Studies*, xiii (1973), pp. 1–20; G. O. Sayles (ed.), *Select Cases in the Court of King's Bench*, 7 vols, Selden Society, vi (1936–71), pp. xvi–xix.

of England down to subtaxers and their clerks. Before the next parliament met in April 1341 trailbaston powers were extended. The justices were given authority to hear cases of offences committed as far back as the start of Edward II's reign, and they were to take wages out of the fines they levied so that they would do their work more 'forcefully'. The king issued public assurances that he would not be reconciled with corrupt officials and a show trial of Richard Willoughby, ex-chief justice of the king's bench, took place to emphasise the seriousness of the king's intent.[56] However, the trailbaston of December 1340 was to prove highly unpopular.

In the parliament of April 1341 commons and lords were united in their opposition to the trailbaston. The commons complained that such burdensome commissions had not been issued before without their consent. Strictly speaking, this was a spurious claim but it was not without foundation in events of the last two decades or more.[57] Most commons complaints centred on the exploitation of the courts by the king and malpractice by the justices of trailbaston, rather than legalistic claims. Before the parliament met the king had authorised the acceptance of fines of up to 2000 marks, and he was also willing to take collective fines from all the officials and ex-officials of a shire to stay further presentments. The acceptance of this in some shires, with, for instance, Essex offering 3000 marks, illustrates the desperation felt in some areas. The commons complained that both individual and apportioned collective fines bore more relation to the wealth of the individual than they did to the scale of alleged offence. In response the king conceded the right of appeal against the size of collective fines and that future assessments would only take account of alleged offences and not personal wealth.[58]

The trailbaston justices engaged in several irregular procedures. They issued a common summons calling all people to come before them and amerced those who failed to attend, irrespective of whether they were usually resident in the county or not. Amercement for failure to attend the common summons had been limited to eyres since 1259, and this practice was clearly onerous and illegal.[59] There were also problems with trial juries. Sheriffs were maliciously nominating non-resident or indisposed men to juries so that they would be amerced in their absence. The justices also allowed men who had served on presenting juries to act as trial jurors. This was not strictly illegal, but it was definitely frowned upon.[60] Furthermore, people

---

[56] *CPR, 1340–43*, pp. 108, 111–13; Sayles, *King's Bench*, v, p. cxxxviii; PRO, SC 1/62/85; Aungier, *Croniques de London*, p. 87; L. O. Pike (ed.), *Year Book of King Edward III*, 15 vols, Rolls Series (1883–1911), Years 14 and 15, pp. 258–262.

[57] See above, nn. 13 to 17.

[58] Hughes, *Constitutional Tendencies*, pp. 167–8, 209–11; *RP*, ii, pp. 128 (14), 133 (63, 64). Suffering was also recorded in private petitions, PRO, SC 8/52/2590.

[59] *RP*, ii, p. 128 (14); Hughes, *Constitutional Tendencies*, p. 169.

[60] *RP*, ii, pp. 128 (14), 134 (66); T. A. Green, *Verdict According to Conscience: Perspectives on the English Criminal Trial Jury, 1200–1800* (London, 1985), p. 22.

were being put in exigent (the first stage of outlawry) by the trailbaston justices for offences which did not strictly speaking constitute felonies or trespasses against the peace, such as fraud in the wool trade.[61] On questions of the composition of juries and the use of outlawry, the king and council agreed a temporary ban on irregular practices until the next parliament. The commons proposed the replacement of the current trailbaston with one composed of lawyers and men knowledgeable about the activities of royal officials, apparently meaning the gentry. A review of the trailbaston commissions in the presence of members of the lords and commons was promised. Ultimately the parliament ended with the trailbaston being allowed to continue, but with its scope, and various of its practices, limited.[62]

From the petitions of 1341 it is clear that the commons did not yet object to trailbaston commissions as such. However, they sought to establish some sort of parliamentary control over their appointment, powers and procedures. Over the following two years the extent to which the commons had failed to achieve this became clear. When the king departed for Brittany, in October 1342, new commissions of oyer and terminer were issued for twenty counties. These 'new inquiries' were primarily concerned with illegal trade in coinage and in wool, but also investigated desertions by archers and the failure of requisitioned ships to aid the king's passage.[63] They were issued without consultation with the commons and the next parliament did not meet until May 1343. The commons took up many of the complaints from 1341 again, but still persisted with attempts to reform rather than replace trailbastons. They sought the selection of new justices in parliament with the consent of the lords and commons, and the declaration of the terms of the commissions. The king and council agreed to part of this request. The main points of new commissions were drawn up in parliament and presented for the approval of the commons. They concentrated on crime in general, conspiracy, tax fraud and the disturbance of royal courts. The agreements of 1341 suspending abuses concerning outlawry and the selection of jurors were renewed. The commons secured various concessions on the levying of common fines, and won a ban on their use in future.[64] By 1343 it was no doubt clear that the common fines were much more burdensome than the ordinary sessions and fines of the trailbastons.

Once parliament had ended the new trailbaston commissions were issued. It is unlikely that the commons exercised any control over the selection of justices, but the men appointed were senior royal judges or had notable local judicial experience. This accorded somewhat with the commons' desires although, perhaps more importantly, it followed recent government practice. The wording of the commissions was less in line with commons thinking:

---

[61] *RP*, ii, p. 134 (65).
[62] Ibid., ii, pp. 128 (14), 131 (40).
[63] *CPR, 1340–43*, pp. 585–6.
[64] *RP*, ii, pp. 136–7 (11), 137 (12), 139 (21), 140 (30), 140–1 (34).

the articles published in parliament had concentrated on crime and the malpractices of officials. However, the commissions concentrated on investigating officials and deserters from the king's forces, and only briefly referred to criminal jurisdiction.[65] Neither did these new commissions replace the old ones of December 1340 and October 1342. In 1343 there was a general intensification of trailbaston activity, rather than an alleviation of this burden on the country.

The parliament of 1344 marked a watershed in commons' attitudes and the policy of the king and council. The parliament had been called to discuss the king's problems with France and the need for taxes to finance the war. The commons were more concerned about the trailbastons. They complained bitterly that fines and ransoms were 'more to the destruction of the people than their amendment'. They called for the removal of the trailbastons and their replacement with new, revitalised peace commissions. They proposed that these should be composed of two of the most notable men of the county, with between two and four other knowledgeable men, presumably meaning knights and lawyers. The new justices were to have full power to hear trials and inflict punishments. The commons had now finally abandoned attempts to regulate trailbaston commissions, and set their face to removing them and creating peace commissions powerful enough to make them unnecessary. Commons success was very mixed. The king and council approved the removal of trailbaston commissions and the 'new inquiries' of 1342 and authorised the issue of new commissions to keepers of the peace. When necessary, lawyers were to be assigned with keepers to try men who had been indicted.[66] Considering that justices of the peace had been operating throughout much of England between 1338 and 1344 with powers to hear and determine felonies and trespasses, the new commissions amounted to demotion for peace commissions. The trailbastons were removed, as the commons wished, but the justices of the peace were not to replace them.

The new keepers of the peace were appointed on 20 July 1344, between three and six keepers being assigned to each county and almost all being drawn from the gentry.[67] Over the following five years, twenty-eight commissions were issued to lawyers and keepers to try the men indicted before the keepers of the peace. These commissions touched only eleven counties and this resulted in a rather haphazard arrangement in peace-keeping.[68] For instance, commissions to hold trials were issued four times in Dorset, Huntingdon and Worcester, but never in Devon, Cambridge or Hereford.

---

[65] *CPR, 1343–46*, pp. 97–8; compare to *RP*, ii, p. 137 (12).

[66] *RP*, ii, p. 148 (12); *Statutes of the Realm*, i, p. 301, cap. 2.

[67] *CPR, 1343–46*, pp. 393–7.

[68] *CPR, 1343–45*, pp. 507, 510, 572–3; *1345–48*, pp. 31, 105–7, 111, 169–70, 175–6, 241, 301, 306, 310, 318, 472; *1348–50*, pp. 64, 75, 79, 235, 457. The number of commissions here does not accord with that given by B. H. Putnam because of different treatment of the parts of Yorkshire and Lincolnshire: Putnam, 'Transformation', p. 42.

A few records that survive from Huntingdon suggest that the frequent issue of trial commissions allowed the keepers and lawyers to act like justices of the peace there. However, this must have been unusual and the known work of the keepers of the peace in Nottinghamshire suggests that in counties where no trial commissions were issued, keepers acted more conventionally.[69]

In trial commissions lay the first stage in the development of the quorum, an arrangement by which one of a specified inner group of justices of the peace had to be present at trials. The trial commissioners, like the quorum justices who were to succeed them, usually featured the justices of assize for the given county.[70] This link between assizes and trials of men indicted before peace commissions was not wholly new. As far back as Edward II's reign men indicted before keepers of the peace had been tried before justices of gaol delivery. Under the statute of Northampton gaol delivery was supposed to be carried out by the justices of assize. During the 1330s, with commons' support, the union of the assizes and gaol deliveries became the norm.[71] In this way the bond between keepers of the peace and justices of assize and gaol delivery had been established before. In 1344 the difference was that, where trial commissions were issued, the gentry keepers were associated with the justices who were to deliver indicted criminals. Elsewhere and in the past this had not been the case. From 1350 the assize justices were usually incorporated in all peace commissions.

If any courts took on the work of the trailbastons it was probably the assizes. In the mid and late 1340s it was these that were relied upon increasingly by the king and council. After 1344 they often heard trials of men indicted before keepers of the peace, either in special commissions alongside the keepers or in their capacity as justices of gaol delivery. In 1346 justices of assize were given authority under an ordinance to hear cases against sheriffs and other shire officials, and to inquire into maintainers and the perversion of juries. In the same year they also received powers to hear and determine cases of the importation and circulation of false money.[72] The accumulation of these powers in 1346 was closely linked to the king's impending departure on campaign in France. Once again he seems to have been taking some precautions concerning maintaining order during his absence.

The commons in the September parliament of 1346 had clearer ideas about how the peace should be kept during the king's absence. The king

---

[69] PRO, KB 145/2/22, mm. 151, 152, 198, 199; KB 145/2/23/1.

[70] Powell, 'Peace sessions and assizes', p. 51; Putnam, 'Transformation', p. 42. Under Edward III the association was only broken in the 1360s: Powell, 'Peace sessions and assizes', pp. 51, 58–9.

[71] *Statutes of the Realm*, i, pp. 257–8, cap. 2 (this confirmed Edward I's statutes unifying the justices of assize and gaol delivery: ibid., i, pp. 129–30 cap. 4); Richardson and Sayles, *Rotuli parliamentorum*, p. 235 (11); M. M. Taylor, 'The justices of assize', in Willard et al. (ed.), *English Government at Work*, iii, p. 238.

[72] *Statutes of the Realm*, i, p. 305, cap. 6; *CPR, 1345–48*, p. 182.

had left the country in July 1346 and the commons proposed that justices of the peace should be appointed to hear and determine offences committed since then.[73] The petition was concise, but subtle. It drew a parallel between contemporary events and those of 1338: in 1338 the king had appointed justices of the peace to deal with crimes committed during his absence. Now that the king had just embarked upon another major campaign in France, the commons sought a repetition of this measure. The widespread and justified fear that crime would rise in the absence of the king had no doubt encouraged the commons.[74] However, the response reiterated the practice begun in 1344: good men would be appointed to keep the peace and lawyers added when cases were to be tried. In the two parliaments of 1348 the commons continued their opposition to trailbaston commissions.

Although no nationwide trailbaston commissions were issued after 1344, there was good reason to be concerned. In 1346 a trailbaston commission was issued to Surrey, in January 1348 another went to Lancashire. Meanwhile in summer 1347 general eyres had been proclaimed in Wales, and in December a forest eyre in Cheshire.[75] Furthermore, many shire communities were still feeling the effects of the commissions of seven or eight years before. Northamptonshire still had more than £337 to pay of their common fine of 1341.[76] In 1348 the commons commented that trailbastons were inclined to be burdensome without being effective against lawlessnes. A tax on moveables was granted in the March parliament and the commons tried to set a condition saying that neither eyres nor trailbastons of the king or prince of Wales should be issued during the three years in which the tax was to be collected. They also petitioned that neither the king nor the prince of Wales should hold eyres and general inquiries during the war.[77] Despite this commons request, the king did proclaim an eyre in Kent in September 1348, following the death of the archbishop of Canterbury. It was cancelled following payment of £1000, and a 200 mark fine for the justices and eyre officials.[78]

The commons petition for the appointment of new justices of the peace in 1346 had been turned down, but in both of the parliaments of 1348 the commons petitioned again, and they were much more precise about what was required.[79] In January they proposed that commissions should be composed

---

[73] *RP*, ii, p. 161 (20).

[74] B. A. Hanawalt, *Crime and Conflict in English Communities, 1300–1348* (London, 1979), pp. 234–5, 238; PRO, C 81/322/18163.

[75] *CPR, 1345–48*, p. 239, *1348–50*, pp. 67, 71; B. H. Putnam, *The Place in Legal History of Sir William Shareshull, Chief Justice of the King's Bench, 1350–61* (Cambridge, 1950), p. 67; P. H. W. Booth, *The Financial Administration of the Lordship and County of Chester*, Chetham Society, 3rd series, xxviii (1981), p. 121.

[76] Ormrod, *Reign of Edward III*, p. 244 n. 92.

[77] *RP*, ii, pp. 174 (70), 200–1 (4), 202 (9).

[78] Crook, 'Later eyres', pp. 265–6.

[79] *RP*, ii, pp. 174 (70), 201 (6); the latter is a very slightly inaccurate version of the original, PRO, C 65/14, m 2.

of two magnates, two lawyers and two of the gentry, and more people if necessary. The local men were to be drawn from the most loyal and worthy of the county. Commissions were to be issued from the chancery giving authority to hear and determine all felonies and trespasses. The request for the inclusion of noblemen and lawyers was not a novelty. Since the 1330s the commons had occasionally requested that magnates be given judicial power and as recently as 1344 they had requested the inclusion of lawyers on peace commissions.[80] The exclusion of lawyers in particular would have been unthinkable if the revitalised peace commissions had been intended permanently to replace trailbastons. In the March parliament the commons made three additional requests. First, they proposed that justices swear in parliament to hold sessions at least three times a year. Regular sessions would have given the counties the easy recourse to justice that was so lacking with irregular visitations by trailbastons and, according to another petition, by the assizes.[81] Swearing in parliament harked back to the previous attempts of the commons to regulate the trailbastons, although here they did not attempt to gain any power over selection. Secondly, the commons proposed that the justices should be paid. The commons had supported the paying of trailbaston justices earlier in the decade, and might have recalled the recent payment of justices of weights and measures. It may also have been that they hoped the justices would have been more diligent and effective through regular payment.[82] Thirdly, the commons requested that justices should be given powers over the circulation of substandard coinage. This was a major economic problem of the time and was largely the preserve of the assizes.[83]

In these two petitions of 1348 the commons outlined the objectives that were to dominate their petitions concerning peace commissions for the rest of the reign. To say that the commons wanted powers of trial to be restored to keepers of the peace would be a major oversimplification. They sought the creation of wide-ranging, permanent justices in the counties, who were paid and had authority over economic and criminal matters. They wanted justices of the peace who could effectively replace trailbaston commissions once and for all. The objectives expressed in the 1348 petitions were so broad that, even after the restoration of powers to hear and determine felonies and trespasses eventually came in 1350, the commons were to submit very similar petitions in 1352 and 1361, the latter of these two forming the basis of the well-known statute of the justices of the peace.[84] Even so the introduction of many of the measures outlined by the commons in 1348 was

---

[80] *RP*, ii, p. 148 (12).

[81] Ibid., ii, p. 167 (19).

[82] Ibid., ii, p. 141 (41); Ormrod, *Reign of Edward III*, p. 157; Sayles, *King's Bench*, vi, p. cxxxviii.

[83] *RP*, ii, p. 167 (19); see above, n. 72.

[84] Ibid., ii, p. 238 (13); *Statutes of the Realm*, i, pp. 364–5, cap. 1. Also see related petitions in 1353, 1354, 1363 and 1365: *RP*, ii, pp. 252–3 (36), 257–8 (17), 277 (19), 286 (15).

piecemeal. Regular sessions were introduced for the enforcement of the labour laws in 1351 and were revised and extended to all business by statute in 1362.[85] Authority over economic legislation came in the 1360s as well: powers to punish weights and measures offences were added in 1361, forestalling and regrating in 1364, and breaches of the labour laws in 1368.[86] Wages began to be paid under statutes of 1388 and 1390.[87]

To return to the late 1340s; no justices of the peace were appointed in 1349 and a parliament was planned for 1349, but cancelled as a result of the Black Death. The next parliament was not to sit until 1351. In February 1350 the king appointed justices of the peace again. The old keepers of the peace were inadequate: their numbers were depleted by the plague, and the process of sending out special commissions to hold trials had always been haphazard in its operation and was time-consuming for the now disrupted chancery.[88] Clearly, if there was to be an effective response to the threat of disorder posed by the Black Death, new measures had to be taken.[89] Although no parliament sat in 1349 or 1350, it would seem that the king and council took note of the commons' opinions expressed in recent sessions, particularly those of 1348. Certainly the blending of noblemen, lawyers and gentry appointed in 1350 roughly fitted with the petitions of that year. Furthermore, the ordinance of labourers, drawn up in June 1349 to deal with the anticipated labour shortage, needed to be enforced.[90] Peace commissions with large proportions of local gentry serving on them were well suited to enforcing this sort of economic legislation. The commons had proposed that justices of the peace have powers against the circulation of false money in 1348, and keepers had enforced other economic legislation under Edward II.[91] In

---

[85] *Statutes of the Realm*, i, pp. 313, cap. 7, 374, cap. 12.

[86] Ibid., i, pp. 365, cap. 5, 388, cap. 6; Putnam 'Transformation', p. 46.

[87] *Statutes of the Realm*, ii, pp. 58–9, cap. 10, 77, cap. 11.

[88] Some disruption in the chancery is evident from the failure to enrol all the peace commissions issued in February 1350. For commissions see Putnam, 'Transformation', p. 43; *CPR, 1348–50*, pp. 526–7, *1350–54*, p. 26; *CCR, 1349–54*, p. 181; *CPR, 1348–50*, pp. 533, 594; Rymer, *Foedera*, iii, p. 211; PRO, KB 27/362, m. 72; B. H. Putnam, *The Enforcement of the Statutes of Labourers during the First Decade after the Black Death, 1349–1359* (London, 1908), p. 11 n. 5, appendix p. 248; PRO, KB 145/2/24; Sayles, *King's Bench*, vi, p. 76. For special trial commissions see above, nn. 66 to 69, and, for a peace commission apparently depleted by the plague, see *CPR, 1348–50*, p. 457; also see W. M. Ormrod, 'The English government and the Black Death of 1348–49', in W. M. Ormrod (ed.), *England in the Fourteenth Century: Proceedings of the 1985 Harlaxton Symposium* (Woodbridge, 1986), pp. 177–8.

[89] Quantifying disorder in the wake of the Black Death is very difficult, but problems flared up in London and York, and on the death of the bishop of Worcester his estates were looted: R. R. Sharpe (ed.), *Calendar of Letter Books of the City of London: F* (London, 1904), p. 210; *CPR, 1348–50*, pp. 497, 530, 584; PRO, SC 8/26/1286; SC 8/162/8089; KB 145/2/23/1, m. 1; E. B. Fryde, 'The tenants of the bishops of Coventry and Lichfield and of Worcester after the plague of 1348–9', in R. F. Hunnisett and J. B. Post (ed.), *Medieval Legal Records Edited in Memory of C. A. F. Meekings* (London, 1978), p. 229.

[90] Putnam, *Statutes of Labourers*, pp. 10–13; idem, 'Transformation', p. 43.

[91] Idem, *Proceedings before the Justices of the Peace*, p. xxviii.

the difficult circumstances of early 1350, the king and council voluntarily conceded peace commissions similar to the ones the commons had pressed for in the late 1340s. Thereafter the justices of the peace began their unsteady progress towards being an established part of the shire administration and judicial system.

The early experimentation with the justices of the peace was not the result of a straightforward clash of ideas and vested interests, between the gentry represented by the commons in parliament and the circle of professional justices around the king. Changes and developments in the use of peace commissions in the years 1327 to 1340 reflected reactions to the various difficulties in government. It was by no means clear in these years that the commons were to favour the use of peace commissions over trailbastons. Indeed, local opinion was more inclined to be guided by the actions of the king and council than to challenge them. The transformation in commons attitudes came in the years 1340 to 1344 as a direct result of the king's acceptance of the abuses and excesses of the justices of trailbaston. Thereafter the commons became more insistent on the use of justices of the peace. Upsetting the commons in parliament certainly did not serve the king's purposes, but the appointment of justices of the peace in 1350 and thereafter was no simple concession. It reflected changing governmental attitudes to maintaining social and economic order in the aftermath of the Black Death and in a period of sustained war. The king and council maintained close control over the selection of the new justices, they altered their powers at will, and the presence of justices of assize limited gentry autonomy. The emergence of the justices of the peace reflected a common current in the interests of the gentry and the king, not a simple shift in power from the centre to the localities. The question remains to what extent this process of development can be traced in the history of other local offices and institutions.

6

The Dissolution of St Augustine's Abbey and the Creation of the Diocese of Bristol

J. H. Bettey

The religious changes in Bristol during the 1530s occurred against a background of violent controversy and public debate, with rival preachers either urging further change or denouncing the new ideas, and this 'battle of the pulpits' stimulated a long period of fierce argument over religious affairs. The survival of a considerable amount of evidence concerning this public controversy means that reactions to the early Reformation in Bristol, including the establishment of the oddly-constituted diocese of Bristol in 1542, can be followed in unusual detail. The ferocity of the debate and the new ecclesiastical organisation which emerged from it illustrates the way in which the church continued to provide a powerful focus for local loyalties and civic pride during this eventful period. As a major port and commercial centre, with influence extending throughout the west country, Bristol was a crucial element in government policy, and the events leading up to the creation of the new diocese reveal the close watch which royal officials kept on events in tne town, their constant fear of civil unrest and the frequently strained relations between central government and the local community.

Throughout much of the middle ages the port of Bristol, with its advantageous geographical position, secure harbour, fertile hinterland, good inland communications, and trade in wool, woollen cloth and wine, remained generally prosperous, and by the time of John Cabot's notable voyage in 1497 the wealth and piety of Bristol merchants had ensured that the town was crowded with religious institutions of all sorts. Eighteen parish churches were crammed within and around the walls of the town, among them such magnificent buildings as St Mary Redcliffe and St Stephen's. These and many other of the others had been expensively rebuilt during the fifteenth century, or had been provided with fine western towers, guild chapels, chantries and elaborate furnishings.[1] There were numerous hospitals, almshouses and chapels, while each of the four major orders of friars had a house in the town. The Benedictine priory of St James was situated on the

[1] J. H. Bettey, 'The medieval churches of Bristol', *Transactions of the Ancient Monuments Society,* xxxiv (1990), pp. 1–27.

northern edge, overlooking the River Frome, while a small house of Augustinian canonesses occupied a site at the foot of St Michael's Hill. By far the richest and most impressive of the religious houses was St Augustine's, which had been founded in about 1140 by Robert fitz Harding on his land just outside the town and overlooking the busy harbour at the confluence of the rivers Avon and Frome.

This house of secular canons, which adopted the Victorine or stricter form of the Augustinian rule, was well-endowed with lands and property in Bristol, Somerset and Gloucestershire. Fitz Harding himself was created first Lord Berkeley, and before his death in 1170 became a canon in his own foundation.[2] Evidence of the wealth of St Augustine's is apparent from the early architecture, particularly in the cloister and chapter house, which contains some of the finest Romanesque work in Bristol. There is also notable Romanesque work in the gatehouse and former monastic precinct. The continuing prosperity of the community is also evident from the early-fourteenth century work in the chancel, aisles and eastern lady chapel. This work, which was undertaken by Abbot Knowle who died in 1332, is Bristol's major contribution to architectural advance, creating a vaulted hall-church with three aisles of equal height. This is clearly the work of outstanding designers and craftsmen of great originality. The complex structure, the delicate manner in which the vault is supported, the feeling of space which is created, and the light which is brought into the whole interior is a remarkable achievement.[3]

By the end of the middle ages, the dominant position of the church in Bristol was everywhere apparent, and the fine buildings and spectacular towers of the parish churches were the principal landmarks on the Bristol skyline. St Augustine's continued to be the best endowed and most splendid of all the religious houses, and during the early sixteenth century considerable work was carried out on the monastic buildings. This included the grandiose plan of rebuilding the nave of the church, a project which had not been completed when the abbey was suppressed in 1539. Late medieval account rolls of the abbey show in detail the wealth of the institution, its income and expenditure, and the way in which its affairs were managed. Annual income came in several ways and from different sources. The abbey received part of the tithes from numerous appropriated churches, including All Saints's, St Nicholas and St Augustine the Less in Bristol, sixteen churches in Gloucestershire, seven in Somerset and one in Dorset. In Bristol it also possessed houses, shops, inns, a rope-walk and a water-mill, from all of which it received rents. However, the abbey's main source of income remained its

---

[2] J. C. Dickinson, 'The origins of St Augustine's, Bristol' in P. McGrath and J. Cannon (ed.), *Essays in Bristol and Gloucestershire History* (Bristol, 1976), pp. 109–26.

[3] B. Little, 'Bristol Cathedral', in A. Gomme et al. (ed.), *Bristol: An Architectural History* (London, 1979), pp. 31–8; M. Q. Smith, *The Art and Architecture of St Augustine's Abbey* (Bristol, 1991).

numerous manors in Gloucestershire and Somerset: from these the revenue came in the form of rents, fines, profits of manorial courts, sales of timber and manorial dues. An indication of the late medieval wealth of the abbey can be seen on its estate at Ashleworth, on the River Severn north of Gloucester, where beside the fifteenth-century church is the manor house and court house, both built during the time of Abbot Newbury in about 1460. Among the farm buildings is the stone-built barn, 125 feet long and with an immense roof of stone slates, erected during the time of Abbot Newland in about 1490. Like most large landowners, St Augustine's had given up direct farming of the demesne on most of its manors. In most places the collection of rents, tithes and other dues was left to receivers, so that there was little contact between the abbey and those who contributed to its maintenance. At Leigh or Abbots Leigh down the Avon from Bristol, where the abbot had a residence, and at Portbury near the mouth of the river, the abbey continued to be engaged in farming. A constant supply of livestock, eggs, wheat, barley and pease came up the Avon by barges to Canons' Marsh for the support of the canons and their servants. Likewise, large quantities of brushwood and faggots were supplied for the kitchens. This produce also provided a small profit, since the abbey made and sold malt from its own barley and also sold second quality bread from the abbey bakery.

Annual expenses included a large allowance for the separate establishment maintained by the abbot, whose household and other expenditure accounted for some 20 per cent of the total income of the abbey. Food, drink and clothing for the canons and the abbey servants, together with the upkeep of the domestic buildings amounted to nearly 30 per cent. A third category of expenditure included the care of the abbey church, provision of the materials for services, care of vestments and ornaments and all other things necessary for the maintenance of worship, as well as the expenses of a school for teaching boys and educating novices. Together these costs amounted to about 8 per cent of the income. A further 6 per cent was spent on alms and hospitality, while a similar amount was accounted for by allowances of money to the individual canons, a practice which persisted in spite of all prohibitions and condemnations. The rest of the income was spent on building work, on business expenses including travel, papal taxes, gifts to royal or local officials and legal expenses.[4]

Having spent many years in the detailed study of the late-medieval records of St Augustine's, the late Arthur Sabin concluded that 'the abbey resources were carefully garnered and controlled' and that 'the abbey rose adequately to contemporary standards of correct conduct even if it did not soar very high in saintliness. It seems reasonable ... to suppose that it was in the main

[4] G. Beachcroft and A. Sabin (ed.), *Two Compotus Rolls of St Augustine's Abbey, Bristol*, Bristol Record Society, ix (1938); A. Sabin (ed.), *Some Manorial Accounts of St Augustine's, Bristol*, Bristol Record Society, xxii (1960).

expending its income according to the wishes of its founders'.[5] But by the end of the middle ages there is little evidence of religious fervour, scholarly work or pastoral endeavour associated with St Augustine's. The number of canons also declined from twenty-four in 1498 to thirteen or fourteen by 1535 and eleven in 1539. During the 1530s there were few among the 10,000 or so people in Bristol who were prepared to defend a system whereby an annual net income of over £670 was used to support the prayers of just over a dozen canons, together with more than forty servants, so when the dissolution came in 1539 no protest was heard from the townsfolk of Bristol. None the less, so wealthy and influential was St Augustine's that it would have seemed incredible to Bristolians during the early sixteenth century that it could so quickly and easily be suppressed.

Not only was St Augustine's an ancient religious institution, it also occupied an important position in the economic and social life of Bristol. Throughout the middle ages Bristol was on the extreme edge of the large diocese of Worcester. The suburbs of Redcliffe, Temple, St Thomas's and Bedminster, across the River Avon, were in the diocese of Bath and Wells. Bristol was therefore remote from episcopal supervision and the abbot of St Augustine's was accordingly the major ecclesiastical figure in the town. It was at St Augustine's that important visitors to Bristol were accommodated: Edward IV stayed there in 1476; and Henry VII and his queen, Elizabeth of York, stayed there and were entertained with great ceremony in 1486 only a few months after his accession.[6] The abbey controlled the patronage of four local churches, as well as owning many properties and providing much employment in the town. With the wealthy property-owning abbey situated so close to the busy, outward-looking port of Bristol, it is hardly surprising that relations should have been strained from time to time. A dispute over rights and jurisdiction over the land around the abbey dragged on for many years from the 1490s, which on one occasion saw a running battle with swords and daggers drawn between the town officials and the abbey servants – apparently oblivious of the mayor who cried 'Keep the Peace!' until he was hoarse.[7] A further quarrel in 1515 led to violence, while during the 1520s a dispute over the non-payment of taxes led to the mayor imprisoning some of the abbey servants, whereupon the abbot and his men stormed the prison in an unsuccessful attempt to release them.[8]

There is some evidence that Bristol became a focus for Lollard beliefs, and during the early sixteenth century there were occasionally trials of Bristolians for heresy. Some members of the merchant community actively favoured religious change, while influential landowners in the neighbourhood such

---

[5] Beachcroft and Sabin, *Two Compotus Rolls*, p. 85.

[6] J. H. Bettey, *Bristol Observed* (Bristol, 1986), pp. 21–2, 32–3.

[7] R. C. Latham (ed.), *Bristol Charters, 1509–1899*, Bristol Record Society, xii (1947), p. 21.

[8] Gloucester Public Library, 'Hockaday Abstracts', 428; VCH, *Gloucestershire*, ii (1907), p. 78; E. Ralph (ed.), *The Great White Book of Bristol*, Bristol Record Society, xxxii (1979), pp. 17–67.

as the Poyntz and Walsh families were advocates of church reform and sheltered William Tyndale, who not only produced an English translation of the New Testament but was also strongly critical of abuses within the church. During the early 1530s heretical literature was widely distributed in Bristol, and banned books were,

> thrown in the street and left at mens' doors by night, that where they durst not offer their poison to sell they would of their charity poison men for naught.[9]

Notwithstanding the critics, however, the fine series of late medieval church-wardens' accounts and other records of Bristol parish churches show that the church continued to play a central part in the life of the community and in the annual round of ceremonies, processions and festivals which were such an important feature of social life in the town.[10]

The stormy process of the Reformation began in Bristol in 1533 with a controversy which followed an invitation from the mayor and common council to Hugh Latimer to deliver three Lenten sermons in the town. Latimer was already well known for his radical opinions and was later to achieve high office as bishop of Worcester, but in 1533 he still occupied a lowly position as rector of the small parish of West Kington, near Castle Combe in Wiltshire. In his sermons Latimer made a vigorous attack on 'abuses' in the church, including pilgrimages, veneration of saints, homage to the Virgin, images and relics. Latimer's homely, direct style of preaching, his ready wit and his denunciation of social, as well as religious, abuses made him an extremely popular preacher. His eloquently expressed views roused a storm of protest in Bristol, where several conservative preachers sprang to the defence of the established order, among them John Hilsey, prior of the Bristol Dominicans, and William Hubberdyne, another popular preacher and staunch defender of the contemporary church. The clash of rival opinions and the discord which this created in Bristol became sufficiently serious for the matter to be brought to the attention of Thomas Cromwell. Cromwell appointed a commission headed by William Burton, abbot of St Augustine's, and including three former mayors to investigate the matter. After several sittings and collecting depositions from numerous witnesses, they condemned all parties for the 'infamy, discord, strife and debate' they had created. Few would testify against Latimer, however, and it was Hubberdyne who was sent to London for further examination and who was later imprisoned in the

---

[9] G. R. Elton, *Policy and Police: The Enforcement of the Reformation in the Age of Thomas Cromwell* (Cambridge, 1972), pp. 112–20; K. Powell, 'The beginnings of Protestantism in Gloucestershire', *Bristol and Gloucestershire Archaeological Society Transactions*, xc (1971), pp. 141–57; J. A. F. Thompson, *The Later Lollards, 1414–1520* (Oxford, 1965), pp. 20–5.

[10] J. H. Bettey, *Bristol Parish Churches during the Reformation* (Bristol Historical Association, 1979).

Tower.[11] In this situation the mayor and common council evidently felt that it was wise to ingratiate themselves with Thomas Cromwell: in August 1533 they invited him to accept the office of recorder with an annual fee of £19 6*s*. 8*d*., assuring him that 'hitt shalbe but to you litell labor'.[12]

Furious religious debate continued to be reported from Bristol during the next few years, as rival preachers proclaimed their views or heaped abuse on the opinions of their opponents. In 1536–7 John Kene, vicar of Christ Church, was denouncing the reformers, calling their new learning 'old heresy new risen':

> They say they have brought in the light into the world; no, no, they have brought in damnable darkness and endlesss damnation. Chose you, go to hell an ye will, for I will not be your lodesman.[13]

Meanwhile the new prior of the Bristol Dominicans, William Oliver, was casting doubt on the whole purpose of the religious orders, declaring that without faith nothing could be gained by 'a whole shipload laden with friars' girdles and a dung-cart full of monks' cowls'.[14]

In August 1535 Hugh Latimer, whose preaching had sparked off the whole controversy, was appointed bishop of Worcester and thus became the episcopal ruler of Bristol. Latimer did not visit Bristol during the four years of his episcopate, but the violent debate continuing in the town led him to appoint one of his principal officials, Henry Holbeche, prior of Worcester, as suffragan bishop of Bristol in March 1538.[15] It was against this background of ferocious debate in Bristol that the suppression of the religious houses was carried out.

In 1534 all clergy and monks were required to take an oath upon the holy scriptures that they accepted the royal divorce from Katherine of Aragon, agreed with the king's marriage to Anne Boleyn and would give allegiance to the children of that marriage, and accepted the royal supremacy over the church. Abbot William Burton of St Augustine's, together with his twelve canons, all took this oath as required, as did most other monks throughout the country. No doubt they saw little alternative in the face of royal power, and some perhaps hoped fervently that time would change the situation. Whatever their feelings, they bowed to the royal will. None could have forseen the full consequences of their action, for they were now left with no defence in all the changes and upheavals which were so swiftly to follow.[16]

[11] PRO, SP 1/119/184–197; SP 2/0/11; M. C. Skeeters, *Community and Clergy: Bristol and the Reformation, c. 1530–1570* (Oxford, 1993), pp. 34–56.
[12] PRO, SP 1/78/110.
[13] *LP, Henry VIII*, xii(i), no. 1147.
[14] Quoted by Elton, *Policy and Police*, pp. 14, 118.
[15] *LP, Henry VIII*, xiii(i), nos 401, 646(2).
[16] Ibid., vii, no. 1216.

The first result of the royal supremacy was the great enquiry into the wealth of the church, the *Valor ecclesiasticus*. Although Bristol is omitted from the *Valor*, the survival of St Augustine's late medieval accounts still makes it possible to calculate its income, as already discussed. Bristol was a county in its own right, and was far from the diocesan centre at Worcester. It was presumably for this reason that it was missed by the commissioners, just as they also failed to include the nearby Cistercian abbey of Kingswood, which was a detached part of Wiltshire within the county of Gloucestershire.

While the material for the *Valor ecclesiasticus* was still being collected, Cromwell launched another enquiry into the state of the religious houses. The second group of commissioners, who visited the monasteries, interviewing all the monks, canons and nuns, was charged with the task of finding evidence of scandal, abuses, neglect of religious vows and waste of resources, which Cromwell could use to justify the suppression of at least some of the houses. In August 1535 the Bristol houses were visited by Richard Layton, a young and energetic priest, who was anxious to rise in Cromwell's service, and whose salacious stories about the monks and nuns in the houses he visited, while often untrue or wildly exaggerated, must certainly have provided Cromwell with a change from the sort of correspondence he normally received. In Bristol, however, Layton appears to have found nothing amiss; or, if he did, his account has not survived. At St Augustine's he contented himself with the usual injunctions ordering the abbot that neither he nor any of his canons should go outside the precincts of the abbey, and that lay persons, especially women, should not be allowed in the abbey. It is a considerable tribute to the Bristol religious houses that Layton apparently could find nothing to criticise, for in other places he found or fabricated evidence of misdemeanors and scandals of all sorts. If anything had been wrong in Bristol he would assuredly have reported it.[17] His injunction to the abbot to remain within the abbey precinct moved Abbot Burton to write an obsequious letter to Cromwell, protesting at the restrictions and asking for permission to visit the abbey estates and to 'walk to my manor places nigh to Bristol for the comfortable health of my body and for the saving of expenses'. The abbot also asked that the canons might have liberty to walk 'three or four together, the juniors with the seniors (refraining the town) about the hills and fields to recreate their minds and lax their veins whereby they may be more apt to continue both day and night in the service of God'. Finally, he asked that the canons might have 'some poor honest woman to keep us if any pestiferous plague or distress of sickness do fall among us, as it hath been there of long consuetude'.[18]

Similar letters were being sent to Cromwell from monasteries all over the country, and no reply appears to have been received by Abbot Burton. The

---

[17] T. Wright, *Letters Relating to the Suppression of the Monasteries*, Camden Society, xxvi (1843), pp. 7–10, 58–9.
[18] PRO, SP 1/96/32–3.

only evidence which has come to light of any laxity or scandal at St Augustine's in the years before the suppression comes from quite a different source.
In 1540, after the monastery had been suppressed, one of the former canons,
John Rastle or Rastall, was nominated to the position of chantry priest in
the parish church at Winterbourne in south Gloucestershire, but the rector
of the parish, John Compton, objected on the grounds that Rastle was
unsuitable. Compton's allegations were made at the diocesan court of the
bishop of Worcester, where he accused Rastle, who had apparently already
been serving in some capacity at Winterbourne, of negligence, preaching
false doctrine, and of being well-known as a player at cards and dice and
an inveterate gambler. Evidence of Rastle's gambling was given by Nicholas
Corbett, vicar of St Philip's, Bristol, who had known Rastle for sixteen years,
having been a canon of St Augustine's with him. Corbett stated that 'he hath
known the said Rastle to have been a great dicer and a carder when they
were both canons dwelling in the monastery of St Augustine, now dissolved,
[where] the said Rastle got at dice and cards of divers men in his chamber
at the said late monastery some x li, v li and v marks, and specially the year
before the dissolution of that monastery ...' Other witnesses gave similar
evidence, one saying that he had known one man who sold the coat off his
back in order to continue playing with Rastle. Some years before the dissolution Rastle had been sent to Oxford, where he had possibly acquired bad
habits; upon his return to Bristol Rastle had set up a gambling den in the
monastery, to which laymen seem to have had ready access. In spite of
the evidence against him and the protests of the parish priest, he was
instituted to the chantry at Winterbourne by the bishop, and remained there
until the suppression of the chantries in 1547. He later became vicar of
St Nicholas in Bristol.[19]

With its annual net income of nearly £700, St Augustine's was far outside
the terms of the act for the suppression of the smaller monasteries in 1536,
and monastic life therefore continued throughout 1537 and 1538 while
many other houses in the region surrendered to the crown and while the
houses of the four orders of friars in Bristol were dissolved and all their
property seized. During the early months of 1539 more and more west
country houses were persuaded by successive visitations by royal commissioners to make a 'voluntary' surrender of all their possessions and accept
the royal offer of pensions. None the less, Abbot Burton seems to have
hoped that St Augustine's could avoid closure, and was at pains to ingratiate
himself with Cromwell. On 21 February 1539 Abbot Burton wrote another
obsequious letter to Cromwell thanking him for his great goodness to the
monastery and sending him twenty nobles, an additional sum to payments
Burton had already made to him.[20] By the summer of 1539, only a few west

[19] Gloucester Public Library, 'Hockaday Abstracts', Winterbourne file.
[20] J. H. Bettey, *The Suppression of the Monasteries in the West Country* (Gloucester, 1989), p. 107;
LP, Henry VIII, xiv(i), no. 33.

country monasteries remained and it must have been obvious that the future for all the rest was very uncertain. At this unfortunate time, in July 1539, William Burton died, having been abbot of St Augustine's since 1525. Incredibly, the crown granted permission for a successor to be elected, and on 24 August 1539 the royal assent was given for the election of the prior, Morgan Gwilliam, as abbot.[21] He was to remain as abbot for little more than three months, for with eleven canons he surrendered the house to the royal commissioners on 9 December 1539.[22] The clear yearly value of St Augustine's was assessed at £692 2s. 7d., besides £70 3s. 4d. 'in fees and annuities granted to divers persons for term of life'. Like the heads of most religious houses, the recently-appointed Gwilliam was awarded a very generous pension. He received eighty pounds p.a., the manor house at Leigh (Abbots Leigh), together with the orchard, garden and dovecote there, as well as twenty loads of firewood each year. The canons received pensions ranging from eight pounds p.a., for the prior and for the gambling expert John Rastle, to six pounds each for the more junior members. Each canon also received an immediate payment of £2 as an additional inducement to surrender their house. Less fortunate were the forty-six servants and officers of the monastic household, who were paid their wages and dismissed by the commissioners. No doubt the loss of regular doles of food and clothing, and other monastic charity, was sorely missed by the poor of the town, but no evidence survives concerning their feelings.[23]

Some indication of the opulence of the abbey, its buildings and furnishings, can be obtained from the inventory prepared by the commissioners. They estimated that there were 130 fodders or fothers of lead on the roofs, that is some 126 tons. There were ten bells in the tower, and 526 ounces of silver plate, as well as 'Mitres garnished with silver gilt, ragged pearls and counterfeit stones. Certain garnishing of vestments of silver gilt duameld and set with small pearls'. All these were reserved to the king's use, but the commissioners also sold ornaments, goods and chattels for £103 13s. 7d. They also paid sundry outstanding debts for victuals, cloth, wax, salt, wine and spices, amounting to £58 10s. 2d.[24] Sadly, we know nothing of the view which the abbot and his eleven canons took of their suppression and dispersal. There is no evidence to show whether they went willingly or reluctantly, whether they signed the surrender and accepted their pensions as a welcome release from the daily round of the offices and the cloister, or because they saw no alternative in the face of royal pressure. Whatever their views, most succeeded in obtaining benefices in and around Bristol. The abbot, Morgan Gwilliam, with one of the canons, Richard Carsy, departed to live on the Isle of Wight, and one other canon, Richard Hughes, moved to a benefice

[21] *LP, Henry VIII*, xiv(ii), no. 113(27).
[22] Ibid., xiv(i), no. 660.
[23] Gloucester Public Library, 'Hockaday Abstracts', p. 428.
[24] Ibid.

in Norfolk, later returning to Bristol. The rest remained in the Bristol region and were thus able to witness the transformation of their abandoned abbey into a cathedral.[25]

The lands and buildings of most of the religious houses in Bristol were disposed of very rapidly by the crown. Much was purchased by courtiers such as Sir Miles Partridge and the king's physician and former Bristolian, George Owen; by officials such as Sir Ralph Sadler and William Popley; and by merchants like Henry Brayne, William Chester and John Smyth. The corporation of Bristol also managed to secure a share of the estates, and in 1541 purchased most of the lands which had belonged to Gaunt's hospital and the Carmelite and the Franciscan friaries. These, together with later purchases of monastic and chantry lands, were to prove so lucrative that Bristol became one of the richest corporations in England.[26] The site of St Augustine's was not sold by the crown, and during 1540 and 1541 the former monastic church, cloister and all buildings lay unused and empty, but in 1542 Bristol became one of six new dioceses created by Henry VIII, with St Augustine's as its cathedral, the abbot's lodging as the palace for the new bishop and the domestic buildings as residences for the canons.

The process of founding new dioceses had started with the Bishoprics Act of 1539 which empowered the king to establish new dioceses; at the outset some eighteen new bishoprics were contemplated, but during 1540 and 1541 only five were founded – Chester, Peterborough, Oxford, Westminster and Gloucester.[27] The large medieval diocese of Worcester was divided by the creation of the Gloucester diocese in September 1541, which included the deanery of Bristol. Only nine months later, on 4 June 1542, the diocese of Bristol was established by royal charter and at the same time Bristol was given the right to the title of 'city': 'the whole of our town of Bristol from now henceforth for ever shall be a city'.[28] This creation seems to have been an ill-conceived afterthought, for the Bristol diocese was poorly endowed and administratively impossible, and there has been much speculation as to why the new diocese should have been so oddly constituted. As well as the parishes within the city and county of Bristol, the diocese included a few parishes in south Gloucestershire, the parish of Leigh or Abbots Leigh in Somerset, and the whole of the county of Dorset, which had previously been part of the huge diocese of Salisbury. This was in spite of the fact that the nearest Dorset parishes were more than forty miles distant from Bristol. The situation in Dorset was further complicated by the fact that fifty-four

---

[25] G. Baskerville, 'The dispossessed religious of Gloucestershire', *Bristol and Gloucestershire Archaeological Society Transactions*, xlix (1927), pp. 63–122. For details of the subsequent careers of the Bristol friars, see Bettey, *The Suppression of the Religious Houses in Bristol*, p. 19.

[26] *LP, Henry VIII*, xvi, no. 878(10).

[27] *Statutes of the Realm*, iii, p. 728, 31 Henry VIII, c. 9.

[28] R. C. Latham (ed.), *Bristol Charters, 1509–1899*, Bristol Record Society, xii, pp. 93–4.

of the parishes in the county remained as peculiars of the dean of Salisbury or of various prebends in Salisbury cathedral, so that for most purposes they were effectively removed from episcopal control.[29]

In a recent study Dr Martha C. Skeeters concluded that the king belatedly agreed to the creation of a Bristol diocese under pressure from the governing class in the town:

> While no direct evidence of this pressure is extant, the context of the creation leaves no other explanation. Local concern with diocesan authority and, more importantly, the rivalry with Gloucester were strong motivations for Bristol's elite to seek a diocese of their own.[30]

This may well be true, although the absence of evidence makes it impossible to be certain of the motivation for the belated creation of this curiously-constituted diocese. But Bristol was a much larger and more important town than Gloucester. As one of the major seaports of the country, it was an obvious candidate for a diocese, especially since St Augustine's provided a ready-made cathedral, although the Bristol governing class can hardly have wanted the inclusion of Dorset in the new diocese. An even stronger motive may well have been the government's belated recognition of the desirability of an episcopal presence in Bristol because of its recent history of religious controversy and the fear of popular uprising. Moreover, it should not be assumed that the religious changes and ecclesiastical provisions of the 1530s and 1540s were carried out according to any rational and pre-conceived plan. Clearly, the creation of the new bishoprics, like so many other changes of the Reformation, was a response to immediate pressures and problems; the six new dioceses left much of the medieval ecclesiastical framework of England untouched and most dioceses remained as unwieldy, inconvenient administrative units for another three centuries.

One small piece of evidence exists to suggest that the new diocese and cathedral may have been welcomed by the governing merchant class in Bristol. In his will dated 10 September 1542, only three months after the creation of the Bristol diocese, Thomas White, one of the leading Bristol merchants and an active figure in the government of the town, left an ornate stone screen which had formerly belonged to the Carmelite friars of Bristol to 'my Cathedrall Church'. This fine screen, still a notable feature of Bristol Cathedral, bears the monogram and merchant's mark of Thomas White and provides the sole link with the former friary church. The date and wording of Thomas White's will suggest that he was pleased by the new diocese and proud of the cathedral and the city status it brought to Bristol:

---

[29] P. Stewart, *Guide to the Records of the Diocese of Salisbury* (Wiltshire County Council, 1973), pp. 138–9.

[30] M. C. Skeeters, 'The creation of the Diocese of Bristol', *Bristol and Gloucestershire Archaeological Society Transactions*, ciii (1985), pp. 175–8.

Also I geve and bequethe unto my Cathedrall Church called the Trynytie of Bristowe, the Quere [Choir Screen] which was somtyme in the White Friers ... and the said Quere for to be sett upp in the said Churche at my coste and Charge.[31]

The cathedral establishment at Bristol was to be very similar to the monastic institution which it replaced, for the charter of 1542 provided for St Augustine's to be the cathedral and to be styled the church of the Holy and Undivided Trinity; it was to have a dean, six canons, six minor canons, a deacon, six lay-clerks, one master of the choristers, two masters of the grammar school, four almsmen, a sexton, a porter and verger, a butler and two cooks. Clearly, a communal life along monastic lines was intended, and the first dean, William Snow, was a former monk who had been prior of the Augustinian house at Bradenstoke in Wiltshire.[32]

The new cathedral consisted only of the choir and transepts of the former abbey church, since the nave had been demolished in preparation for rebuilding on a grander scale, leaving the fine gateway to the precinct isolated at the west end, but the work of reconstruction had proceeded slowly, and at the time of the dissolution only the lower parts of the walls had been constructed. These were subsequently demolished and tenements were built which remained there until the nave was finally rebuilt during the later nineteenth century. A more serious problem than a little cathedral was the poor endowment of the new diocese. The properties granted to the new cathedral and bishopric included many of the former lands of St Augustine's abbey, together with parcels of land that had belonged to the houses of Muchelney, Bruton, Shaftesbury, Bath, Bradenstoke and St Oswald's, Gloucester. Also included in the endowments of the new diocese were annual pensions from several parish churches, among them St Nicholas, St Augustine-the-Less and All Saints' in Bristol, as well as rents from properties in the town such as St Augustine's Green, Brandon Hill, the mill house and three mills called Trevill Mills in Redcliffe, a pasture and barn called Cantocks, and an inn called the Boarshead and Raven in High Street.[33] These produced a net income of £697 3s. 11d. per annum which was very similar to the sum in the region of £690 per annum enjoyed by the abbot and canons of St Augustine's; but when divided among the bishop, dean, cathedral clergy and other staff the income for each meant that Bristol was the most poorly-endowed of all bishoprics. This poor endowment was recognised by the fact that the first bishop, Paul Bush, was allowed to keep the canonry which he already held in Salisbury Cathedral 'with the house

---

[31] E. W. W. Veale (ed.), *The Great Red Book of Bristol*, Bristol Record Society, xvi (1951), pt iii, pp. 130–3; R. H. Warren, 'The choir screen of Bristol Cathedral', *Clifton Antiquarian Club Proceedings*, vi (1908), pp. 6–10.

[32] J. Britton, *The History and Antiquities of the Abbey and Cathedral Church of Bristol* (London, 1836).

[33] *LP, Henry VIII*, xvii, no. 1154.

in the cathedral close in which he still dwells'.[34] The result was that few bishops stayed long at Bristol but sought more lucrative sees elsewhere. Few visited the Dorset part of their diocese, and several scarcely had time to come to Bristol. Not surprisingly the absence of episcopal supervision had damaging consequences for church life in Dorset, where as late as 1577 two of the leading gentlemen in the county, Sir John Horsey and George Trenchard, justified to the privy council their inability to obtain information about Catholic recusants on the grounds that 'it was uncertain in whose diocese the shire was'.[35]

The administration of the new diocese was the responsibility of the chancellor, John Cotterell, who continued to hold ecclesiastical office through all the religious changes from 1543 until his death in 1572. He was also archdeacon of Dorset and a canon of Wells. The career of the first bishop, Paul Bush (1542–53) will be examined shortly; he was followed by John Holyman (1554–58), a zealous Catholic who had vigorously opposed the royal divorce. Thereafter, Richard Cheney (1558–79) held Bristol *in commendam* with Gloucester; the see was then vacant until the appointment of Richard Fletcher, chaplain to Queen Elizabeth in 1589, and after his translation to Worcester in 1593 it again remained vacant for another ten years. During the early decades of the seventeenth century bishops seldom remained at Bristol for more than three or four years, and the low esteem in which the see was held as the most poorly-paid of all bishoprics is reflected in the remark of Anthony Wood in 1661 when the rich landowner and cleric, Gilbert Ironside, was created bishop of Bristol, that 'being wealthy, he was looked upon as the fittest person to enter upon that mean bishopric'.[36]

Few of the subsequent bishops of Bristol had a career as full of unexpected changes and alterations or as greatly affected by contemporary upheavals as the first holder of the office. Paul Bush was born at Dilton, near Westbury in Wiltshire around 1490.[37] His father, William Bush, leased a farm and fulling mill from the Bonhommes priory at Edington, and it was there that Paul Bush, as the younger son, was sent to receive an education. Clearly he was a clever boy, being sent from Edington to study at Oxford. He graduated in 1518, and remained at Oxford, acquiring a reputation both for his medical and theological writing and as a poet. Early in the 1520s Paul Bush was ordained priest and returned to Edington to join the community of Bonhommes. At this well-endowed house in its remote situation he might have expected to live out the rest of his days in the ordered round of the monastic life. His reputation as a scholar and theologian was recognised by his appointment as canon of Salisbury. Soon, however, he became deputy to

[34] Ibid., appendix 12.
[35] PRO, SP 12/117/21.
[36] A. Wood, *Athenae Oxoniensis*, ii, pp. 939–40.
[37] For fuller details of the career of Paul Bush, see J. H. Bettey, 'Paul Bush, the first bishop of Bristol', *Bristol and Gloucestershire Archaeological Society Transactions*, cvi (1988), pp. 169–72.

the head of the house, John Ryve, and was called upon to face the increasing pressures put upon the religious during the 1530s. In May 1538 John Ryve died, and Paul Bush was appointed 'rector' or head of the house. A year later he and his twelve brethren were persuaded to surrender their house into the hands of Sir John Tregonwell, the king's commissioner.[38] Paul Bush received a handsome pension of £100 per annum, together with the manor house at Coleshill in Berkshire, so that from a career as an Oxford scholar, and then as a monk withdrawn from the world, he had now become a wealthy country gentleman. He also retained his canonry at Salisbury and a house in the cathedral close.

The next twist in his story followed shortly: in 1542 Paul Bush was chosen to be the first bishop of Bristol. As bishop his religious views seem to have been moderate, and he accepted the Henrician changes, the English Bible and (later) the English Prayer Book. In the House of Lords he voted against the bill to legalise clerical marriage in 1549, but when the clergy were permitted to marry Paul Bush was quick to take advantage of the new freedom. His wife was Edith Ashley, daughter of Henry Ashley, from Monkton Up Wimborne in Dorset; her brother was already married to Paul Bush's sister, Margaret. Following his marriage, his wife moved into the bishop's palace in Bristol. As bishop he also possessed the manor house at Leigh (Abbots Leigh) and several episcopal documents were issued from there. His background as a monk hardly fitted Bush to cope with the pressures put upon him as a bishop, and he was unable to resist the demand from the royal government for the manor of Leigh. At first, Bush tried to retain the manor, but the royal council, led by the duke of Northumberland, refused to be diverted and wrote from Greenwich:

> Wee do therefore desire and pray you with convenient diligence to procede thereunto. And advertising us of your doinges we shall not fayle to make report to his Highness of your redy mynde and good disposition to the satisfaction of his Majesties requests accordingly
>
>   Your loving Friendes ...

The deed of surrender was signed by the bishop and ratified by the dean and chapter in the presence of Edmund Gorges and Hugh Denys, acting as agents for the privy council, on 25 May 1551. Shortly afterwards the manor of Leigh was granted by the crown to Sir George Norton.[39]

The next revolution in Paul Bush's life came in 1553 with the death of Edward VI and the accession of Queen Mary. From his writings it appears that Bush may have welcomed the restoration of Catholicism, but as a married bishop he was in an impossible position and had no alternative but to resign. He retired with his wife to become rector of Winterbourne in

---

[38] *LP, Henry VIII*, xiv(i), no. 635.
[39] *APC*, 1551, 186, 210.

south Gloucestershire, where Edith died in October 1553. Paul Bush continued to live at Winterbourne in considerable style. He evidently resumed a
life of scholarship, one of his writings being an *Exhortation* addressed to
Margaret, wife of John Burgess, clothier of nearby Kingswood. This was a
spirited defence of the mass against the 'rash fantastycall myndes of the
blynde and ignorante'.[40] Paul Bush died at his manor house, Gastlings Court
at Frampton Cotterell, near Winterbourne, on 11 October 1558. His will,
which was couched in thoroughly Catholic terms, included bequests to former
servants at Edington, Bristol and Winterbourne, to his own family and to
that of his wife. It also ordered that his body should be buried close to his
wife in the north aisle of Bristol cathedral. His tomb was erected according
to his instructions in classical style, demonstrating the artistic influence of
the Renaissance: it shows him as an emaciated figure, his head resting on
a mitre and holding a pastoral staff. The Latin inscription can still be read
and describes him as *primus huiis ecclesiae episcopus*. Nearby was a slab to his
wife which is no longer legible but which bore the inscription, 'Off your
charitye pray for the soul of Edith Bush, otherwise Asheley, who deceased
8 October 1553'.[41]

---

[40] *Wiltshire Notes and Queries*, iv (1902–4), pp. 104–7; A. B. Emden, *Biographical Register of the
University of Oxford, 1501–1540* (Oxford, 1974), p. 552.

[41] J. F. Nicholls and J. Taylor, *Bristol Past and Present*, ii (Bristol, 1881), pp. 67–8.

7

Sir Thomas Cheyne, Lord Warden of the Cinque Ports, 1536–1558:
Central Authority and the Defence of Local Privilege

Peter Fleming

The Cinque Ports – Dover, Sandwich, Rye, New Romney, Hastings, Hythe and Winchelsea – rarely claim the attention of historians. They were no longer the mainstay of royal navies after the thirteenth century, and their economic decline set in soon after.[1] By the 1530s Dover and Sandwich were still reasonably prosperous, and the silting at Rye and Hastings had not yet ruined their harbours, but Hythe was fighting a losing battle against the shingle that had already blocked New Romney and Winchelsea.[2] The maritime activities of the portsmen were confined largely to fishing, with most seaborne trade in the hands of foreign merchants.[3]

The constitutional history of the ports, particularly for their period of relative greatness during the middle ages, has been well covered, but far less attention has been paid to other aspects of their history.[4] Perhaps this is because the necessary records for the detailed study of political, social and economic activity within the ports are extant only from the later middle ages, partly as a result of the greater elaboration of administrative machinery which, ironically, accompanied the ports' drift into decay.[5] Historians tend to be more interested in the growth of institutions than their decline, and so the post-medieval history of the Cinque Ports has aroused little interest.

---

[1] K. M. E. Murray, *The Constitutional History of the Cinque Ports* (Manchester, 1935), pp. 27–46, 205–25.

[2] Ibid., p. 209.

[3] Ibid., pp. 209–16.

[4] See ibid., and F. Hull (ed.), *Calendar of the White and Black Books of the Cinque Ports*, Kent Archives Society/Historical Manuscripts Commission (1966), Introduction, for the constitutional history and administrative structure of the ports. In addition, J. L. Gillespie, 'Dover castle: key to Richard II's kingdom?', *Archaeologia Cantiana*, cv (1989), pp. 179–95, deals with the political significance of the wardenship at the end of the fourteenth century, as does J. K. Gruenfelder, 'The Lord Warden and elections, 1604–1628', *Journal of British Studies*, xvi (1976), pp. 1–23, for a later period. S. T. Bindoff (ed.), *The History of Parliament: The House of Commons, 1509–1558* (London, 1982), i, pp. 253–64, contains useful short accounts of each of the ports.

[5] Murray, *Constitutional History*, pp. 217–19.

But the fact that the ports maintained their privileged status into the Tudor period and beyond suggests that they were still reckoned to be of some value even in their twilight years, at least in part because the territory which fell within the liberty of the Cinque Ports included the most strategically important coastline in England.[6] It is the contention of this essay that the Cinque Ports in the early modern period should not be written off as an anachronism or as constitutional oddity, but can provide material for a useful case study in the relationship between central and local authority in sixteenth-century England.

The crown's agent in the Cinque Ports was the lord warden. His position within the liberty can be likened to that of the medieval sheriffs before their powers were eroded by the rise of JPs and lieutenants of counties: he had sole responsibility for the return of writs to the crown, the collection of taxes and the arrest of criminals. Through his court held in the church of St James below Dover castle he exercised jurisdiction broadly equivalent to that of chancery (and commonly referred to as such within the Cinque Ports), and he also exercised admiralty jurisdiction along the south-east coast. He had a lieutenant's powers of muster, and his constableship of Dover castle furnished him with a garrison and imposing accommodation for his staff, led by the clerk and the lieutenant of the castle.[7] The Cinque Ports made much of their liberties; in fact, the powers of the lord warden had the potential to place these communities in a uniquely subservient relationship with central government. But the sixteenth-century lord warden was not simply the crown's representative, and his loyalties were divided. Appointed by a crown increasingly intolerant of rival jurisdictions, he was none the less bound by his oath of office to maintain and defend the ports' liberties. As their individual political influence declined, the ports looked to their lord warden to champion their cause at the centre; and while the lord warden's first loyalty had to be to the sovereign, he could not afford to ignore threats to what was after all his power base.[8] The lord warden was the ports' viceregal governor; he was also their protector from external pressures, not least those exerted by the crown. This essay examines how one lord warden attempted to balance these competing demands while at the same time developing his own power base within the liberty. By so doing, the nature of the Cinque Ports themselves, and their relationship with the crown, will also be explored.

Sir Thomas Cheyne was appointed lord warden on 17 May 1536, on the same day that the previous holder of the office, Viscount Rochford, was

---

[6] Despite Murray's verdict, ibid., pp. 217, 225–30. For a description of the privileges, see ibid., pp. 1–8.

[7] Ibid., pp. 77–119. For a general account of Cheyne's activities as lord warden, see R. E. Brock, 'The courtier in early Tudor society' (unpublished university of London Ph.D. thesis, 1964), pp. 101–5.

[8] Murray, *Constitutional History*, pp. 77–119.

executed; his tenure ended with his death on 16 December 1558, a month into the reign of Elizabeth. Cheyne's term of office coincided with the so-called 'Mid Tudor Crisis': a period of intense political, religious and social tensions, combined with a series of foreign threats culminating in the loss of Calais and the invasion scare of 1558. These crises were felt as strongly along the south-east coast as anywhere else in provincial England. If the nature of political and social relationships is most clearly illuminated in the stark light cast by dissension and crisis, then Cheyne's wardenship should offer a rewarding period for study.

Thomas Cheyne was born about 1485 into a gentry family which had been prominent in Kent since the fourteenth century. From the beginning he had links with the Tudor dynasty: his uncle and guardian was John, Lord Cheyne of Berkshire, Henry Tudor's standard bearer at Bosworth. As a youth Thomas Cheyne is said to have been among Henry VII's henchmen; he was a squire of the body at the king's funeral, and as the step-son of Isabella, daughter of Sir Geoffrey Boleyn, he would become a distant relative of Henry VIII.[9] Cheyne served all five Tudor monarchs, his career showing the classic renaissance mix of courtier, soldier and diplomat. He was an esquire of the body from 1509, knighted in 1512/3, a gentleman of the privy chamber from 1526 to 1539, and thereafter privy councillor and treasurer of the household. In his military capacity he commanded a ship against the French in 1513, served in France from 1523 to 1525, and again in 1544 and 1545; he led forces against Wyatt in 1554, was constable of Queenborough, Rochester, Saltwood and Dover castles, and as lord warden and lord lieutenant of Kent (1551 to 1553) he was much involved with musters and coastal defence. As a diplomat he was sent to the papal curia in 1513, was present at the Field of Cloth of Gold in 1520 and was three times ambassador to France under Henry VIII and to Charles V in 1549 and in August 1553.[10] Above all he possessed the ability to survive: while there were fluctuations in his career, Cheyne managed to retain his position amid all the vicissitudes of the mid Tudor period.

Cheyne was already a prominent figure within Kent when he became lord warden, but it was from this point in the mid 1530s that he built up his power base to become one of the most powerful men in the south east. He was a Kentish JP from 1526, and from at least 1539 he represented Kent in every parliament with the single exception of 1555 (in 1557 the council seems to have taken steps to ensure that this unfortunate occurrence would not be repeated, and Cheyne was duly elected to his final parliament the following year).[11] Cheyne's wealth matched his public position. To the family

---

[9] This paragraph is based on Bindoff, *History of Parliament*, i, pp. 634–8; Brock, 'Courtier in early-Tudor society', passim; S. B. Wyatt, *Cheneys and Wyatts: A Brief History in Two Parts* (London, 1960), pp. 28–30.

[10] Brock, 'Courtier in early-Tudor society', pp. 82–5, 171–2, 217–19.

[11] Bindoff, *History of Parliament*, i, pp. 112–14.

estates in Kent he added property in Berkshire and Middlesex through his marriage to Frideswide, daughter of Sir Thomas Frowick (by 1515), but probably the larger share of Cheyne's wealth in later life derived from his acquisition of former monastic property and from the fruits of office. In his will of 1558 Cheyne mentioned various properties which together gave him an annual net rental income of over £950, and this was in addition to the sizeable jointure lands provided for his second wife and his daughter-in-law, as well as numerous generous bequests to family, servants and friends; after his death it was estimated that he kept between two and three hundred people in his service.[12]

In 1536 the Cinque Ports received this courtier-soldier-diplomat as their new 'good lord', and Sir Thomas Cheyne acquired a new affinity. But the ports had a recent history of unrest: in 1526 an attempt by the king's bailiff at Sandwich to extend the crown's rights led to serious dissent from jurats (councillors) and communalty (burgesses), while Wolsey may have encouraged communal strife as part of his policy of increasing royal control through the lord warden.[13] The disturbances of the 1520s came on top of the ever-present rivalries between individual ports, the underlying social tensions between rich and poor, and the growing religious frictions. So Cheyne's new affinity required careful management.

The Cinque Ports were always jealous of their privileges, but under the Tudors these were coming under increasing pressure, and Cheyne was often called upon to help defend them. The lord warden's monopoly on the return of writs came under increasing pressure during the 1540s and 1550s. In 1541 Thomas Birchet of Rye was commended by the Brotherhood for ignoring a *sub poena* from chancery because it arrived without a letter of attendance from the lord warden. He was advised to procure a letter from Cheyne to the lord chancellor notifying him of this decision.[14] Six years later the exchequer was the offending department, when representatives of Rye, Hastings and Sandwich met with Sir James Hales, the ports' retained

---

[12] The Elizabethan writer of an anonymous memorandum on the decline in Kent's defensive capacity looked back fondly to the greater security which Cheyne's private resources had brought to the county, and maintained that he generally kept in his household 160 serving men, together with retainers, gentlemen and others who were ready to attend upon him at times of special need, numbering in total at least 300 men: PRO, SP 12/75/43. For Cheyne's acquisitions of former monastic property, see: *LP, Henry VIII*, x, no. 176 (Davington priory, 25 January 1536); xv, g. 436, nos 44–5 (Faversham abbey, Ludgate friary and Morton, Surrey, 16 March 1540), no. 1032 (St Sexburgh, Minster, 5 June 1540); xvi, g. 379, no. 58 (Syon, Middlesex, 25 December 1540), no. 1500, p. 725 (St Augustine, Canterbury, 16 February, 1541). For his will see PRO, PROB 11/42b, ff. 2–7.

[13] P. Clark, *English Provincial Society from the Reformation to the Revolution: Religion, Politics and Society in Kent, 1500–1640* (Hassocks, 1977), pp. 13–14, 20.

[14] Hull, *White and Black Books*, p. 227. The brotherhood was the representative assembly of the ports, and its main purpose was to guard against infringements of the liberties, Murray, *Constitutional History*, pp. 188–9.

legal counsel, to discuss the best way to secure Cheyne's assistance.[15] This particular abuse of the ports' privileges seems to have increased under Edward VI: in 1550 the mayor and jurats of Dover refused to accept a royal writ because it was not accompanied by a letter of attendance from the lord warden. Two years later the brotherhood complained of the many writs and processes that had recently been issued directly to portsmen rather than via the lord warden, and it was decided to draw up a petition, to be circulated around the ports and then presented to Dover castle for Cheyne's inspection.[16] These incidents involved portsmen and resulted in appeals made on their behalf to the lord warden.

When officers of Dover castle suffered from infringements of the ports' liberties, Cheyne himself took the initiative. In May 1556 Joseph Beverley, clerk of Dover castle, and William Crispe, lieutenant of the castle, were arrested by the lord chancellor's sergeant at arms; their offence may have related to the muster they had taken on the day of their arrest, or to a royal demand for the delivery of prisoners held on suspicion of piracy.[17] Beverley and Crispe appealed to Cheyne for help, who, after taking legal advice, replied that he would complain to the lord chancellor that the warrant for their arrest was invalid since it had not been addressed to the lord warden's office, and so infringed the liberties of the Cinque Ports:

> I trow thys ys the ffyrste lord Chancellor that ever sent any such offysur to areste any man with in the ports onles he cam ffyrste to the Warden of the ports ... I wyll styk wythe the Ryght to the utter moste of my power, I meane to the libertyes of the ports, as ffar as there charters wyl bere.[18]

Beverley and Crispe regained their freedom but were shortly to appear in court when Cheyne wrote to advise them that they should request every port to 'make serche for suche presidentes as they have to maynteigne their said liberties', and to send representatives to a meeting at Dover to discuss tactics; he closed the letter by restating his determination to 'stand by you and them for the maynteininge of their said liberties asfar as their charters will beare to thuttermoost of my po[w]ore'.[19] Clearly, Cheyne did not hesitate to appeal to the liberties of the Cinque Ports when his own rights were

[15] Hull, *White and Black Books*, p. 237.

[16] 1550: BL, MS Egerton 2094, f. 28.1552: Hull, *White and Black Books*, p. 257.

[17] BL, MS Add. 34150, f. 55; Bindoff, *History of Parliament*, i, p. 428. In May 1556 Cinque Ports delegates met at Dover to discuss a demand from the king's admiralty court for the delivery of prisoners held on charges of piracy, which demand it was claimed infringed the liberties, Centre for Kentish Studies, Maidstone (CKS), Sa/Ac4, f. 85. Four years previously Cheyne had raised doubts about the competence of a commission which had been appointed to try portsmen accused of piracy following the request of William Thomas to the lord chancellor, *CSPD, 1547–1580*, xiv, no. 69; *APC*, iv, p. 130. For tensions over musters see Clark, *English Provincial Society*, p. 104.

[18] BL, MS Add. 34150 ff. 55–6.

[19] CKS, Sa/ZB/3/59, f. 102v.

infringed, but his second letter suggests that he expected the portsmen would regard this incident as an infringement of their liberties as well.

The lord warden's monopoly on the return of writs was not an unmixed blessing. Failure to return writs within the allotted time rendered him liable to amercement, whatever the reason for delay. When sending some exchequer writs under the lord warden's precept to Sandwich in 1558 Joseph Beverley warned the recipients to deal with them speedily and lawfully, so that his master would:

> be not therupon amersed as of late tyme he hath byn and moche adoe to escape the danger therof wherof I have thought good to advertyse you so as therby ye maye the rather kepe yorselves and the said office from perill.[20]

The Cinque Ports were traditionally granted exemptions from fifteenths and tenths and subsidies, ostensibly in recognition of the contribution they made to the king's navies; this had been recognised in a charter of 1465, despite the fact that by then their contribution to the navy was largely confined to a handful of transport ships.[21] At the granting of an exemption to the ports from a fifteenth and tenth the usual procedure was for each head port on behalf of itself and its members to draw up billets or receipts for the sums exempted, and these were given to the collectors for presentation to the exchequer.[22] But these exemptions were not given automatically, and the portsmen had to work hard for them in the face of increasing royal fiscal demands.

In 1538 Cheyne helped to secure a respite from subsidy payments for Dover's members.[23] In May 1540 a guestling (a meeting of the Cinque Ports' representatives) appointed solicitors to put the ports' case for an allowance from the fifteenth to the lord warden and to the Council, in July Sandwich sought Cheyne's assistance in securing its allowance, and by November 1541 continued representations to the Council had achieved a hearing in the exchequer. In the meantime, collectors were to cease their demands within the liberty and upon the 'advocantes' (portsmen living outside the liberty).[24] The immediate result of this process seems to have been favourable to the ports, for by June 1542 they were making out new billets to claim their exemptions.[25] But the following month further action was being discussed and in December the ports agreed to follow Cheyne's advice on a petition to be presented to the king.[26] Similar appeals appear to have worked in 1544, when Sandwich, Dover and their members were released from all sums

---

[20] CKS, Sa/ZB/3/39, f. 124v.

[21] Murray, *Constitutional History*, p. 219.

[22] Ibid., pp. 219–21.

[23] BL, MS Egerton 2093, ff. 312, 314.

[24] Ibid., ff. 386–7, 392, 394; Hull, *White and Black Books*, p. 225, 227; *LP, Henry VIII*, xvi, no. 672.

[25] Hull, *White and Black Books*, p. 228.

[26] Ibid., pp. 229–30; BL, MS Egerton 2093, ff. 402, 406.

due from them for all fifteenths and tenths and subsidies granted since 1534.[27] In April and May 1546 the collectors of the subsidy and of the fifteenth were forbidden to extend their activities into the liberty, and this followed lobbying of the council by Cheyne and three representatives of the ports.[28] But in June Cranmer was discussing with the council ways of making the Cinque Ports contribute, and in December the portsmen were once again petitioning for a pardon from the fifteenth and tenth, with some success.[29]

These efforts to secure exemption show the ports working closely, and it seems, successfully, with their lord warden, on an issue which was always of great importance to them. The ports claimed that taxation would exacerbate their decline, leading to depopulation and the weakening of the south east's coastal defences.[30] Cheyne's help was readily given when requested, suggesting that he saw this as part of his exercise of lordship, and as protecting his power base. His seat on the council made him a particularly effective mediator.[31]

In the autumn of 1556 the ports faced a challenge that potentially struck at the root of their privileges, in the shape of a writ of *quo warranto* which called into question the legal foundations of the liberty.[32] The help of the lord warden was essential in this matter, and so at the special guestling called on 10 September the ports decided to send elected representatives to Cheyne, explaining the situation and requesting him to act as a 'meane' between themselves and the queen; meanwhile each port was to seek legal advice.[33] While the ports were in no doubt as to the importance of this issue, this was not reflected in the timetable they had set themselves: the representatives were not to meet among themselves until the 22nd, by which time Cheyne had already received a writ demanding the appearance in king's bench of the bailiff, jurats and commonalty of New Romney to answer the *quo warranto* for their claim to be a corporate body.[34] The *quo warranto* touched the interests of the lord warden as well as those of the ports, and so his assistance was eventually forthcoming: in April and September 1557

[27] *LP, Henry VIII*, xix, pt 2, no. 527.

[28] Ibid., xxi, pt 1, nos 698, 870; CKS, NR/FAc/25.

[29] *LP, Henry VIII*, xxi, pt 1, no. 1041; CKS, Sa/AC 3, f. 192. The petition was successful: in March 1547 the barons of the Cinque Ports were given exemption from the fifteenth and tenth and the subsidy, East Sussex Record Office, Lewes (ESRO), RYE/57/1 f. 66.

[30] Murray, *Constitutional History*, pp. 222–3.

[31] Cheyne was not always approached directly. From 1554 Dover retained his secretary, Henry Tennant, at 40s. per annum as its solicitor in all its business with the lord warden or with the council, BL, MS Egerton 2094, ff. 107, 117v.

[32] For the use of *quo warranto* under the early Tudors see H. Garrett-Goodyear, 'The Tudor revival of *quo warranto* and local contributions to state building', in M. S. Arnold, T. A. Green et al. (ed.), *On the Laws and Customs of England: Essays in Honor of Samuel E. Thorne* (Chapel Hill, North Carolina, 1981), pp. 231–95.

[33] Hull, *White and Black Books*, p. 254.

[34] CKS, NR/CPW/20. Sandwich sent its representative to discuss the *quo warranto* with Cheyne on 18 September 1556, CKS, Sa/AC4, f. 95.

Joseph Beverley, clerk of Dover castle, accompanied Thomas Menys the mayor of Sandwich in discussions with the ports' counsel Roger Manwood on this matter.[35]

Another aspect of the lord warden's relationship as patron to the ports was his role as arbiter and general facilitator of business. For example, in 1540 Cheyne was approached by Dover regarding a debt of £44 which Sandwich allegedly owed to the port, and the following year he arbitrated between Hastings and Pevensey over the annual payment owed by the latter as a 'limb' of the head port, and helped the two communities to come to an agreement.[36] Cheyne also occasionally acted in disputes between individuals and corporations: the brotherhood wrote to him in 1546 and 1551 requesting him to exert pressure on behalf of individuals in dispute with Dover and Sandwich, while in November 1536 Richard Dering, the lieutenant of Dover castle, acted with the mayor of Dover in giving arbitration between two residents of the port.[37] The lieutenants of Dover castle could also be found sitting alongside the mayor and jurats of Dover in the borough, or hundred, court.[38]

The lord warden's chancery court of St James acted as a court of appeal: in the 1550s a plaintiff before the general court of New Romney petitioned Cheyne to summon the jurors in the case to St James to explain why they had awarded what the petitioner claimed were insufficient damages.[39] In 1547 Cheyne wrote to the bailiff and jurats of New Romney requiring them to see that justice was done to a suitor in their court of record.[40]

Clearly, the lord warden's appellate jurisdiction had the potential for causing friction between Dover castle and the ports. In 1542 Cheyne summoned a number of unruly Sandwich residents to appear before his court of St James, an act which the common council of Sandwich complained was in breach of their charter.[41] Nine years later John Monynges, the lieutenant of Dover castle, summoned some Dover men accused of causing an affray; the mayor of Dover demanded that he appear before the corporation to answer for this alleged breach, to which Monynges haughtily replied that if the mayor and jurats wanted to discuss the matter they would have to do so at the castle.[42] Meanwhile the accused found themselves doubly rebuked: Dover corporation proceeded to make a demonstration of its right to pass judgement by imposing fines on them, in the king's name, while – also in

[35] CKS, NR/CPC, ff. 16, 18. The process continued into the following year. In July 1558 the mayor and jurats of Fordwich were summoned to Sandwich to discuss their authority for the various privileges they held, CKS, Sa/AC 4, ff. 128–128v.

[36] BL, MS Egerton 2093, f. 353; ESRO, PEV 816.

[37] BL, MS Egerton 2093, ff. 292–3, 372; Hull, *White and Black Books*, pp. 235, 245.

[38] BL, MS Egerton 2093, ff. 328, 369.

[39] CKS, NR/CPL 4.

[40] CKS, NR/JBF 3.

[41] CKS, Sa/AC3, ff. 143–143v.

[42] BL, MS Egerton 2094, f. 40v.

the king's name – they received further writs demanding their appearance at the castle.[43]

In 1542 the mayor of Sandwich met with his counterpart at Fordwich – one of the head port's limbs – to discuss the writs of *certiorari* which had been used to bring cases from the borough courts to the lord warden's court of St James, and ten years later the Sandwich common council noted that parties in the court of record before the mayor and jurats had been procuring writs of *certiorari* in order to impede the process of justice, and therefore proclaimed that any person guilty of this tactic would now be liable to a £10 fine, loss of freedom and banishment.[44] A writ of *habeas corpus* from the lord warden provided another means by which individuals could evade the justice of the borough courts: in 1543 two jurats of Sandwich and two brewers who had been imprisoned for an unspecified offence procured a writ of *habeas corpus* under the lord warden's seal, and broke free, brandishing the writ as their justification.[45] The mayor claimed that the writ was contrary to the charter, and that the four 'had not done like honest men in the opteyninge of the same'; in consequence, the common council agreed that their legal counsel should send a letter of complaint to Cheyne on behalf of the town.[46]

In disputes with the lord warden the ports' usual recourse was to the charters that guaranteed their privileges; the incumbent of Dover castle had a larger armoury, ranging from threats to withdraw his protection to the use of force. When Sandwich failed to elect Cheyne's nominees for the March 1553 Parliament he sent two of his officers to tell the town's council that 'they shuld loke out for them selfes for they shuld get no aide and helpe at his handes'; but the mayor and council were obdurate, and their rather arch response was that:

they had don nothing but according unto the kinges magesties writt & his lordshipes precept and that they cannott ne yet could not do otherwise than according unto the kinges lawes & usages & privileges unles his lordship could purchase a newe writte for the same.[47]

On this occasion Sandwich got its way, and their two elected burgesses took their places in parliament.[48]

Behind the lord warden loomed a still greater presence. On 11 September 1555 Sandwich was required to supply two ships for the transport of King Philip and his retinue across the Channel.[49] Three days later the council required Cheyne to supply a further twenty-five or twenty-six ships from the Cinque Ports, observing that it was thought best to require a smaller

[43] Ibid.
[44] CKS, Sa/AC3, f. 169v; Sa/AC4, ff. 27v–28.
[45] CKS, Sa/AC3, f. 155.
[46] Ibid.
[47] CKS, Sa/AC4, f. 31v.
[48] See below, p. 140.
[49] CKS, Sa/AC4, f. 73.

number than their customary contribution, in order that they be well equipped; Cheyne's opinion was sought on this matter.[50] Accordingly Cheyne sent a copy of the council's letter to the Cinque Ports with a demand that this be done.[51] The Cinque Ports then protested to the council that this was the second time in a year that they had been required to supply ships, and that their charter bound them to supply ships once a year only; after examining the records of the liberty the council found that this claim could not be substantiated, and so wrote back to Cheyne, instructing him to repeat the demand for twenty-five ships, adding ominously, 'and therefore we cannot but thynk it very straunge that they aunswere the matter so slenderly', and had so hesitated to do their duty, particularly since they had for so long been spared the burdens imposed on other communities.[52] This letter, with for good measure an endorsement from Cheyne that if the Cinque Ports did not comply it would be to their 'greate hyndraunce hereafter', was circulated to the ports, who were instructed to reply without delay.[53] The letter prompted a circular from Dover to the other Cinque Ports observing that their answer had been 'wonderfully evyll taken' and that to avoid 'further inconvenyence' they should hasten to supply the best fleet they could.[54] Faced with the combined displeasure of the council and the lord warden the ports could do nothing else but comply: by 6 October Dover castle had received certificates listing the ships they were preparing to send.[55] However, William Crispe, the lieutenant of Dover castle, had to request that the ports resubmit their certificates, this time omitting any mention of the fact that they were responding to circulated copies of a confidential letter sent from the council to Cheyne: it seems that the ports had made one last defiant gesture by registering the forced nature of their compliance and by so doing, knowingly or not, might have caused their lord warden some embarrassment, had it not been for his diligent lieutenant. In their haste, or ill temper, the ports had also neglected to address the lord warden by his full title, an omission which Crispe huffily required to be supplied in the returned certificates and in all subsequent letters.[56]

The mayor and jurats of Sandwich appealed to their privileges again in November 1556 when Cheyne demanded that they supply twenty men to go to Portsmouth for Philip's long-awaited crossing of the Channel. Anticipating Sandwich's claim that this went beyond their accustomed service of ships, Cheyne's officers warned that, if they did not comply, 'his lordship wold not faile to send thaunsweres of the said maior & jurates unto the

---

[50] CKS, Sa/ZB/3, f. 96.
[51] Ibid., f. 96v; *APC*, v, p. 184.
[52] CKS, Sa/ZB/3, f. 98v; another copy in CKS, NR/CPW 16.
[53] Ibid.
[54] CKS, NR/CPW 16.
[55] CKS, NR/CPW 17.
[56] Ibid.

quenes majestie, for a contempte, to whome the said maior shuld aunswere for the same accordingly'. To this the mayor and jurats replied that they were willing, if need be, for this case to go before the council.[57] Despite this brave posturing, the following summer Sandwich and its limbs agreed to supply a handful of infantry and cavalry, although the jurats made it clear that they made this concession freely, out of consideration for the lord warden's obvious need of troops, and that this was not to establish a precedent.[58] Their generosity was to some degree reciprocated when they found themselves unable to raise the requisite number of men and instead offered the lord warden £40 towards the costs of equipping his troops: Cheyne replied that 'consydering the premysses' he would not require this, and so the money was spent on the town's defences.[59]

At times Cheyne went beyond threats. In 1539 he imprisoned Thomas Birchet, the mayor of Rye, in Dover castle, after complaints against him to the comptroller of the household by John Fletcher, the king's purveyor. Fletcher claimed that Birchet had so set the Rye fishermen against him that he would be unable to procure fish for the household.[60]

It would not be surprising if Cheyne did act with particular assiduousness when it came to enforcing royal demands. He could never forget that for all his lording it over the Cinque Ports he was still the crown's servant: in February 1557 Cheyne wrote to William Crispe, the lieutenant of Dover castle, that the provision of ships and men for Philip's anticipated crossing had to be effected 'to thuttermost of your poure aswell for your discharge as for myne'.[61]

These incidents remind us that relations between the lord warden and the ports cannot be studied in isolation. The lord warden was the ports' formal channel of communication with the crown and its agents, but there were many other influences on the political life of the liberty, and many other points of contact with national and regional politics. A detailed account of all aspects of Cheyne's political career would be neither possible nor appropriate within the scope of this essay, but some attempt must be made to locate him in his wider political context before moving on to discuss the Cinque Ports' position within the networks of regional and national power in mid Tudor England.

Cheyne is usually regarded as a religious conservative.[62] He probably owed

[57] CKS, Sa/AC4, f. 97.

[58] Ibid., ff. 109v–110.

[59] Ibid., ff. 111v–112. Further negotiations followed in August 1557 when Cheyne demanded twenty men from Sandwich to defend the queen, and Sandwich replied that he could have ten, ibid., f. 104v.

[60] PRO, SP 1/154, pp. 35–6 (*LP, Henry VIII*, xiv, pt 2, no. 341); PRO, SP 1/155, pp. 1–2 (*LP, Henry VIII*, xiv, pt 2, no. 546).

[61] CKS, NR/CPW/21.

[62] Unless otherwise stated, the following is based on Bindoff, *History of Parliament*, i, pp. 634–8, and Brock, 'Courtier in early Tudor society', passim.

his appointment as lord warden to Cromwell, and appears to have enjoyed his favour until 1537; thereafter relations may have cooled, but not necessarily as a consequence of Cheyne's religious position.[63] In any case, Cheyne's command of the royal archers who arrested Cromwell and made an inventory of his goods in 1540 hardly suggests a warm relationship between the two.[64]

Cheyne's relations with another leading figure in the English Reformation were also ambiguous. In 1537 Cranmer entered into an acrimonious correspondence with an unnamed Kentish potentate, whom he accused of disrupting the progress of religious change in the county: the recipient of Cranmer's vitriol could have been Cheyne, but there are other candidates.[65] Cranmer's assurance to Cecil of his good will towards Cheyne over a decade later strongly suggests a history of strife between the two.[66] This presumed hostility may have stemmed from religious differences alone, but there were more mundane bones of contention between them. In November 1546 the council required Cheyne to submit to their arbitration his dispute with Cranmer over their respective rights to the goods from a Spanish vessel wrecked the previous year.[67] Cheyne and Cranmer were also rivals for influence within the Cinque Ports.[68] Cheyne's acrimonious dispute with

---

[63] John Husee reported to Lord Lisle that some thought Cheyne's appointment was by Cromwell's preferment, M. St Clare Byrne (ed.), *The Lisle Letters* (6 vols, London and Chicago, 1981), iii, p. 695. For Cheyne's appointment, see *LP, Henry VIII*, x, no. 1015, g. 16. There were signs of friction from 1538: in March Cromwell countermanded Cheyne's order to the mayor and jurats of Rye to confiscate six tuns of wine rescued from a wreck (PRO, SP 1/130, p. 55; *LP, Henry VIII*, xiii, pt 1, no. 513); in the same month Cromwell was watching carefully Cheyne's negotiations for the purchase of lands of Faversham abbey (PRO, SP 1/130, p. 120; *LP, Henry VIII*, xiii, pt 1, no. 585); in November Jane Roper complained to Cromwell that her son Christopher, one of Cromwell's servants, had been kept out of his lands by Anthony Auger, paymaster of the king's works at Dover, and Nicholas Finch, Cheyne's servant (PRO, SP 1/139, p. 137; *LP, Henry VIII*, xiii, pt 2, no. 857). However, Cheyne and Thomas Cromwell's son Gregory sat for Kent in 1539, and the latter may have owed his seat partly to Cheyne's influence, Bindoff, *History of Parliament*, i, p. 728.

[64] *LP, Henry VIII*, xv, no. 804.

[65] PRO, SP 6/2, pp. 171–182 (*LP, Henry VIII*, xii, pt ii, pp. 297–9); Clark, *English Provincial Society*, p. 48. Bindoff, *History of Parliament*, i, p. 635, unhesitatingly identifies Cranmer's correspondent as Cheyne, but J. Ridley, *Thomas Cranmer* (Oxford, 1962), pp. 154–5, suggests Sir John Baker or possibly Sir Christopher Hales as alternatives. Cheyne was high steward of the archbishop's lands until 1540, *LP, Henry VIII*, xvi, no. 271.

[66] '... ther is no man more loth to be in contention with any man, than I am, specially with my Lorde Warden, my nere neighbour, dwellynge both in one contray, and whose familier and entier frendeshippe I most desier, for the quyetnes of the hole contray. For the example of the rulers and heades wil the people and membres followe', J. Strype (ed.), *Memorials of the Most Reverend Father in God, Thomas Cranmer, Sometimes Lord Archbishop of Canterbury* (Oxford, 1840), ii, p. 1037.

[67] *LP, Henry VIII*, xxi, pt ii, no. 390. This probably relates to goods taken by Anthony, Cheyne's servant, among others, from certain Spaniards, under the pretence of a wreck, in May 1545, ibid., xx, pt 1, no. 732. In November 1546 Anthony was ordered to bring books relating to the dispute to the council, ibid., xxi, pt ii, no. 390.

[68] See below, p. 138–9.

Cardinal Pole in 1558 over a number of issues, including fowling on the archbishop's liberty, further suggests that quarrels between the county's potentates need not always have had theological causes.[69]

Cheyne enjoyed a greater prominence at court during the short-lived conservative reaction of the early 1540s: he had been treasurer of the household since March 1539, and he is recorded as being present at over half of the council meetings between 1540 and 1543, as compared to less than a third during the remainder of his career.[70] In July 1540 he led the delegation from the commons that requested the king to put the question of his marriage to Anne of Cleves to convocation.[71] He also received a flurry of grants of former monastic properties in 1540 and 1541.[72] It may have been due to his influence at court at this time that his son John was pardoned in June 1541 for the murder of a gamekeeper during Lord Dacre's poaching expedition.[73] John Cheyne's unsubstantiated accusation in November 1541 that his father was a closet papist suggests that there were rumours abroad about Sir Thomas's religious predilections. So also do the unspecified, and equally unsuccessful, accusations made against him by Richard Cavendish, comptroller of king's works at Dover in January 1543, a minstrel in July 1545, and by his own lieutenant of Dover Castle, John Monynges, in September 1552.[74]

The nature of Cheyne's involvement with the Prebendaries' Plot against Cranmer in 1543 is also problematic: his chaplain was approached by some of the plotters to ask his master to use his influence with the archbishop to procure the release of Robert Serles, the conservative vicar of Lenham. This certainly suggests that the chaplain was thought to be sympathetic to the conservative cause, but the part that Cheyne himself was expected to play would have relied on his having had some sort of working relationship with Cranmer.[75]

Whatever his religious position may have been in the early 1540s, at

---

[69] *APC*, vi, p. 327.

[70] Brock, 'Courtier in early Tudor society', pp. 42, 50–1.

[71] Bindoff, *History of Parliament*, i, p. 635.

[72] See above, n. 12.

[73] *LP, Henry VIII*, xvi, g. 947, no. 53, nos 931–2, 954. John Cheyne's pardon, and Lord Dacre's execution, was reported as shocking the populace, Brock, 'Courtier in early Tudor society', pp. 141–2. Clark suggests that the incident gave Henry VIII the excuse to dispose of the last vestiges of the troublesome Neville affinity, *English Provincial Society*, pp. 53–4.

[74] John Cheyne's accusation, *LP, Henry VIII*, xvi, no. 1375. Cavendish's accusation, ibid., xviii, pt 1, no. 18; *APC*, i, pp. 73–4. The minstrel's accusation (Edmund Finch), *LP, Henry VIII*, xx, pt 1, nos 1083 & 1140. Cheyne and Monynges were summoned to appear before Northumberland in September 1552 to settle their dispute, *APC*, iv, p. 127. Cavendish had been in dispute with Cheyne in 1542 over the division of their responsibilities in Dover, and this may have encouraged his subsequent denunciation, ibid., i, p. 61.

[75] *LP, Henry VIII*, xviii, pt 2, no. 546; Ridley, *Thomas Cranmer*, pp. 231–6; Brock, 'Courtier in early Tudor society', p. 74. For the local background to the plot, see Clark, *English Provincial Society*, pp. 57–66.

Henry's death Cheyne was high in the king's favour.[76] He was accepted by Somerset's regime, but after Warwick's coup he feared that he would be branded as a conservative.[77] He opposed the adoption of Jane Grey and while he was forced to acquiesce in Northumberland's scheming he pledged his support for Mary as soon as he felt that it was safe to do so.[78] Despite his early show of support Cheyne was distrusted by Mary, at least initially, as she confessed to the imperial ambassador.[79] The court could not be certain of his loyalty at the outbreak of rebellion under his erstwhile friend and neighbour Sir Thomas Wyatt in 1554: later that year he was among those considered for exclusion as part of an unsuccesful plan to reduce the size of the council.[80] The reasons for Cheyne's lukewarm relationship with the Marian regime are unlikely to have been theological. Perhaps he feared for his holdings of former monastic estates, or his association with Warwick (now Northumberland) may have counted against him – although neither of these factors would have differentiated him from several other courtiers who were readily accepted into the fold – or it may be that Cheyne's francophile predilictions set him against closer imperial ties.[81]

Cheyne's will and the elaborate proceedings at his funeral were entirely consistent with orthodox Catholicism, but this is hardly surprising given that he died only a month into Elizabeth's reign.[82] It would be unwise to accept the Elizabethan William Darell's description of Cheyne as a well-wisher to the Reformation whose radicalism estranged him from Mary (and who died

---

[76] W. K. Jordan, *Edward VI: The Young King* (London, 1968), p. 64; Brock, 'Courtier in early Tudor society', p. 52. According to Paget, Cheyne was to have been raised to the peerage, but the king changed his mind before producing the final version of his will; however, he was left £200 and made an assistant executor, ibid.; Bindoff, *History of Parliament*, i, p. 636.

[77] Cheyne was among those councillors entrusted with the government of the realm during Somerset's Scottish campaign of 1547, Brock, 'Courtier in early Tudor society', pp. 66–7. He was among those who sanctioned Gardiner's imprisonment in June 1548, and he was involved in the interrogation of Sir Thomas Seymour in 1549, ibid., pp. 67–8; Bindoff, *History of Parliament*, i, p. 636.

[78] Brock, 'Courtier in early Tudor society', pp. 68–9; Bindoff, *History of Parliament*, i, p. 636; J. Loach, *Parliament and the Crown in the Reign of Mary Tudor* (Oxford, 1986), p. 4.

[79] Brock, 'Courtier in early Tudor society', pp. 174–5. But Cheyne retained his position as treasurer of the household when Mary replaced other household officers, D. Loades, *The Reign of Mary Tudor* (2nd edn, London, 1991), pp. 19–21, 42.

[80] Brock, 'Courtier in early Tudor society', pp. 69, 215; Bindoff, *History of Parliament*, i, pp. 636–7; Wyatt, *Cheneys and Wyatts*, p. 30; D. Loades, *Two Tudor Conspiracies* (Cambridge, 1965), pp. 57–64. In October 1554 the mayor of Canterbury told the council of 'a leud feallowe that hath bruted there the Quene to be apprehended and kept [in] the Lord Treasourer's house', *APC*, v, p. 79. Despite these doubts and rumours Cheyne was still given a pension of 1000 crowns by Philip, Brock, 'Courtier in early Tudor society', p. 637. See also, A. Weikel, 'The Marian council revisited', in J. Loach and R. Tittler (ed.), *The Mid Tudor Polity, c. 1540–1560* (London, 1980), pp. 52–73.

[81] Brock, 'Courtier in early Tudor society', p. 17; Bindoff, *History of Parliament*, i, pp. 634, 636.

[82] PRO, PROB 11/42b. His funeral is described in J. G. Nichols (ed.), *The Diary of Henry Machyn, Citizen and Merchant Taylor of London*, Camden Society, xlii (1848), pp. 184–5.

from an excess of joy at the news of the accession of her sister). The imperial ambassador's estimate of him in 1549 as a true Catholic willing to spend his fortune in the good cause also seems at odds with the facts of his career.[83] Perhaps the other part of the ambassador's judgement on him also needs to be taken into account: 'a timid man, much addicted to worldly possessions'.[84] Cheyne's conservatism was evidently of the milder sort, well tempered with pragmatism.

One gauge of political influence within the Cinque Ports is provided by the returns of burgesses to parliament. In accordance with his monopoly on the return of writs, the lord warden received the writs for parliamentary elections. It was through him that the returns were made, which gave him the potential for exerting considerable influence over the ports' representation.[85] In the four parliaments between 1536 and 1545 there were probably no more than three Cinque Ports burgesses with particular Cheyne connections, but in the parliaments of 1547 and March 1553 there may have been as many as ten Cheyne associates, and in the five elections under Mary possibly as many as forty-two. This would give averages of less than one 'Cheyne' burgess for each election under Henry, five under Edward and over eight (making an average of more than one per port) under Mary.[86] While in some cases the relationship between a burgess and the lord warden may have been entirely irrelevant to his election, the overall pattern is clear, and in many instances Cheyne's influence on elections is beyond doubt. Cheyne's interference under Mary represents a new peak in the lord warden's influence on Cinque Ports' elections, establishing, de facto, his nomination of one of the two burgesses for each of the ports; this precedent was to haunt the portsmen in their struggles with Dover castle for generations to come.[87] The above evidence suggests a steady accretion of power throughout Cheyne's wardenship, culminating in his supremacy under Mary, but the reality was more complex, as the lord warden's influence was subject to periodic checks both from within the ports and by outsiders.

In April 1545 Cheyne fell ill, and he was temporarily relieved of his duties

---

[83] W. Darell, *The History of Dover Castle* (London, 1786), pp. 66–7; Brock, 'Courtier in early Tudor society', p. 74; *Calendar of State Papers, Spanish*, ix, no. 462, x, no. 8.

[84] Ibid.

[85] Bindoff, *History of Parliament*, i, p. 253; J. E. Neale, *The Elizabethan House of Commons* (London, 1949), pp. 213–4.

[86] Bindoff, *History of Parliament*, i, p. 254.

[87] Neale, *Elizabethan House of Commons*, pp. 216–21; Gruenfelder, 'Lord warden and elections', pp. 1–23. In 1571 Sandwich claimed this precedent as a safeguard against still further encroachments by the then lord warden, Lord Cobham: in 'all Sir Thomas Cheyne's time and in all your Lordship's time also we have had both or one at the least of our own inhabitants, according to the Queen's writ and our liberties; and by our customs and liberties, always used, one at the least must be such as was sworn to our liberties', Neale, *Elizabethan House of Commons*, p. 216.

as lord warden by Sir Thomas Seymour, Hertford's brother.[88] For the next four months Cheyne shared his responsibilities in the Cinque Ports and Kent with Seymour.[89] This association may have helped Seymour to develop his interest in the Cinque Ports after his brother, subsequently duke of Somerset, rose to power in 1547, for in the parliament of that year both members for Winchelsea, John Rowland and John More, were outsiders who probably owed their elections to the influence of the Seymour-Somerset circle.[90] In August Seymour had been granted most of the former Howard baronies of Bramber and Lewes, and seems to have been flexing his muscles in Sussex, while his position as lord admiral since 1544 would also have brought him into contact with the ports.[91]

The new Somerset court circle also seems to have been responsible for the return of the religious radical William Brooke (later Lord Cobham) at Hythe. Seymour may have persuaded Cheyne to have another radical outsider, Sir William Stafford, returned for Hastings.[92] Cheyne appears to have been deprived of the wardenship soon after Edward VI's accession, but was granted it back in April: it probably took him some time to find his feet under the new regime. At this point his personal influence in the ports may have been in danger of being subsumed into that of the radical court connection.[93] In April 1547, solicitors appointed by the Cinque Ports to help procure a new general charter were instructed to make their suit directly to the council: Cheyne does not appear to have been involved in this.[94] By July Cheyne was once again acting as a mediator between the ports and central government, but the Seymours' influence in the Cinque Ports remained strong: in August 1548 Somerset's support of the radical Thomas Birchet resulted in his election as mayor of Rye.[95]

Cheyne was unable or unwilling to prevent the encroachment of the Seymours, but he showed himself determined to meet the challenge from another representative of the radical new order. Cranmer attempted to have up to three of his men elected in 1547: Peter Hayman at New Romney and John Seer at Sandwich were definitely his clients; Thomas Pinnock at

---

[88] On 27 April the council sent Seymour to be Cheyne's deputy, in view of the latter's 'naughty whoreson ague', PRO, SP 2/5200, f. 74 (*LP, Henry VIII*, xx, pt 1, no. 584). Two years previously Seymour had served under Cheyne in France, PRO, SP 1/179, f. 116 (*LP, Henry VIII*, xviii, pt 1, no. 773).

[89] Ibid., xx, pt 1, g. 846, no. 13, no. 1313; pt 2, no. 94; *APC*, i, p. 226.

[90] Bindoff, *History of Parliament*, ii, pp. 618–9; iii, p. 223. For the local background to this period, see Clark, *English Provincial Society*, pp. 69–86.

[91] R. J. W. Swales, 'The Howard interest in Sussex elections, 1529 to 1558', *Sussex Archaeological Collections*, cxiv (1976), pp. 49–60, 54–5; Jordan, *The Young King*, pp. 368–83.

[92] Bindoff, *History of Parliament*, i, pp. 512–13; iii, pp. 364–5.

[93] *CPR, Edward VI*, i, p. 103.

[94] Hull, *White and Black Books*, p. 236.

[95] Ibid., p. 237; ESRO, RYE/60/6, f. 167v. A further indication of the challenge to Cheyne's hegemony may be the increasing number of royal writs directed straight to portsmen, bypassing Dover castle and infringing the lord warden's right of monopoly: see above, pp. 126–7.

Sandwich is very likely to have been.[96] Archiepiscopal involvement in the Cinque Ports was nothing new: Hythe was part of the manor of Saltwood and most of New Romney lay in the manor of Aldington, both of which had been held by the archbishops until Cranmer was forced to surrender them in 1540. New Romney at least had probably returned a Cranmer client to every election since 1535.[97] But Cranmer's intervention in Sandwich was a new development.[98] In September John Seer and Thomas Pinnock were elected for Sandwich, but the mayor, John Stile, refused to accept their return and called another election, which returned Thomas Arden, who had been in Cheyne's service since 1541 (and the first non-jurat to be returned for the port since at least the fifteenth century), and the royal bailiff of Sandwich, Thomas Patche. Both were almost certainly Cheyne's placemen, and Stile was probably acting on Cheyne's orders, or at least with his approval.[99] But the proceedings at Sandwich came to the attention of the council, which forced the readoption of the original members, and in May 1548 the common council of Sandwich fined Stile £10 for his action the previous year in breaking open the common chest in order to falsify the election returns.[100] The council's intervention on behalf of what may have been the 'Cranmer Party' no doubt alarmed Cheyne, who had also suffered a rebuke from the same quarter for his clumsy handling of the Kent election, where Cheyne failed to have returned John Baker, the council's chosen candidate.[101] Further humiliation came in 1548, when Thomas Pinnock secured Cranmer's help in Sandwich's campaign for government assistance with harbour improvements.[102]

The growing confusion of authority within the liberty evidently concerned a number of the leading portsmen. In August 1550 a brotherhood proposed that the franchise for the election of the ports' head officers – mayors, jurats and bailiffs – be restricted to thirty-seven people in each port, to be chosen by the mayors and jurats and that the views of the commons be sought on this. Cheyne was requested to help in the consultation process.[103] Cheyne's officers actively promoted the proposal to turn the ports into closed corporations, but Sandwich at least decided not to adopt it and Dover's franchise was not restricted until September 1556.[104] The apparent failure of a measure

[96] Bindoff, *History of Parliament*, ii, pp. 325–6; iii, pp. 109–10, 288.

[97] Ibid., i, pp. 257–9.

[98] Cranmer seems to have been making deliberate efforts to establish himself at Sandwich: in March 1547 Sandwich common council agreed to make a freeman at Cranmer's request, CKS, Sa/AC 3, f. 194v.

[99] Bindoff, *History of Parliament*, i, pp. 263, 328–9; iii, pp. 69, 109–10, 288.

[100] Ibid., i, p. 262; CKS, Sa/AC 3, ff. 207–207v.

[101] Bindoff, *History of Parliament*, i, p. 367.

[102] Ibid., iii, pp. 109–10; CKS, Sa/AC 3, ff. 204–204v, 206v.

[103] This was based on the precedent of an act passed in a brotherhood of 1525, CKS, NR/CPc/9. See also Murray, *Constitutional History*, p. 92, and Clark, *English Provincial Society*, p. 80.

[104] CKS, Sa/AC 3, ff. 238v, 244v; BL, MS Egerton 2094, ff. 154–5.

that would have greatly increased the lord warden's ability to control the Cinque Ports corporations is another indicator of Cheyne's difficulties under Edward VI. Cheyne's appointment as lord lieutenant of Kent in April 1551 made a valuable addition to his powers, but his authority within the Cinque Ports was still being contested: it was in September 1551 that lieutenant Monynges made his accusations against Cheyne.[105]

Elections for the March 1553 parliament were the occasion for further conflict. At New Romney the chamberlain noted that William Tadlow (almost certainly Cranmer's choice) and Richard Bunting were 'put awaye by our lorde warden frome [their] electon' and replaced by Simon Padyham and another unnamed Cheyne client, 'contrarye to our eleccon'.[106] Cheyne's high-handed action in an area of traditional archiepiscopal influence may be a reflection of Cranmer's declining political capital under Northumberland.[107] Cheyne acted likewise at Rye, whose elected burgesses, Robert Wood and the radical Alexander Welles, appear to have been turned away at the parliament door in favour of the lord warden's men, Richard Fletcher and John Holmes.[108] Cheyne's client Henry Crisp was returned at Dover, and only Sandwich appears to have successfully resisted pressure from the lord warden.[109] The appointment of Cheyne as bailiff of Sandwich in June 1553 may have been an attempt to buttress his authority in the most independent and troublesome of the Cinque Ports.[110]

Before Mary's first parliament the Cinque Ports attempted to challenge the legality of the lord warden's interference in elections. New Romney and Rye considered the possibility of holding a guestling at which a suit against Cheyne would be discussed, and Dover and Sandwich were also involved in legal proceedings, but nothing came of it, apart from an increasing tension between the lord warden and the ports.[111] At the elections in Autumn 1553 the burgesses for Dover, Thomas Colly and Thomas Portway, were set aside in favour of Joseph Beverley (the clerk of Dover castle) and John Webbe, another Cheyne client; John Peyton at Hastings, William Oxenden (Cheyne's servant) at Hythe, Clement Heigham and John Holmes at Rye were all probably returned as the result of pressure from the lord warden.[112] At Winchelsea, John Guildford, the sheriff of Kent, and William Egleston were set aside by Cheyne in favour of Henry Crisp and William Roper, but

---

[105] *APC*, iii, p. 258; Clark, *English Provincial Society*, pp. 78–81. For the lieutenant's accusations see above, p. 135.

[106] CKS, NR/FAc 7, f. 80v; Bindoff, *History of Parliament*, i, p. 546; iii, pp. 40, 418–19.

[107] Ridley, *Thomas Cranmer*, pp. 318, 322, 340–2.

[108] Bindoff, *History of Parliament*, ii, pp. 153–4, 379–80; iii, pp. 572–3.

[109] Ibid., i, pp. 722–3; for Sandwich see above, p. 131.

[110] *CPR, Edward VI*, v, p. 78; and see Clark, *English Provincial Society* p. 80.

[111] CKS, NR/FAc 7, f. 82v; Sa/AC 4, ff. 35–35v; BL, MS Egerton 2094, f. 90v.

[112] Bindoff, *History of Parliament*, i, pp. 428–9; ii, pp. 329–30, 379–80; iii, pp. 39–40, 100–1, 140, 564–5.

Guildford was then placed at New Romney, only to be removed when the council decided that he could not represent a seat within the county of which he was sheriff.[113] Sandwich elected two men of Protestant sympathies, Simon Linch and Thomas Menys. Cheyne had strongly objected to Menys' election for the previous parliament, and this time he succeeded in having him replaced by John Perrot, Cheyne's son-in-law.[114]

Linch was allowed to sit, but in December the council informed Sandwich that his recent election as mayor could not stand since he was already custol ier of the port. The real reason lay, of course, with his political symp.thies.[115]

Menys and Linch were part of a radical group in Sandwich, the former appearing to have been their leader and a particular thorn in Cheyne's side. Menys and Linch were elected by Sandwich to bear the canopy at Mary's coronation – the traditional right of the portsmen. This was not a happy choice, since they stole the canopy and sold it.[116] The pair appear to have escaped serious punishment for this calculated insult, being merely required to pay for a replacement.[117] But in July 1554 Menys was granted a reduction on his contribution towards a new canopy in recompense for the time he had spent in the Marshalsea, having been put there on the orders of the lord warden while on the port's business: the nature of his transgression is not known.[118]

The spring 1554 elections seem to have been relatively uneventful, but by the November parliament Cheyne's influence on the elections was openly acknowledged throughout the ports: it appears that for this election each port – with the predictable exception of Sandwich – accepted the principle that one of their two burgesses was to be chosen by the lord warden.[119] Sandwich elected its mayor, John Tysar, and a jurat, William Lathebury, but then was forced to accept the latter's replacement by Cheyne's son-in-law, Nicholas Crispe.[120] For each of the two remaining parliaments of Mary's reign, in 1555 and 1558, Cheyne maintained his new-found right to nominate one member for each port. He felt no qualms about introducing

---

[113] This was probably the result of political considerations. Guildford had been linked with Northumberland and may have been a Protestant, Bindoff, *History of Parliament*, i, pp. 722–3; ii, pp. 87–8, 265–6; iii, pp. 215–7.

[114] Ibid., ii, pp. 532–3, 595–6; iii, pp. 86–8.

[115] Ibid., ii, pp. 532–3; CKS, Sa/AC 4, ff. 37, 39. Linch's name was on a list of MPs drawn up in 1553, probably indicating those opponents of some aspects of Mary's religious policies, Loach, *Parliament and the Crown*, pp. 83–90, 239–40.

[116] CKS, Sa/AC 4, ff. 55v–56.

[117] Ibid., f. 58.

[118] Ibid., f. 71.

[119] Bindoff, *History of Parliament*, i, p. 254. In September New Romney wrote to Cheyne asking him to inform the chancellor that they had granted him the nomination of a burgess to parliament, CKS, NR/CPW 16.

[120] Bindoff, *History of Parliament*, i, p. 262.

complete outsiders, members of his family and household, and apparently, clients of his friends.[121]

Cheyne's period of greatest intervention in elections was also a time of great unrest in the ports, particularly at Sandwich. Here prominent inhabitants were showing greater reluctance to accept election as jurats and mayors.[122] There was also a spate of outbursts against the mayor and jurats during the mayoralty of John Master in 1557–8.[123] Master had radical associations, and his religious and political sympathies may account for the opposition to him, but he was also a friend of Thomas Menys, Cheyne's bête noire, and so dissension may have been encouraged from Dover castle.[124] Menys had been mayor the previous year, and in October 1557 he was summoned to appear before the council, together with Nicholas Peake, another of Master's associates, over an offensive letter – whose contents are unknown – that had been sent from Sandwich to the lord warden.[125] Menys was ordered to bring before the council the five 'chiefelie doers in the devising of the said lettres', while Peake was to remain in attendance, reporting daily to one of the clerks.[126]

Throughout Mary's reign a radical group managed to survive among the Sandwich jurats. Cheyne's opposition to the religious positions of a number of its leading inhabitants undoubtedly exacerbated his stormy relationship with Sandwich, but he did not completely disassociate himself from religious radicals. Sir John Perrot, his son-in-law, had radical leanings, as had Thomas Arden. Thomas Randolph, who probably had Cheyne to thank for his return for New Romney in 1558, may also fall into this category, while Reginald Mohun, burgess for Rye in 1555 – probably again at Cheyne's behest – was unable to secure election in his native Cornwall because of his radical sympathies.[127] The Marian council instructed the returning officers to secure

[121] In 1558 Henry Tennant, MP for Hastings, was Cheyne's secretary; Richard Daper for Hythe was Cheyne's servant. Cheyne's sons-in-law Perrot and Crispe sat for Sandwich in 1555 and 1558 respectively. John Herbert, member for New Romney in 1555, was a cousin of Cheyne's associate the earl of Pembroke. Reginald Mohun owed his return for Rye in the same parliament to his links with the earl of Bedford, another of Cheyne's associates. A Bedford connection may also have eased Thomas Randolph's passage to parliament as burgess for New Romney. Bindoff, *History of Parliament*, i, pp. 723–4; ii, pp. 13, 339, 609; iii, pp. 86–8, 176, 436.

[122] For example Thomas Manwood, April 1557, CKS, Sa/AC 4, ff. 106v, 109, and John Sayn, ibid., f. 108v. In July 1557 jurats were to be fined if they failed to appear with the mayor at borough courts, ibid., f 110v. During his mayoral year in 1557–8 John Master asked to be excused from any other offices in the future because of his age, ibid., f. 117v. In April 1558 Simon Linch also asked to be excused office as mayor or bailiff to Yarmouth for two years, ibid., f. 125v.

[123] Ibid., ff. 123, 123v, 124v, 125.

[124] Bindoff, *History of Parliament*, ii, pp. 587, 595–6.

[125] Ibid., iii, pp. 77–8 (Peake was Menys' father-in-law, and was related by marriage to the Manwoods); *APC*, vi, p. 189.

[126] Ibid.

[127] See above, nn. 99, 121; and for Perrot's opposition to Marian policy, see Loach, *Parliament and the Crown*, pp. 211–13, 229.

the return of members of the 'wise, grave and catholic sort'. As these examples suggest, Cheyne occasionally allowed other factors to override his aversion to religious radicalism, and by so doing preferred his own interests before the demands of the crown.[128]

No doubt much of the tension within the Cinque Ports at the end of Mary's reign was a local manifestation of general dissatisfaction with the crumbling regime, intensified by the particular demands and fears to which the south coast was subject as the borders of the realm shrank across the Channel.[129] But the difficulties between Cheyne and Sandwich may have had more to do with an attempt by the port to resist the encroaching power of the lord warden. Religious differences do not seem to have been the only root of this struggle, although they were certainly a very important element. Sandwich was still prosperous enough to feel able to resist. Unlike Dover, which might also have felt itself strong enough to make a stand, it was far enough distant from Cheyne's administrative base to maintain some degree of independence. Cheyne's growing control over the ports was not merely one among many examples of interference in local politics by the crown and its agents; in fact his success in this regard contrasts sharply with the Marian regime's generally 'perfunctory and ineffectual' attempts to control elections.[130]

The liberty of the Cinque Ports began as a royal initiative – the product of crown expediency – but by the sixteenth century it had evolved into a community with a sophisticated administrative system, including the brotherhood (a common assembly for its own defence) and a certain common sentiment among its elite that this heterogeneous affiliation was theirs, was something to which they owed a degree of loyalty, and which was worth fighting for. Through the institutions of the brotherhood, the guestling, the shared benefits guaranteed by charters granted to the ports collectively rather than individually, a fund of common interests, and intermittently through the figure of their lord warden, the portsmen maintained this sense of belonging to a community that cut across county boundaries. Despite royal encroachments, it was the crown, through the lord warden, which ultimately safeguarded this identity.

For the crown, the liberty provided a valuable reserve of patronage. The lord wardenship was naturally regarded as a particularly valuable reward for good service, but it was much more than this. The lord warden enjoyed a pivotal position in the politics of the south east, and was in possession of a power base that enabled him to develop his own policy within the

---

[128] Ibid., pp. 30–1; Loades, *Reign of Mary Tudor*, p. 216.

[129] Ibid., pp. 304–39; Clark, *English Provincial Society*, pp. 98–107.

[130] Loades, *Reign of Mary Tudor*, p. 399. Crown influence was mainly used to secure seats for 'useful' candidates, rather than to prevent unsympathetic men from sitting, Loach, *Parliament and the Crown*, pp. 27–32.

region.[131] This was a potentially threatening situation for the crown.[132] That the crown was willing to live with the risks suggests the scale of the advantage it expected to derive from this arrangement. Sir Edward Coke made clear the nature of this advantage when he wrote that the Cinque Ports, 'do lie towards France and therefore prudent antiquity provided that they should be vigilantly and securely kept'; the lord warden, 'in former times was ever a man of great fidelity, wisdom, courage, and experience, for that he had the charge of the principal gates of the Realm'.[133]

The Cinque Ports were strategically important not for their own military resources – the men and ships of the ports never made an impressive display – but for the infrastructure they provided. The staff of Dover castle supplied the nucleus of a command structure, the chain of ports gave ready communications along the south-east coast, and the ports' fishing fleets provided a reasonably effective watch on events in the Channel.[134] For this reason the crown was willing to suffer the presence of an 'anachronistic' liberty, to allow its exemption from taxation and, for the sake of having this strategic infrastructure under firm, unified control, it was prepared to devolve such powers into the hands of the lord warden.

[131] In 1597 there was a fierce struggle between Essex and the Cecils to place their respective clients in the vacant post, Neale, *Elizabethan House of Commons*, pp. 214–15.

[132] The court's unease over Cheyne's loyalties at the outbreak of Wyatt's rebellion is a case in point, see above, p. 136.

[133] E. Coke, *Fourth Institute* (London, 1669), pp. 222–4, cited in Neale, *Elizabethan House of Commons*, p. 213.

[134] For the portsmen's reconnaissance in the Channel, see *LP, Henry VIII*, xiii, pt 1, nos 206, 217; xx, pt 1, no. 1144, pt 2, no. 94; *APC*, iii, p. 118; iv, p. 79. In July 1548 Cheyne replied angrily to a request from the commissioners of muster that he allow some of his servants to lead the Kentish forces. He refused on the grounds that, 'I have the cure of the whole shire methinkes yee should consider that it is meete and beside requisit that I should have my owne men about me', BL, MS Add. 37668 f. 15v. This could be dismissed as bluster, but the anonymous Elizabethan writer on the state of Kent's defences attributed the county's past security to the presence of Cheyne's household, PRO, SP 12/75/43. Tudor governments realised the importance of maintaining the coastal defences, Clark, *English Provincial Society*, pp. 47, 72. In 1548, when Sandwich corporation petitioned Somerset for help with the rebuilding of their coastal defences, they included a short account of the defensive role the port had played over the previous two hundred years, W. Boys, *History of Sandwich* (2 vols, Canterbury, 1792), ii, p. 733.

8

Purveyance and Politics in Jacobean Leicestershire

Richard Cust

Recent work by historians of Jacobean England has demonstrated the very considerable political significance of purveyance. Purveyance was the prerogative right claimed by the crown to buy provisions for the royal household at well below market prices. The purchasing was done by purveyors, who were notorious for extorting goods and draining local markets of produce. Steps were taken at the end of Elizabeth's reign to remedy these abuses through a series of composition agreements, whereby counties themselves undertook to provide goods by particular dates at specified prices and covered the difference between the purchase price of these goods and the price paid by the crown by levying a county rate. However, although these agreements removed some of the worst grievances associated with purveyors, they failed to get rid of the purveyors themselves, since many reappeared, acting as undertakers for those supervising the compositions. They also created a new source of resentment in the form of an annual levy which had to be paid by everyone down to the lowliest property owner.[1]

Complaints about purveyance were voiced in the later parliaments of Elizabeth's reign, but opposition to it came to a head soon after the accession of James I. The king had aroused expectations of a reform of purveyance only to disappoint his subjects by imposing still heavier burdens as a result of his enlarged household and frequent progresses. Hostile grumblings developed into a direct challenge to the royal prerogative in the parliaments of 1604 and 1606, when, as Eric Lindquist and Pauline Croft have shown, MPs discovered that purveyance was explicitly prohibited by a whole series of medieval statutes. The commons proposed legislation which would not only have remedied the abuses of purveyors, but also abolished altogether the king's right to take goods at reduced prices. When this was blocked by the crown and the house of lords they negotiated to 'buy' the king out of his prerogative. This culminated in the bargaining over the 'Great Contract'

[1] I am grateful to the Huntington Library, California, and the British Academy for awarding me a Huntington-Exxon grant which made possible much of the research on which this essay is based. A. Woodworth, *Purveyance for the Royal Household in the Reign of Queen Elizabeth*, Transactions of the American Philosophical Society, new series, xxxv, pt 1 (1945).

in the parliament of 1610.[2] Lindquist has argued that the reason why parliament paid so much attention to purveyance in these sessions – especially in 1606 when it dominated the commons agenda – was because it was a genuinely popular grievance. The heaviest burden fell not on the gentry, who were exempt from certain sorts of purveyance and could defend themselves against the excesses of purveyors, but on ordinary taxpayers, who bore the main cost of the compositions through county rates, and also the high food prices which resulted when purveyors visited local markets. There are indications that taxpayers followed the commons proceedings over purveyance closely; and after the 1604 session MPs went home to consult their constituents and take advice on what was to be done next. Lindquist argues that the pressure which this generated accounts for the alacrity with which the commons took up again in 1606 the bill against purveyance which had foundered in 1604. Similar consultations also took place in the summer of 1610 when MPs canvassed opinion amongst constituents about the terms of the 'Great Contract'.[3] From the beginning of James' reign, then, the whole legal basis of purveyance, as well as the particular abuses to which it gave rise, were widely discussed and widely questioned. Of all the subjects' current grievances this was the one which had most impact and caused most annoyance at a local level, particularly in the home counties and the midlands where the burdens tended to be heaviest.[4]

But what effect did all this have on local politics? We are used to looking at the way in which royal levies of the 1620s and 1630s, such as the forced loan or ship money, disrupted local politics and furthered the process of politicising local taxpayers; and in the heavily burdened and divided county of Norfolk such developments have been traced back as far as the 1590s.[5] But what of James' reign, when the country as a whole was relatively lightly burdened with taxes and the monarch rarely needed to resort to prerogative levies because the country was at peace? This study of Leicestershire seeks to throw some light on the impact of purveyance, and to illustrate the complex and contradictory ways in which local politics could become entangled with national issues.

---

[2] E. N. Lindquist, 'The king, the people and the House of Commons: the problems of early-Jacobean purveyance', *HJ*, xxxi (1988), pp. 549–70; E. N. Lindquist, 'Supplement: the bills against purveyance', *PH*, iv (1985), pp. 35–43; E. N. Lindquist, 'The failure of the Great Contract', *Journal of Modern History*, lvii (1985), pp. 617–51; P. Croft, 'Parliament, purveyance and the City of London, 1589–1608', *PH*, iv (1985), pp. 9–34.

[3] Lindquist, 'The problem of early-Jacobean purveyance', pp. 550–64; A. G. R. Smith, 'Crown, parliament and finance: the Great Contract of 1610', in P. Clark, A. G. R. Smith and N. R. N. Tyacke (ed.), *The English Commonwealth, 1547–1640* (Leicester, 1979), pp. 120–2.

[4] G. E. Aylmer, 'The last years of purveyance, 1610–1660', *Economic History Review*, 2nd series, x (1957–8), p. 86.

[5] R. P. Cust, *The Forced Loan and English Politics, 1626–1628* (Oxford, 1987); T. G. Barnes, *Somerset, 1625–1640* (Oxford, 1961); P. Clark, *English Provincial Society: Religion, Politics and Society in Kent, 1500–1640* (Hassocks, 1977), chapters 11–12; A. Hassell Smith, *County and Court: Government and Politics in Norfolk, 1558–1603* (Oxford, 1974).

Since the mid sixteenth century Leicestershire had been involved in composition agreements by which the county itself undertook to supply various provisions in return for being freed from the visits of purveyors. The agreement which operated for most of James' reign had been drawn up after negotiations between the Board of the Greencloth, the household department responsible for supervising purveyance, and the fourth earl of Huntingdon, sometime between 1596 and 1600. No copy of this agreement has been found, but the evidence of its workings suggests that it was rather more flexible than most of the others drawn up in this period. It listed the provisions due from the county – forty oxen, 600 mutton, 400 lambs and 120 dozen poultry and fowl – and the dates by which these were to be delivered to the Greencloth; however, it also seems to have included some allowance whereby the county could simply send the money it raised to cover the composition to the Greencloth, which would then make the purchases itself. Gerald Aylmer has suggested that such a system was not operating before James's reign, but there is evidence that it was being applied in Leicestershire as early as February 1599/1600.[6]

Presumably the county's decision on which way to proceed was based on the availability and prices of particular goods in local markets, which could fluctuate from year to year. In the absence of accounts it is not possible to calculate precisely how much the purveyance composition cost Leicestershire. In 1611, when the county was negotiating over the introduction of a fixed monetary payment to replace the earlier composition, Lord Grey suggested that they offer £500, which can be presumed to be the minimum they thought they could get away with. In 1621, on the other hand, prior to similar negotiations, the Greencloth calculated the difference between the prices paid for goods by the king and their cost to the county at £983 17s. 4d. The annual demand probably fluctuated between these two amounts, depending on food prices.[7] This made purveyance the heaviest annual demand from the crown which Leicestershire had to bear during James' reign. The total levied might still fall short of the sums raised by parliamentary subsidies or benevolences; but such demands were occasional and irregular, and anyway were paid only by the wealthier taxpayers.[8] The purveyance composition,

[6] Woodworth, *Purveyance in the Reign of Elizabeth*, pp. 39–41, 54, 79, 81; Huntington Library, California (HL), HA Correspondence, 4127, 4129, 4130; HMC, *Report on the MSS of Reginald Rawdon Hastings* (4 vols, 1928–47), iv, 189–90; Aylmer, 'Last years of purveyance', p. 82.

[7] Bodleian Library, Oxford, MS Carte 78, f. 321; PRO, LS 1/279, f. 73v. It is probable that the cost of purveyance in Leicestershire rose considerably during the course of James's reign as it did in Kent, where there was a considerable increase after 1610, in part because of an extra two shillings in the pound levied to cover the treasurer's fee: J. J. N. McGurk, 'Royal purveyance in the shire of Kent, 1590–1614', *BIHR*, cxxi (1977), p. 66. In 1620 the Leicestershire JPs warned Huntingdon that because of high food prices the county was due to pay £120 more than previously to cover the cost of the purveyance composition: HL, HA Correspondence, 8534.

[8] In 1620 the county paid £1558 as a voluntary contribution for the defence of the Palatinate and between April 1621 and February 1622 approximately £1500 on the grant of two subsidies

although in practice an annual tax, was treated by the county justices as a local rate, and therefore had to be paid by all ratepayers – which in Leicestershire at this time meant almost anyone owning land or more than a few animals. When divided up between parishes the cost of purveyance was considerable, usually amounting to over 10 per cent of the total collected by parish constables, and more when the king was on one of his hunting trips to the east midlands.[9] Moreover there was the added inconvenience with a local rate that its division between the parishes had to be determined by the local justices, which led to friction and disputes, particularly where extra rates were levied to cover defaults.

High cost and administrative inconvenience were not the only problems which purveyance brought to Leicestershire. It also led to frequent contact with the Board of the Greencloth, whose heavy-handed methods caused further annoyance. The Greencloth had the power to act as a prerogative court and summon and pass judgement on individuals who were in dispute with purveyors or compounders. It could also issue commissions to allow purveyors to make the original levies if the county fell into arrears with its composition. These powers were invoked repeatedly in the early years of James's reign and caused considerable ill-feeling. For much of the period the Greencloth employed as their purveyor in Leicestershire Christopher Walton, a hard-headed businessman who also acted as undertaker for the justices in providing the goods due under the composition agreement.[10] His methods were clearly not popular. Complaints were voiced against him in 1608 by the MP for Leicester, Sir William Skipwith; and in 1611 it was said that 'the countrey doth greatlie dislike him' and that if anyone refused to meet his demands he had with him a messenger from the Greencloth, named Kite, 'who doth not only compell and inforce the people to present payment, but doth also exact many great fees'.[11] The composition agreement had therefore failed to free the county from the abuses of purveyors and Greencloth pursuivants. Indeed in some respects it had probably made the situation worse, because the statutory restrictions which had previously been imposed on purveyors no longer applied to compounders and their undertakers.[12]

---

made by the 1621 Parliament: T. E. Cogswell, '"Skrued out of our money at every becke": the Leicestershire ratepayers and the burden of war' (unpublished paper). I am much indebted to Professor Cogswell for allowing me to cite these figures and for many enjoyable discussions about early Stuart Leicestershire.

[9] In Waltham, near Melton Mowbray, the constable's accounts show a regular bill for purveyance in the latter half of James's reign of £1 15s. 6d., rising to between £3 and £4 when the king was in the county. This compared with a total annual levy by the constables of £12 15s. 10d. – £17 18s. 0d.: Leicestershire Record Office (LRO), DE 625/60.

[10] HL, HA Correspondence, 4122; Woodworth, *Purveyance in the Reign of Elizabeth*, pp. 50–1.

[11] HL, HA Correspondence, 8093; Bodleian Library, MS Carte 78, ff. 321, 361.

[12] Hassell Smith, *County and Court*, pp. 292–302.

The onus of defending the county's interests fell on the local justices, but in the face of the prerogative powers wielded by the Greencloth they had little scope for effective action. Their habitual response when the Greencloth harassed them over defaults or arrears was to try to break off the existing agreement and renegotiate it. This the Greencloth resisted with threats that it would issue commissions for purveyors to take extra provisions and would also inform the king that Leicestershire was setting a bad example to other shires. There would then follow an exchange of letters between the two sides and local meetings at which the justices sought the advice and support of local taxpayers. This procedure was followed in 1607, 1610, 1611, 1617, 1618, 1619 and probably on other occasions; but each time the result was the same: the county, under pressure, eventually agreed to continue with the agreement reached under Elizabeth.[13] Whilst the king clung to his prerogative in the face of protests from the commons, and the Greencloth remained adamant, there was little else they could do.

After December 1622 the crown attempted to do away with the whole process of compositions in kind and introduce a system of fixed annual monetary payments. The Leicestershire JPs agreed to this, presumably because it would help to avoid uncertainty over the amount – and wrangling with the Greencloth. The scheme was abandoned early in 1625, however, because some counties refused to participate, and of those which did several were behind on their payments.[14] So purveyance remained a source of friction into Charles's reign, although by this stage it was coming to be overshadowed by other, more pressing, grievances.

In the meantime the constant complaints and repeated meetings and negotiations ensured that the issue of purveyance remained high on the agenda of local politics. The prevailing view amongst local taxpayers was doubtless that expressed in 1611 by Sir George Belgrave, a former justice of the peace: 'The provision money', he declared, 'hath been and is yerely levied with much greevance and offence to the people, especially in rating and taxing the county for perticuler defaultes.'[15] This meant that those local governors entrusted with managing the service were in a peculiarly fraught position. They were under intense pressure from their neighbours to mitigate its worst effects, but at the same time were being continually harassed by the Greencloth to collect in the money and meet deadlines. It was out of these difficulties that the conflicts over purveyance in Leicestershire arose.

Leicestershire in the early part of James's reign was a divided county. The origins of this can be traced back to the death of the third earl of Huntingdon, the redoubtable 'Puritan Earl', in 1595. In spite of being absent from the county for much of Elizabeth's reign, serving as president of the council of

---

[13] HL, HA Correspondence, 4120, 4121, 4122, 4127, 4129, 4130, 8532.

[14] Aylmer, 'Last years of purveyance', pp. 86–8; HL, HA Correspondence, 4134, 5502.

[15] Bodleian Library, MS Carte 78, f. 361.

the north, Huntingdon dominated most aspects of county life. Operating through the agency of three of his brothers, Sir George, Sir Edward and Sir Francis Hastings, he directed the bench, supervised the affairs of Leicester corporation, controlled county elections and established a vigorous Protestant preaching ministry. Because of his massive prestige, this dominance was largely accepted by the local gentry.[16] He was succeeded by his brother, George, who, insofar as he lacked the third earl's integrity and reputation for godliness, found it that much harder to maintain his family's local hegemony. He became involved in quarrels with several leading magistrates, including his own brother, Sir Francis Hastings; he faced allegations of corruption over his appointment of local officials; and he had to endure some spectacular slights and insults, most notably at the hands of Sir George Belgrave after the 1601 Leicester election.[17] While this inevitably led to friction and division amongst the county gentry, what made the whole situation potentially explosive was the reemergence into county politics of the Grey family.

Since the attainder of Thomas Grey, marquis of Dorset, in 1554, the Greys had been living in exile in Essex. Through careful cultivation of Elizabeth and the Cecils, however, and service at court, culminating in the lieutenancy of the Band of Gentleman Pensioners, Sir Henry Grey had regained most of his ancestral lands.[18] By the late 1590s the family was ready to make its mark in Leicestershire once more. Initially Sir Henry entrusted responsibility for this to his son, Sir John, who can be seen taking a prominent role on the commission of the peace soon after his appointment as a justice in 1598; however, following defeat in the 1601 shire election, Sir John seems to have decided to seek his fortunes elsewhere, as a soldier and courtier, and it was his father who eventually came to reside at the family seat at Bradgate Park, taking the local title of Lord Grey of Groby soon after the accession of James.[19]

Rivalry between the Greys and the Hastingses was one of the fixed points of Leicestershire politics. Beginning during the Wars of the Roses, when the

[16] M. C. Cross, 'The Third Earl of Huntingdon and Elizabethan Leicester', *Transactions of the Leicestershire Archaeological Society*, xxxvi (1960), pp. 6–21; idem, 'Noble patronage in the Elizabethan church', *HJ*, iii (1960), pp. 1–16; P. W. Hasler (ed.), *The House of Commons, 1558–1603* (3 vols, 1981), i, p. 192.

[17] For suspicions about the fourth earl's godliness, see M. C. Cross, *The Puritan Earl* (London, 1966), p. 31; HL, HA Correspondence, 4714. For his quarrels with the Leicestershire gentry, see M. C. Cross (ed.), *The Letters of Sir Francis Hastings, 1574–1609*, Somerset Record Society, lxix (1969), pp. xxiv, 70–1; Bodleian Library, MS Carte 77, ff. 518–19; 78, ff. 319, 361; BL, MS Lansdowne 83, f. 65; PRO, STAC 5/A54/2; J. E. Neale, *The Elizabethan House of Commons* (Glasgow, 1976), pp. 167–9.

[18] *DNB*, sub tit. Grey, Lord John; Hasler, *House of Commons, 1558–1603*, ii, pp. 203–4, 376–7.

[19] Ibid., pp. 223–4; PRO, C 231/1, ff. 52, 110; M. Bateson (ed.), *Records of the Borough of Leicester, 1509–1603* (Cambridge, 1905), pp. 339, 348, 385–6, 393, 414; Bodleian Library, MS Carte 77, ff. 518–19; BL, MS Lansdowne 89, f. 44; W. J. Tighe, 'The Gentlemen Pensioners in Elizabethan politics and government' (unpublished University of Cambridge Ph.D., 1983), pp. 72–3, 376–7; Hasler, *House of Commons, 1558–1603*, ii, pp. 222–3.

families found themselves on opposite sides, it had flared up again under Henry VIII and Mary.[20] The old animosities revived soon after the Greys' return to the shire. At the 1601 shire election, Sir John Grey threw himself into a vigorous campaign for the principal county seat and seemed assured of victory, having apparently secured the backing of the earl of Huntingdon, when, at the last moment, he was opposed, and eventually defeated, by Henry Hastings, the earl's nephew.[21] With his credit fully extended, this defeat was profoundly humiliating for Grey and, not surprisingly, he blamed Huntingdon. The episode was later recognised as the point at which the traditional rivalry revived. Soon after, Sir John was joining with other justices to criticise Huntingdon's appointments to local offices.[22]

The main cause of contention between the two families, however, arose when the fourth earl of Huntingdon died in December 1604. He was succeeded by a grandson who was a minor, and therefore ineligible to fill the family's traditional offices of lord lieutenant and custos rotulorum. Lord Grey, who seems to have been waiting for such an opportunity, pressed Robert Cecil to award the offices to him, along with the Hastingses' other crown offices of receiver of the duchy of Lancaster and lieutenant of Leicester forest; however, the new earl responded with a vigorous counter-petition, pleading the damage that would be inflicted on his family's reputation in the shire. Cecil came down on his side: Huntingdon was granted the forest and duchy offices, whilst the lord lieutenancy was left in abeyance until his coming of age.[23] An accommodation was arranged soon after to bring the two families back on speaking terms but, the old wounds having been reopened, it would take more than this to overcome feelings of hostility and mutual distrust.[24] These were to overshadow events relating to purveyance.

During the early 1600s responsibility for administering purveyance was divided between the leading justices. As lord lieutenant and custos rotulorum, the fourth earl of Huntingdon had negotiated the county's composition and

[20] VCH, *Leicestershire* (5 vols, 1907–64), ii, pp. 98–9, 101, 105, 109; L. Fox and P. Russell, *Leicester Forest* (Leicester, 1948), pp. 77–82; D. M. Loades, *Two Tudor Conspiracies* (Cambridge, 1965), pp. 25–34. The Suffolk author of the *Vita Mariae Reginae* in Mary's reign referred to the 'perpetual enmity' between the Greys and the Hastingses as an established fact: D. MacCulloch (ed.), 'The *Vita Mariae Reginae* of Robert Wingfield of Brantham', in *Camden Miscellany*, xxviii, Camden Society, 4th series, xxix (1984), p. 280 (I am grateful to Diarmiad MacCulloch for this reference).

[21] Bodleian Library, MS Carte 77, ff. 518–19; Hasler, *House of Commons, 1558–1603*, i, pp. 192–3; ii, p. 224.

[22] Bodleian Library, MS Carte 77, ff. 518–19; 78, f. 361.

[23] BL, Microfilm of the MSS at Hatfield House, 189/57; 197/14; PRO, SO 3/2, 11 February 1604/5; J. C. Sainty, *Lieutenants of Counties, 1558–1642*, BIHR, Special Supplement, 8 (1970), p. 26.

[24] Bodleian Library, MS Carte 77, ff. 518–19. These feelings are apparent in the various memoranda drawn up by the fifth earl, *c.* 1611–13, including his advice to his son: Bodleian Library, MS Carte 77, ff. 518–19; 78, ff. 308–11, 318–19, 325–6; HL, HA Personal, box 15, nos 7 and 8.

was responsible for overseeing the service; but other local governors at odds with the earl, such as Belgrave and Sir John Grey, were also involved, particularly when it came to the delicate business of collecting arrears.[25] Between the death of the fourth earl and the fifth earl's coming of age in May 1607, the situation was less clear. The leading role on the bench passed to the Greys and their allies, the Beaumonts: Lord Grey took the role of unofficial spokesman for the county justices in their dealings with the centre and with Leicester corporation; Sir Henry Beaumont of Coleorton became custos rotulorum and, at a by-election in 1606, was chosen to serve alongside his brother, Sir Thomas Beaumont of Stoughton, as knight of the shire; and Sir John Grey, now a gentleman of the privy chamber, provided the all-important link with the centre.[26] Who was responsible for administering purveyance at this time is uncertain as no letters or warrants relating to the service have been found; however, it is clear that as soon as the fifth earl succeeded to the lord lieutenancy (and also, by dint of Sir Henry Beaumont's death, to the office of custos rotulorum) he took over the supervision of this, as well as all the other administrative and political responsibilities of local officeholders.[27] His approach throughout was notably partisan.

During the Hastings interregnum, the Greys and the Beaumonts made a start in revising the commission of the peace – the key to local power. Sir John Grey's opponent in the 1601 election, Sir Henry Hastings of the Abbey, found himself demoted in the order of precedence from second to sixth place amongst the county knights, a significant snub; whilst Sir Henry Beaumont's twenty-three-year-old son, Sir Thomas of Coleorton, and Matthew Saunders, an ally of the Greys and the Beaumonts, were brought into the commission.[28] From the start of his term of office the young earl was determined to reverse this trend and repair the damage done to his family's influence. This was nowhere more apparent than in his appointment of deputy lieutenants. The claims of long-established and experienced county leaders linked with the Greys, such as Sir Thomas Beaumont of Stoughton or Sir William Skipwith, were ignored and Huntingdon chose instead Sir Thomas Cave, a long-established Hastings client, his cousin Henry Cave, and another Hastings ally, Sir William Turpin. When Henry Cave died in 1609 he was replaced by the earl's kinsman, Sir Henry Hastings of the Abbey.[29] Huntingdon

---

[25] HMC, *Hastings MSS*, iv, pp. 189–91; PRO, C 231/1, f. 110; LS 13/168, f. 32.

[26] H. Stocks (ed.), *Records of the Borough of Leicester, 1603–1688* (Cambridge, 1923), p. 21; BL, Microfilm of the MSS at Hatfield House, 103/100; LRO, Borough of Leicester, Hall Papers, vii, f. 618; PRO, C 66/1662; C 219/35, pt 1, no. 44; J. Nichols, *The History and Antiquities of the County of Leicester* (4 vols, London, 1795–1811), i, p. 456; BL, Microfilm of the MSS at Hatfield House, 24/54; LRO, Borough of Leicester, Hall Papers, vii, f. 349.

[27] HMC, *Hastings MSS*, i, pp. 364–6; iv, pp. 192–6; HL, HA Correspondence, 4120, 5425.

[28] BL, MS Add. 38,139; PRO, C 66/1662, 1682. For Saunders' connections and allegiances, see PRO, PCC Wills, PROB 11/125/34, Rudd; HL, HA Correspondence, 4328.

[29] HL, HA Correspondence, 5419, 1283; Bodleian Library, MS Carte 78, f. 309; HL, HA Financial, box 6, no. 7; Bodleian Library, MS Carte 77, ff. 518–19.

followed a similar course in recommending appointments to the bench, over which, as custos rotulorum, he had considerable influence. Those appointed after May 1607 were either established allies of his family, such as Sir Thomas Compton, or capable men-of-business who were unconnected with the Greys, such as Sir Thomas Haselrigg.[30]

The most controversial of these new appointees was his great-uncle, Walter Hastings esquire. Walter came on to the bench in May-June 1607 at the unusually late age of sixty, having, so he claimed, never previously served in local office.[31] This was remarkable enough, but what staggered the local gentry was the fact that he was a notorious Catholic who, less than two years previously, had been suspected of having a part in the Gunpowder Plot.[32] He may also have been regarded as an unhealthy influence on his young grand-nephew. When Huntingdon succeeded to his title in 1604, uncle Walter offered himself as a guide and counsellor in restoring the Hastings family fortunes, and thereafter became something of an *eminence grise*.[33] Finally, to rub salt into the wound, Walter, as the brother of an earl, was ranked at the head of the local gentry in the commission, directly above Sir John Grey.[34] The Hastingses' opponents did their best to block the appointment, Sir Thomas Beaumont protesting to Huntingdon that 'he knew that could not be by lawe, his wyfe being a recusant and that he knew it to be against the mynd of the parliament and yf he lyved to the next session it should be amended';[35] but this was simply ignored, and the earl caused further outrage late in 1609 when he made Walter a deputy lieutenant in succession to Sir Thomas Cave.[36] This ruthlessly partisan approach was carried over into purveyance. Apart from Huntingdon, responsibility for issuing warrants and making ratings was confined to the deputy lieutenants, Sir Thomas Compton and Sir Henry and Walter Hastings.[37]

[30] Bodleian Library, MS Carte 78, f. 308; HL, HA Financial, box 6, no. 3; PRO, C 66/1748, 1786, 1822, 1898. For the Comptons' friendship with the fifth earl, see J. Knowles, 'WS MS', *Times Literary Supplement*, 29 April–5 May 1988, pp. 472, 485. For the fifth earl's efforts to block Lord Grey's recommendations in 1614, see HL, HA Correspondence, 2513.

[31] Although there is no surviving commission of the peace for Leicestershire between March 1606 and May 1608, it is clear that the appointment of Walter Hastings esq took place between 2 May 1607, when Huntingdon was appointed custos rotulorum, and 25 June 1607, when he is described as JP in a letter from the Greencloth: HMC, *Hastings MSS*, i, p. 364; HL, HA Correspondence, 4120; Bodleian Library, MS Carte 78, f. 318. Walter Hastings' claim that he had never served in office prior to 1607 was not strictly true, since he had acted as a subsidy commissioner in 1605, PRO, STAC 8/55/26.

[32] Cross, *The Puritan Earl*, p. 34; PRO, SP 14/16/71; BL, Microfilm of the MSS at Hatfield House, 214/ 54; VCH, *Leicestershire*, ii, p. 58.

[33] J. Thompson, *A History of Leicester* (Leicester, 1849), pp. 330–2; *Records of Leicester, 1603–1688*, pp. 33–6; HL, HA Financial, box 6, nos 3 and 4; box 7, no. 3.

[34] PRO, SP 14/33.

[35] Bodleian Library, MS Carte 78, ff. 325–6.

[36] Bodleian Library, MS Carte 78, ff. 308–9.

[37] HL, HA Correspondence, 4120, 8093; Bodleian Library, MS Carte 77, f. 518; 78, f. 318.

This had serious implications. If the magistrates were unable to maintain a united front over purveyance, the county was liable to be hampered in its negotiations with the Greencloth and local resentment and opposition would probably increase. Already there were signs of problems in the shire. In 1606 the Greencloth issued the first of a series of commissions empowering purveyors such as Walton to go into Leicestershire and levy goods in lieu of the arrears caused by local dragging of feet.[38] Then in 1607 Huntingdon was involved in extensive negotiations to renew his grandfather's composition agreement, which was running into difficulties. Again the main problem seems to have been footdragging on the part of taxpayers, but there were also hints that some of the justices were becoming hostile to the whole idea of compounding.[39] In 1608 Sir William Skipwith, MP for Leicester, delivered a public attack on 'some ... intollerable abuses [by] Walton and others committed to the great impoverishment of some poore inhabitantes there'.

The Greencloth ordered an enquiry, as a result of which it appears that the local justices extracted an undertaking from Kite, Walton's messenger, that he would not charge excessive fees for his work; however, this seems to have had little effect because there were still complaints about both Walton and Kite in 1611.[40] It is hard to detect any clear pattern to this early unrest over purveyance beyond the sense that it was a miserable and unwelcome burden. The hints of hostility to compounding may indicate a desire on the part of some justices to embarrass Huntingdon, but it is unlikely that there was any sinister motive behind Skipwith's denunciation of Walton. Although he had clashed with the Hastingses in the past, and was close to Sir John Grey, Skipwith was also on notably friendly terms with the fifth earl.[41] His action was probably intended as no more than that of a conscientious local governor, discharging his duty towards his fellow 'countrymen' and perhaps drawing encouragement from the royal proclamation of 1606 which commended those who acted against abuses by purveyors.[42] None the less the very fact that purveyance was being opposed locally put pressure on those local governors entrusted with its supervision. This exacerbated the divisions as purveyance became caught up with the faction struggles in the shire.

This happened in 1610 with the revival of the feud between Sir John Grey and Sir Henry Hastings of the Abbey, which had been rumbling on since the 1601 election. Why it broke out again at this point is unclear. One cause was probably Sir Henry's efforts to obstruct Lord Grey when he tried

[38] PRO, C 231/2, pp. 20, 21, 24, 26, 30, 37, 57.

[39] HL, HA Correspondence, 4120, 5425; Bodleian Library, MS Carte 78, f. 318.

[40] HL, HA Correspondence, 8093; Bodleian Library, MS Carte 78, ff. 318, 321, 361.

[41] Bodleian Library, MS Carte 78, f. 361; BL, Microfilm of the MSS at Hatfield House, 214/54; HL, HA Financial, box 6, nos 3 and 4; Knowles, 'WS MS', pp. 472, 485.

[42] Skipwith's funeral monument described him as someone who 'can when need requires with courage bold / To publicke eares his neighbours grieves unfold': Nichols, *County of Leicester*, iii, p. 359; P. L. Hughes and J. F. Larkin (ed.), *Stuart Royal Proclamations* (2 vols, Oxford, 1973–83), i, pp. 136–42.

to investigate a murder, allegedly committed by one of Hastings' servants, in January 1610; another may well have been the 'ill offices' performed by Sir George Belgrave, who had been quarreling with Sir Henry since the 1590s and was apparently doing his best to sow dissension between the two men.[43] Whatever the reason, Grey challenged Hastings to a duel and in May 1610 the two men travelled to Flushing to fight.[44] Bloodshed was apparently avoided, but the quarrel did not die down and when, a few weeks later, Sir John received a warrant from Sir Henry and Walter, requiring him to help raise purveyance arrears, he exploded. He refused point blank to cooperate and, picking on the more vulnerable of the two deputy lieutenants, announced that 'neither himself, his friends, servants, nor doggs should be under the command of Mr Walter Hastings'. This was followed by a very unsatisfactory interview with Huntingdon at which he was told that 'it was the manner of the countie so to gyve notice to men as well borne as himselfe and that they being at difference, he cold not looke to be sent to in anie other fashion then the rest'. Perhaps not surprisingly, after this Sir John and the earl were said to have never exchanged a civil word again. As far as Grey was concerned, the battle lines were drawn.[45]

His outburst also had a wider significance. It was symptomatic of a determination on the part of some gentry to challenge the whole administration of purveyance within the shire. This challenge took two directions. First of all there was pressure on Huntingdon, early in 1610, to break off the composition agreement. This was only overcome through forceful counter-pressure from the Greencloth.[46] Secondly there were allegations of corruption over the assessment of arrears, directed mainly against Sir Henry Hastings of the Abbey who was said to have reapportioned the money due from his division to cover the whole shire.[47] Those named as leading the challenge were Sir George Belgrave and Sir Thomas Beaumont of Stoughton, which suggests that the main objective was to embarrass the earl and his two principal lieutenants; however, their efforts were given broader legitimacy and essential popular support through the groundswell of opposition to purveyance within the shire. By 1610 the composition was becoming harder to collect and causing greater resentment than ever. Moreover, doubt was thrown on its legal basis at meetings which took place between Sir Thomas Beaumont and the local taxpayers in the autumn of 1610.[48] These meetings arose out of the negotiations taking place in parliament over the Great Contract. During the summer recess MPs were sent home to their shires

[43] PRO, STAC 8/54/13; *APC, 1595–6*, p. 216; Bodleian Library, MS Carte 78, f. 373.

[44] HMC, *Report on the MSS of Viscount De L'Isle* (5 vols, 1925–62), iv, pp. 200, 204–5.

[45] Bodleian Library, MS Carte 77, ff. 518–19.

[46] HL, HA Correspondence, 4121; Bodleian Library, MS Carte 77, ff. 518–19; 78, f. 318.

[47] Bodleian Library, MS Carte 77, ff. 518–19; 78, f. 361; PRO, STAC 8/54/13. For arrears in Sir Henry Hastings' West Goscote division, see PRO, C 231/2, p. 26.

[48] PRO, C 231/2, p. 57; HL, HA Correspondence, 4122.

with instructions to consult local subsidymen about whether they would
consent to an annual tax in return for the king surrendering his feudal
rights to wardship and purveyance.[49] In Nottinghamshire, Sir John Holles
held a series of meetings in September, at which he found the mood of the
taxpayers ambivalent; nevertheless he was able to report that 'they bitt
sumwhat eagerly at the taking away all maner of purveiance ...'[50]

Leicestershire's response was analysed in less detail; however, it is clear
from a parliamentary speech by Beaumont in November that discussions
had been held and that the taxpayers were broadly in favour, provided
certain conditions were met. 'When I went home into my country', he told
the house of commons,

> I did (according to the trust reposed by them in me) acquaint them with
> what we had done, and withal required their advice, telling them the sum
> offered and withal that some gratuity must come. Their answer was they were
> glad that the sunshine of his Majesty's favour should come so far as to reach
> them. But they pressed me particularly to tell them whether the impositions
> which were resolved in parliament to be unlawful, were determined by the
> king to be laid down; and then they said so as the levy might be in a
> reasonable manner, which they hoped should not be all upon land and all
> our grivances drawn in together in the contract, they would be willing to
> give £200,000 a year and also to give some present supply.[51]

In this account of the speech Beaumont did not refer specifically to
purveyance, but from the general context of the debate it is evident that
'impositions' was intended to cover all levies considered legally questionable,
which given the previous discussions in parliament clearly included purveyance.[52] This suggests the issue of purveyance was certainly raised during
Beaumont's local consultations; and once raised it was something on which
he had strong opinions, as he explained in the same parliamentary speech:

> Is it now held inconvenient to speak for confirmation of that Charter which
> our ancestors got with much sweat and blood? Notwithstanding so many laws
> as have been made that no impositions shall be set without assent of parlia-
> ment, are not impositions set voluntarily and maintained to be just? In the
> case of purveyance wherein thirty-six laws were made to restrain it, is it now
> an undutiful speech to name the word law? I was glad from my heart when

---

[49] Smith, 'The Great Contract', pp. 121–2.

[50] P. R. Seddon (ed.), *Letters of John Holles, 1587–1637*, 3 vols, Thoroton Society, record series,
xxxi, xxxv–vi (1975–86), iii, pp. 513–15.

[51] E. R. Foster (ed.), *Proceedings in Parliament, 1610* (2 vols, New Haven, 1966), ii, p. 318.

[52] Ibid., ii, pp. 316–20. In another report of the same speech Beaumont was said to have
described the 'country's' readiness to offer supply 'so that impositions and our other grievances
may be cast in', S. R. Gardiner (ed.), *Parliamentary Debates in 1610*, Camden Society, lxxxi (1862),
p. 130. 'Impositions' was also used in a general sense in a statement of grievances drawn up by
the Leicestershire JPs in 1611, to which Beaumont subscribed, Folger Shakespeare Library,
Washington, V. a. 402, ff. 3–4.

this purveyance was first taken into the bargain even for the salvation of the souls of so many of our countrymen as are used as ministers therein; for if oppression and injustice be a crying sin and be not recompensed or punished in this world as it is not like to be, certainly 'tis to be feared the punishment must be in another world.[53]

In the house of commons in November, Beaumont was ready to make an explicit connection between purveyance and a general challenge to Magna Carta and the liberties of the subject, in the process invoking the 'Form of Apology and Satisfaction of 1604'. Given the complaint made by Huntingdon that he had always opposed the purveyance composition locally,[54] and also the terms in which he described the subsidymen's response, it seems unlikely that he would have neglected to make the same point in Leicestershire a few weeks earlier. If so, this could only have strengthened the impression amongst local taxpayers that the whole legal basis of the service was questionable; and this, in turn, would have further legitimised opposition and undermined those identified with its supervision. All this made life extremely difficult for Huntingdon and his allies, something which the Greys were quick to exploit.

The opportunity for this was provided by the privy council, which in March 1611 encouraged the counties to alter their existing compositions to fixed annual monetary payments. Sir Thomas Beaumont and Sir Henry Hastings of the Abbey, representatives of the opposing viewpoints on purveyance, were summoned to London, apparently to discuss the scheme.[55] There was broad support for it in Leicestershire, but time was needed to consult taxpayers and justices and this was something the Board of the Greencloth (which may not have been entirely happy about the council's initiative) was not prepared to grant.[56] On 27 April they wrote to Huntingdon warning that unless the terms of the existing composition were fulfilled immediately Walton would be sent down to levy provisions.[57] At this point, rather unexpectedly, Sir John Grey came to the rescue and, using his contacts at court, gave an undertaking to deliver the provisions himself. The offer was gratefully accepted by the earl, giving him, as it did, the breathing space needed to complete his negotiations, but this proved to be a big mistake. Once Grey had his foot in the door, and was empowered to act on the

---

[53] Foster, *Proceedings in Parliament, 1610*, ii, p. 318.

[54] Bodleian Library, MS Carte 77, ff. 518–19. In March 1611 Francis Beaumont, who lived with his brother, Sir Thomas, at Stoughton, expressed the view, presumably shared by his brother, that 'this countie hath bene often and for many yeares grievouslie trobled' by the burden of purveyance: Lady Newdegate-Newdigate, *Gossip from a Muniment Room* (London, 1897), p. 107.

[55] Aylmer, 'Last years of purveyance', p. 82; HMC, *Report on the MSS of Lord Montagu of Beaulieu* (1900), p. 86; HL, HA Correspondence, 4122, 4327; Newdegate-Newdigate, *Gossip Fom a Muniment Room*, pp. 107, 109.

[56] This was suggested by Lord Grey: HL, HA Correspondence, 4327.

[57] Ibid., 4122.

county's behalf, he exploited this to embarrass the earl. Sometime during June or July a deputation of local gentry, authorised by Huntingdon and the quarter sessions, met with the council, but was unable to agree a suitable annual payment. Grey took this as a pretext for broaching the subject with the king and extracted from him a sharp rap across the knuckles for those gentry responsible for purveyance. James instructed Grey to

> tell the gentlemen of Leicestershire that he tooke yt in ill parte the breach of composicon, and the rather because yt was at such a time that the whole kingdom tooke notice of yt to the crossing of his further purposes and that hee lived with the lawe on his side and wished the gentlemen to doe soe to, otherwise his Majestie knew what he had to doe …[58]

This must have been particularly wounding to the fifth earl who was acutely sensitive to the nuances of royal favour. Not only did his own local position depend on it, but he also subscribed to the contemporary aristocratic ethos that honour derived from the approval of the monarch.[59] Small wonder that he later described Sir John's initiative as a move 'to crosse me'.[60] For their part the Greys could barely conceal their glee. Lord Grey let slip a reference to the king's words in a letter to Huntingdon in August in which he urged politely, but with more than a hint of blackmail, that another meeting of the justices was needed to finalise the new composition. This the earl agreed to: new proposals were put forward, a fresh deputation was prepared and significantly, for the first time, the Greencloth began addressing its letters to 'Lord Grey' as well as 'the earl of Huntingdon'.[61] Huntingdon was clearly on the run, assailed on all sides and facing the prospect of recriminations from local taxpayers, as well as royal disfavour, as his botched negotiations threatened to make matters worse than ever.

At this point the Greys decided to throw everything behind their offensive. Early in September 1611, Sir John came down to the shire to direct operations. His first move was to join with Beaumont and Belgrave in writing to Cecil to assure the council that Leicestershire wanted to agree to a monetary composition. This was to outflank some of the other justices – presumably Huntingdon and his allies – who were attempting to retrieve their credit by communicating the offer of an annual payment directly to the king.[62] It was probably also Sir John who came up with the scheme for a full-scale indictment of Huntingdon's management of local affairs in the form of a complaint to the lord chancellor and accusations at quarter sessions. The main thrust

[58] Ibid., 4123; Bodleian Library, MS Carte 77, ff. 518–19; 78, f. 316.

[59] M. E. James, *English Politics and the Concept of Honour, 1485-1642, Past and Present,* supplement 3 (1978), particularly pp. 72–92. For evidence of Huntingdon's views on the role of an aristocrat, see his advice to his son, HL, HA Personal, box 15, no. 8.

[60] Bodleian Library, MS Carte 78, ff. 325–6.

[61] HL, HA Correspondence, 4327; Bodleian Library, MS Carte 78, ff. 316, 321; HL, HA Correspondence, 4124.

[62] PRO, SP 14/66/9, f. 17.

of these was against the appointment to the bench of John Bale esquire, a long-established Hastings family retainer who had an unsavoury reputation for suborning jurors and a history of quarrelling with Beaumont, Belgrave and others. There were also allegations about the misuse of funds set aside for repair of Leicester castle, unfair assessments for plague relief and abuses in alehouse licensing, as well as a reiteration of the earlier complaints about unjust apportionment of purveyance arrears, in which the main targets were Sir Henry and Walter Hastings; however the ultimate objective was Huntingdon himself, whose prestige and integrity would be damaged, possibly beyond repair, if the complaints were upheld. The partisan nature of the complaints explains why only five justices and a sprinkling of other gentry, most of them known allies of the Greys, actually signed the letter to the lord chancellor.[63] Nevertheless, even with such limited support there was probably still sufficient to prompt a central government enquiry: everything depended on having the right backing and contacts at court. But here the whole strategy of the Grey camp was suddenly undermined by a cruel stroke of misfortune. At the beginning of October 1611 Sir John Grey contracted smallpox and died.[64]

Sir John Grey's death removed the linchpin of the campaign against Hastings influence and effectively destroyed any hopes of success. The disputes over Bale's appointment dragged on for another six months before his appointment was confirmed and the earl was triumphantly vindicated by the assize judges.[65] Belgrave brought separate charges against Sir Henry Hastings in Star Chamber, but again to no avail.[66] And Walter Hastings, who had been the object of so much revulsion, went from strength to strength, becoming the dominant influence on the bench and the leading deputy lieutenant until his death in 1616.[67] Lord Grey and Sir Thomas Beaumont both died in 1614 and, with the passing of his main antagonists, Huntingdon's dominance of the shire was secure until the late 1630s.[68] As for purveyance, things continued much as before: the proposal for a new monetary composition collapsed, the justices carried on trying to operate the old scheme and the taxpayers continued to feel aggrieved.[69] With the extra

[63] HL, HA Correspondence, 4328; Folger Library, V. a. 402, ff. 3–5; Bodleian Library, MS Carte 78, f. 322.

[64] N. E. MacLure (ed.), *The Letters of John Chamberlain* (2 vols, Philadelphia, 1939), i, p. 314; Hasler, *House of Commons, 1558–1603*, ii, p. 224.

[65] The Bale case and its ramifications are discussed in R. P. Cust, 'Honour, rhetoric and political culture: the earl of Huntingdon and his enemies', in S. Amussen and M. Kishlansky (ed.), *Political Culture and Cultural Politics in Early Modern England* (Manchester, 1995).

[66] PRO, STAC 8/54/13.

[67] LRO, Hall Papers Bound, vol. 11, ff. 115, 120, 131, 199, 214; HL, HA Manorial, box 53, no. 6 (earl of Huntingdon's lieutenancy book 1614–27).

[68] Nichols, *County of Leicester*, ii, pp. 851–61; Hasler, *House of Commons, 1558–1603*, ii, p. 223; J. K. Gruenfelder, 'The electoral influence of the earls of Huntingdon, 1603–1640', *Transactions of the Leicestershire Archaeological Society*, xix (1974–5), pp. 17–29.

[69] HL, HA Correspondence, 4127, 4129, 4130, 8532, 8534; HA Manorial, box 53, nos 7 & 9.

ingredient of gentry factionalism removed, however, it never again produced the conflicts and divisions of 1610 and 1611.

What conclusions can be drawn from this study of a relatively obscure episode in Jacobean local politics? The most straightforward concerns the way in which service to the state could become caught up with local feuds. Efficient administration invariably took second place in early modern England to the pursuit of honour, prestige and local power. As far as Huntingdon was concerned, the main objective of his activities in local politics was to re-establish the power and eminence of the Hastingses.[70] In the context of purveyance this meant entrusting the service exclusively to his kinsmen and adherents, and then demonstrating, to both his neighbours and the king, that they could manage it fairly and effectively. For the Greys and their supporters the aim was just the opposite, to undermine the earl by demonstrating as publicly as possible that his administration was incompetent, ineffectual and ultimately corrupt. In the process the service itself suffered. Purveyance was not one of those central government demands which benefited from the spirit of competition sometimes produced by divisions amongst local officeholders. To manage it successfully required unity and cooperation on the part of the justices; otherwise negotiations with the Greencloth would be hampered, ratings would become contentious and both taxpayers and the king would suffer, as ultimately happened in Leicestershire. All this is much as one might expect, since we have become familiar with the disruptive effects of gentry feuds through the work of Hassell Smith on Elizabethan Norfolk and Tom Barnes on Caroline Somerset.[71] Their research, however, also suggests another aspect of factionalism which has barely been touched on here, the way in which it could lead to the development of a broader political consciousness outside the ranks of the leading gentry.

In Elizabethan Norfolk the rival gentry factions divided between those acting as agents of the central government, who gave backing to patentees, purveyors and deputy lieutenants, and those who sought to defend the autonomy of the local bench. The latter sought support from freeholders, quarter sessions and, ultimately, the house of commons, and, using arguments drawn from the common law, generated a debate which heightened the political awareness of local inhabitants. Similar developments can be seen during the Phelips versus Poulett feud in Somerset, particularly over the issue of billeting. It is worth investigating how far something like this also occurred in Jacobean Leicestershire.

---

[70] For an excellent study of the political attitudes and concerns of the fifth earl of Huntingdon, focusing particularly on his relations with Leicester corporation, see C. F. Patterson, 'Leicester and Lord Huntingdon: urban patronage in early modern England', *Midland History*, xvi (1991), pp. 45–62.

[71] Hassell Smith, *County and Court*; Barnes, *Somerset 1625–1640*.

To start with it has to be said that circumstances here were much less conducive to the 'court' versus 'country' divide which can at times be seen in Norfolk or Somerset. Neither side in the Leicestershire quarrel found itself shut out from the court in the way Sir Robert Phelips was during the late 1620s.[72] Indeed an important part of the Greys' strategy for undermining the court's main representative in the shire was to use their own influence at court to prompt a royal reprimand. It was therefore unlikely that Huntingdon's opponents would risk going too far down the road of stirring up popular opposition to purveyance lest this damage their standing at court. Nor did local sentiment require such an approach. Purveyance was not an issue like, for example, the forced loan of 1626–7, where opposition in some quarters was so intense that any compromise could be regarded by local taxpayers as a betrayal of trust.[73] Local politicians could still fudge and manoeuvre, and, to some extent, play both ends against the middle. Hence Beaumont could denounce purveyance in highly principled terms in parliament (and, one presumes, also locally) in 1610, yet a year later write to Cecil assuring him that he was doing his best to arrange a new composition. So purveyance was less politically charged than some of the issues which faced local governors in the 1620s and 1630s. None the less there are indications that it still served to encourage local inhabitants to think about their immediate grievances in a broader context, and consider how these might be linked to the subject's liberties being debated in parliament. This is, perhaps, the most significant point to emerge from this essay. It gives us a new perspective on the growth of a broader political consciousness in early Stuart England. We are familiar with the processes by which this emerged in the 1620s and 1630s, and (thanks to the work of Hassell Smith) the way in which it could develop in a politically precocious and heavily burdened county in Elizabeth's reign.[74] What we do not know much about is what was happening under James or in less advanced areas which escaped the worst effects of war in the 1590s. This essay can offer some pointers.

What purveyance provided was a high-profile issue affecting most local taxpayers which, over a period of about eight years, was repeatedly debated both in parliament and in the localities. In Leicestershire it was kept at the forefront of the local political agenda, not only because of the burdens and inconveniences to which it gave rise, but also because a group amongst the local governors was determined to challenge the way it was administered.

---

[72] Cust, *The Forced Loan*, pp. 108–10, 204–5.

[73] Ibid., pp. 221–6.

[74] Ibid.; R. P. Cust, 'Politics and the electorate in the 1620s', in R. P. Cust and A. L. Hughes (ed.), *Conflict in Early Stuart England* (Harlow, 1989), pp. 134–67; D. Hirst, 'Court, country and politics before 1629', in K. Sharpe (ed.), *Faction and Parliament* (Oxford, 1978), pp. 105–37; Barnes, *Somerset, 1625–1640*; K. Fincham, 'The judges' decision on ship money in February 1637: the reaction of Kent', *BIHR*, lvii (1984), pp. 230–7; N. J. Jackson, 'The collection of ship money in Northamptonshire, 1635–40' (unpublished University of Birmingham M. Phil. thesis, 1987); Hassell Smith, *County and Court*, particularly pp. 333–40.

In addition to this there were numerous occasions on which it was discussed at local public meetings, often in the presence of those equipped and motivated to bring out its wider constitutional implications. All this helped to develop a sense amongst taxpayers that crown demands like this were linked to a general threat to the liberties of the subject and could therefore legitimately be resisted.

In the nature of the evidence it is hard to find conclusive proof of this, but one indication is the way in which those who can be described as 'patriots' or 'public men' latched on to purveyance as an issue. These were a new breed of local politician, emerging in the latter part of Elizabeth's reign and familiar by the 1620s, whose reputation and status depended on their capacity to give voice to the grievances of their neighbours and link these up with the concerns associated with 'the country'. Like good constituency MPs, which was what many of them were, they had to be sensitive both to the attitudes of their neighbours and to the broader climate of national politics. It is therefore of some significance that the two foremost 'patriots' in early Jacobean Leicestershire, Sir Thomas Beaumont and Sir William Skipwith, both spoke out publicly in the county against purveyance.[75] They evidently felt that it mattered to their neighbours and, perhaps, also that these neighbours could appreciate why parliament was making such a fuss about it.

To conclude, I would argue that in Leicestershire purveyance marked an important stage in the development of a broader political consciousness amongst local taxpayers and freeholders. As such it can be ranked alongside the resistance to muster masters' fees in Somerset and Wiltshire in 1602–6, the campaign against the deprivation of puritan ministers in 1605 and the opposition to the royal benevolence of 1614.[76] These rather neglected episodes in the local politics of James' reign did much to prepare the ground for widespread resistance to royal demands in the 1620s and 1630s.

---

[75] Cust, 'Politics and the electorate', pp. 134–67. For Beaumont, see R. P. Cust, 'Honour and politics in early Stuart England: the case of *Beaumont* v. *Hastings*', *Past and Present*, cxlix (1995), pp. 57–94. For Skipwith, see above n. 42, and Hasler, *House of Commons, 1558–1603*, ii, pp. 392–3. It is worth noting that the emotive term 'tribunes of the people' was used to describe those MPs most active in the purveyance debates of 1606, one of the earliest references to the notion that some MPs were motivated by the desire to appeal to a 'popular' following: Lindquist, 'The problem of early Jacobean purveyance', p. 564.

[76] On the Somerset and Wiltshire lieutenancy, see W. P. D. Murphy (ed.), *The Earl of Hertford's Lieutenancy Papers, 1603–1612*, Wiltshire Record Society, xxiii (1969), pp. 11–13, 102–4; D. H. Willson (ed.), *The Parliamentary Diary of Robert Bowyer, 1606–1607* (London, 1931), pp. 130, 154–6; Hassell Smith, *County and Court*, pp. 336–7. On the puritan ministers in 1605, see S. B. Babbage, *Puritanism and Richard Bancroft* (London, 1962), chapter 6. For the Leicestershire petition, signed by Skipwith, see BL, Microfilm of the MSS at Hatfield House, 103/100; and for proceedings in Northamptonshire, see W. J. Sheils, *The Puritans in the Diocese of Peterborough, 1558–1610*, Northamptonshire Record Society, xxx (1979), pp. 110–12; Northamptonshire Record Office, Montague MSS, vol. 186, unpaginated. For opposition to the benevolence, see Cust, *The Forced Loan*, pp. 151–7.

Index

Abbots Leigh, 109, 115–6, 119
Abinton in Lavendon, 43
agriculture, 34
Alan, family, 33 n. 19
    Robert fitz, 30 n. 8, 31 n. 11
Aldington, 139
Amiens, 71
    Mise of, 80–1
Annales school, 1
Anthony, servant of Thomas Cheyne,
    134 n. 66
Arden, Thomas, 139, 142
Arms, College of, 4
Ash, Alexander, 30 n. 8
Ashbourne, 21 n. 20
Ashendon, 46 n. 82
Ashley, Henry, 120
    Edith, daughter of, 120, 121
Ashleworth, 109
Aslak, Walter, 18
Aslocton, Simon de, 71 n. 58, 73 n.
    65, 76, 79 n. 96
Aston Clinton, 44 and n. 77
Audley, family, 85
    James de, 81
Auger, Anthony, 134 n. 63
Augustinians, 108
Aumale, earl of, *see* Fors
Avon, river, 108, 110
Aylesbury, Walter de, 49
    Philip, son of, 49

Bagingden, Richard de, 69 and n. 45,
    77, 82, 83
    Richard, son of, 83
Bagot, Bagod, William, 66 and n. 34,
    69, 70 and n. 49, 72, 77, 81
Baker, John, 134 n. 65, 139
Bale, John, 159 and n. 65
Balliol, John, 76

Bamburgh, castle, 66 n. 32, 69 n. 45
Barons' Wars, 29, 52 and n. 114, 63,
    69 and n. 47, 70, 79
Baret, Ralph, 30 n. 8
Barnwell Priory, 49
Barry, family, 31 n. 11, 33 n. 19, 35 n.
    31, 38 n. 45, 39
    Robert, 33 n. 22, 54, 54 n. 121,
    123, 55 n. 124
Basset,
    Philip, 74 n. 68
    Ralph, of Sapcote, 78 n. 91
'bastard feudalism', 85
Bataile, family, 33 n. 19, 37 n. 41
    Richard de, 31 n. 11
Bath Abbey, 118
Bath and Wells, diocese of, 110
Beachampton, 46 n. 85
Beachampton, family, 33 n. 19, 36 n.
    40, 38 n. 45
    William de, 31 n. 11
Beauchamp, family, 46, 48 n. 93, 64
    Richard de, 30 nn. 8, 9
    William de, 30 n. 8, 45 n. 82,
        46, 54 n. 123
    William (II) de, baron of
        Bedford, 45 n. 82
    Beatrice, daughter of, 45 n. 82
    John, son of, 45 n. 82
    of Drayton, family, 33 n. 19, 36
    of Salwarpe, William, 65
Beauchamp, honour of, 46
Beaumont, family, 152
    Francis, 157 n. 54
    Henry de, 95
    Henry of Coleorton, 152
        Thomas, son of, 152–3
    Thomas of Stoughton, 152, 155–6
        and n. 52, 157 and n. 54,
        158–9, 161

Bedford, barony of, *see* Beauchamp,
Bedford, earl of, *see* Russell
Bedfordshire, 33, 36 n. 38, 39, 41, 69,
    71 n. 58, 72 and n. 5, 73 and n.
    63, 80, 125
Bedyngfeld, Edward, 22
Belgrave, George, 149, 152, 154, 158–9
Belper, 21 n. 20
Benedictines, 107
Berkhamsted, honour of, 34
Berkshire, 47, 62 n. 14, 67 and n. 36,
    69 n. 46, 71 n. 58, 73 n. 65, 126
Beverley, Joseph, 127–8, 130, 140
Beza Theodore 3
Bicester Abbey, 38 n. 45
Biddlesden Abbey, 38 n. 45
Bidun, family, 42 and n. 62
    Isbella, 42
    John, 31 n. 11
Birchet, Thomas, 126, 133, 138
Black Death, the, 88, 105 and nn. 88,
    89
Blackwell, family, 33 n. 19, 37 n. 41
    William de, 31 n. 11
Bledlow, 39 n. 47, 45 n. 82
Blosseville, family, 33 n. 19, 45 n. 78
    Simon de, 31 n. 11
Bodannan in St Endellion, 46 n. 83
Bolbec, family, 33 n. 19, 38 n. 45, 40,
    48 n. 93, 50, 52 and n. 113, 54
    and n. 122
    Gilbert de, 31 n. 11, 54 n. 121
    Henry de, 40 and n. 53
    Simon de, 40
Boleyn, Geoffrey, 125
    Isabella, daughter of, 125
    Thomas, viscount Rochford, 124
    see also Henry VIII
Bonet, Ralph, 78 n. 94
Bonhommes Priory, Edington, 119
Bordesley Abbey, 38 n. 45, 51
Bosworth, battle, 125
Bottle Claydon, 47
Botyller, William le, 70, 79
Bracy, family, 33 n. 19, 38 n. 45, 48
    n. 93
    Robert de, 31 n. 11
    Roger de, 48
Bradenstoke Priory, 118

    prior of, *see* Snow, William
Bradgate Park, 150
Bradwell Priory, 38 n. 45
Bramber, 138
Bray, 43 n. 71
Brayne, Henry, 116
Breaute, Fawkes de, 52
Breton, Manno le, 34
Bridgnorth, castle, 66 n. 34
Bristol, 12, 107–21
    Augustinian canonesses in, 108
    bishops of,
        see Bush, Paul;
        Holyman, John;
        Cheney, Richard;
        Fletcher, Richard;
        Ironside, Gilbert
    Boarshead and Raven inn, 118
    Cantocks pasture, 118
    cathedral of, Holy Trinity, 116–8,
        121
    dean of, *see* Snow, William
    churches,
        All Saints, 108, 118
        Christ Church, 112
        St Augustine the Less, 108, 118
        St Mary Redcliffe, 107
        St Nicholas, 108, 118
        vicars of, *see* Rastall, John
        St Philip, 114
        vicars of, *see* Corbett, Nicholas
        St Stephen, 107
    Carmelites in, 116
    corporation of, 116
    deanery of, 116
    diocese of, 116–7
        chancellor of, *see* Cotterell, John
    Dominicans in, 111–2
    Franciscans in, 116–7
    High Street, 118
    St Michael's Hill in, 108
    suburbs,
        Bedminster, 110
        Redcliffe, 110
        Trevill Mills in, 118
        St Thomas's, 110
        Temple, 110
Brittany, 100
Broke, Lawrence de, 31 n. 11, 44 n. 73

Brooke, William, lord Cobham, 137 n.
87, 138
Broughton, 53 n. 119
Broughton, family, 33 n. 19, 38 n. 45,
53 nn. 118, 119
John de, 53 n. 119
Robert de, 31 n. 11
Brun, John le, 73 n. 65, 75, 79 n. 96
Bruton Abbey, 118
Buckingham, archdeacon of, *see* Stratton
Buckinghamshire 7, 29–57, 69, 71 n.
58, 72 and n. 58, 73 and n. 63, 80
Burnham plateau in, 34
Bulley, 46 n. 83
Bunting, Richard, 140
Burgess, John, 121
Margaret, wife of, 121
Burton, family, 33 n. 19, 36 n. 40, 48
n. 93
Ingeram de, 36 n. 40
John de, 31 n. 11, 36 n. 40
Maud de, 36 n. 40
William, abbot of St. Augustine's
Bristol, 111–3
Bush, Paul, 119–21
Exhortation of, 121
William, 119
Bushmead Priory, 38 n. 45

Cabot, John, 107
cadets, 39
Caldwell Priory, 38 n. 45
Cainhoe, 46
barony, 46 n. 82
Calais, 125
Calvin, John, 3
Cambridge,
sheriff of, *see* Picot
Cambridgeshire, 31 n. 11, 44 n. 73, 49,
62 nn. 14, 17, 70 n. 49, 72, 75, 77
n. 89, 81 and n. 107, 82, 101
Camden, John, 7
Canon's Ashby Priory, 38 n. 45
Canon's Marsh, 109
Canterbury, 21
archbishops of, 103, 139; *see also*
Cranmer, Thomas, Gardiner,
Stephen
mayors of, 136 n. 80

Cantilupe, William, 41 and n. 57
Carsington, 44 and n. 77
Carsy, Richard, 115
Carun, family, 33 n. 19, 36, 45 n. 78,
48 n. 93, 50, 53 n. 118
Humphrey, 30 n. 8
John, 42
Ralph de, 31 n. 11
of Sherington, 40
Castle Combe, 111
Catholicism, 119, 121, 136, 137, 153
Cauerswall, William de, 71 n. 58, 73 n.
66, 74 and n. 67, 81
Cave,
Henry, 152
Thomas, 152
Cavendish, Richard, 135 and n. 74
Cecil, family, 144 n. 131, 150
Robert, earl of Salisbury, 151, 158,
161
William, lord Burleigh, 134
Cerne,
Philip de, 72 and nn. 61–2, 77, 79
n. 96
Rannulf de, 72 n. 61, 73 n. 66
Chadwick, Sir Edward, 17
Chalcombe Priory, 38 n. 45
Chalfont St Giles, 44
Channel, 131–2, 143–4 and n. 134
Charles I, 149
Charles V, emperor, 125
Cheetham, Geoffrey de, 71 n. 58, 73
n. 65, 75 n. 74, 79 n. 96
Chekers, family, *see* Scaccario
Cheney, Richard, 119
Chesham, 50
Cheshire 2, 4, 18, 65, 103
Chester, bishopric of, 116
Chester, earls of, 35 n. 33
Chester, palatinate of, 64, 65 and n.
27, 66
Chester, William, 116
Chesterfield, 21 n. 20
battle of, 79
Chetwood, family, 33 nn. 19, 22, 38 n.
45, 53 n. 118
John de, 54–5 n. 123
Robert de, 31 n. 11, 45 n. 82, 54–5
n. 121

Cheyne, John lord, 125
  Thomas, 124–44
    secretary of *see* Tennant, Henry
    servants of, *see* Anthony, servant
      of Thomas Cheyne
    Daper, Richard, Finch, Nicholas
    John, son of, 135 and nn. 73, 74
Chilton, 41 n. 57, 46 n. 82
cinque ports, 123–44
  barons of, 129 n. 29
  brotherhood(s) of, 126 and n. 14,
    127, 130, 139 and n. 103, 143
  liberty of 12, 124, 126–8, 132, 139,
    143
  Lord Warden 13, 124–31, 137 and
    n. 87, 138, 140–4
Cistercians, 113
Clare,
  Richard de, earl of Gloucester, 69
    and n. 47, 74, 77 and n. 90, 78
    and n. 91, 79 n. 94, 83
  Gilbert de, 69, 80
Clewer, 50
Clifton Reynes, 47
Clifford, Roger de, 69 n. 47
Climden, Joan de, 46 n. 83
Clinton, 31 n. 11
Clinton, family, 33 n. 19, 36 n. 40, 38
  n. 45, 42
  William de, 31 n. 11, 44 and n. 77
Cobham,
  John de, 71 n. 58, 72, 75, 80
  Reginald de, 62, 72
  see also Brooke
Coke, Edward, 144
Colchester, 67 n. 38
Colne, river, 34
Colly, Thomas, 140
Compton,
  John, 114
  Thomas, 153 and n. 30
confirmatio cartarum, 9
Corbet, family, 85
Corbett, Nicholas, 114
Cornwall, 46, 64, 65 n. 30, 66, 97, 142
  countess of, 36
  earls of, 36 n. 38, 48
    Richard, 34–5, 64–5 and n. 30,
      70, 82 n. 119

Edward son of, 34
coroners, 55, 68–9
Corp, family, 33 n. 19, 35 n. 33, 37 n.
  41, 38 n. 45, 45, 48 n. 93
  Andrew le, 31 n. 11
  Henry, 35 n. 33
Cotterell, John, 119
council of the north, 149
county 15
  hierarchical structure within, 32
  nomenclature of, 24
  office holding in, 24–5, 30, 33, 42,
    44, 51, 54, 57 *see also*
    origins of, 16
  quarter sessions in, 20–1, 24, 27
  taxation in, 25, 128–9, 146–9, 157–8
county community, concept of, 5–10,
  12–13, 15, 27, 32–4, 56–7, 161
county courts 10, 18, 22, 63, 68
'county gentry', 5, 20, 32
Courtenay, family, 74 n. 67
  John de, 70
  William de, 70, 79 n. 96
Cowley, family, 55 n. 125
  John de, 31 n. 11, 55
Cranmer, Thomas, 129, 134 and n.
  65, 135, 138–9 and n. 98, 140
Crawley, 53 n. 119
Crisp, Henry, 140
Crispe,
  Nicholas, 141
  William, 127, 132, 133
Cromwell, Thomas, 111–4, 134 and n.
  63
  Gregory, son of, 134 n. 63
Culvere, hundred, 77
Cumberland, 65, 71 nn. 54, 58, 76,
  82, 97
Curtfalun, family, 36 n. 40, 42–3, 45
  n. 78
  Robert de, 42
    Henry son of, 42–3
    Alice, niece of, 43
  Simon de, 31 n. 11

Dacre, lord, *see* Fiennes
Dairel, family, 33 n. 19, 39, 43, 53 n.
  118, 54 nn. 120, 2
  Henry, 45 n. 82, 46, 51

Henry son of, 51
Ralph, 31 n. 11
Damory, family, 33 nn. 19, 20, 21, 34, 35 n. 31, 46, 47 n. 87, 48 n. 93, 53 n. 118
Robert, 31 n. 11, 54 n. 123
Darches, family, 35 n. 31, 38 n. 45, 52 n. 114, 53 n. 118
Alan, 39
William, 31 n. 11
Darrell, William, 136
Daubigny, Isobel, 46 n. 82
Davington Priory, 126 n. 12
Denham, 43 n. 72
church, 54 n. 120
Denys, Hugh, 120
Derby 19, 21 n. 20
earls of, 70, 74
Derbyshire 2, 5, 19, 21 n. 20, 22, 23, 37 n. 44, 62 n. 14, 69, 71 n. 58, 73 n. 65, 75 n. 77, 76, 81 and n. 107
Dereham, 21 n. 20
Dering, Richard, 130
Devereux, Robert, earl of Essex, 144 n. 131
Devonshire, 62 n. 17, 70, 72, 74 n. 67, 97, 101
stannary in, 74 n. 67
Dialogue of the Exchequer, 32
Dictum of Kenilworth, 52 n. 114
Dilton, 119
dissolution of the monastaries 12, 111–116, 126 and n. 12, 134 n. 63, 135
Doddiscombe, Ralph de, 72 and n. 61, 74 n. 67, 79 n. 96
Dominicans, 111–2
Dorset. 54 n. 123, 62 nn. 14, 17, 67 n. 36, 69, 72 and n. 62, 77, 101, 108, 116, 119, 120
Dover, 123, 127 n. 17, 128, 130, 132, 139, 140, 143
castle, 124–5, 127, 132–3, 135 and n. 74, 137, 138 n. 95
clerk of, *see* Beverley, Joseph
constableship of, 124
lieutenants of, *see* Crispe, William; Dering, Richard; Monynges, John

churches,
St James, 124
comptroller of the king's works at, *see* Cavendish, Richard
corporation, 130
jurats of, 127, 130
mayor of, 127
paymaster of the king's works at, *see* Auger, Anthony
Doynton, family, 33 n. 19, 36 n. 40, 38 n. 45, 48 n. 93
Thomas de, 31 n. 11, 49
Drayton, William fitz Luke of, 30 n. 8
Dudley, John, earl of Warwick, duke of Northumberland, 120, 135 n. 74, 136, 141
Dun, family, 33 n. 19, 36 n. 40, 37
William le, 31 n. 11
Dunstable Priory, 38 n. 45
Duredent, family, 33 n. 19, 38 n. 45, 53 n. 118, 54 n. 123
Philip, 43 n. 72
Thomas, 54 n. 120
Walter, 31 n. 11

East Claydon, 47
Edgcott, Paris of, 30 n. 8
Edington, 121
Edlesborough, Oliver of, 30 n. 8
Edward I, 59, 85, 102 n. 71
as prince, 64–5 and n. 27, 73 n. 63
Edward II, 12, 87, 89–90, 92–3, 99, 102, 105
Isabella, queen of, 92–4 and n. 34
Edward III, 87–9, 92–4, 98 and n. 70
son of, *see* Edward, prince of Wales
Edward IV, 23, 27, 110
Edward VI, 120, 127, 137, 138, 140
Edward, prince of Wales, the Black Prince, 103
Egleston, William, 140
Elizabeth I, 11, 25, 136, 145, 149, 150, 161–2
chaplain to, *see* Fletcher, Richard
Emberton, family, 36 n. 40
William de, 31 n. 11
England
admiralty court, 127 n. 17
bishoprics 12, 116–9

cathedral chapters 12
chancellor, 68, 141 n. 119
    and *see* Wengham
chancery 19, 104, 105 n. 88, 124
    crown of, 9, 49, 51
    as agent of central authority
        16–17, 20, 25, 27, 59–86,
        87–9, 92–106, 112–5, 124–8,
        143–5, 160
    exchequer, 43, 47, 60, 62, 63, 70
        and n. 54, 71, 74, 75, 128
        Pipe and Memoranda rolls of, 1,
        70 n. 54, 71, 75 n. 70
    government records of, 32
    justiciar, 68, 70 n. 54, 71, 76
    kings bench, court of, 1, 47, 88, 94,
        98
    local government in, 17–18, 33, 44,
        47, 124
    lord chancellor, 126–7, 158–9
    monarchs,
        Anglo-Saxon, 25
        Anglo-Norman, 16
        Angevin, 16, 44
        Stuart 1, 2, 17
        Tudor 1, 11, 17, 124–6
    privy council, 125, 157
    Saxon peoples of 8
    treasurer, 68
Engleby, William de, 70 n. 53, 73 n. 66
English Bible, 120
English language 3
English Prayer Book, 120
escheator, 68, 98
Escudamore, Godfrey de, 68, 69 n. 43,
    70, 71 n. 58, 77, 83 and n. 121
    Peter, son of, 83
Essex, 41, 62 n. 17, 66, 67 and n. 38,
    71 nn. 54, 58, 74, 77, 80, 99, 150
Estleye, Thomas de, 78 n. 91
Eure, Hugh de, 30 n. 7
Europe 1
Everard, William, 69, 70 n. 53, 73 n.
    66, 77, 81
Evesham Abbey, 38 n. 45
Evesham, battle of, 52 n. 114, 81
Exeter, castle, 69 n. 45
exigent, 100
eyre, 88, 94, 99, 103

Eythrope and Cranwell, 39
Eyville, John de, 78 n. 94

Faversham Abbey, 126 n. 12, 134 n. 63
Ferrers, Robert de, 79
Field of the Cloth of Gold, 125
Fiennes, Thomas lord Dacre, 135 and
    n. 73
Fileby, Master Robert, 43 n. 72
Finch,
    Edmund, 135 n. 74
    Nicholas, 134 n. 63
fitz Ellis, family, 33 nn. 19, 20, 35 n.
    31, 46, 53 n. 118
    William, 31 n. 11, 46
        Emma, mother of, 46
fitz Hamo,
    Simon, 30 n. 8
    William, 35 n. 33
fitz Harding, Robert, Lord Berkeley,
    108
fitz John, family, 33 n. 19, 37 n. 41,
    45 n. 78
    Ralph, 42 and n. 62, 51
        of Merston, 42 n. 62
    Roger, 40 and n. 53
    Simon, 43
fitz Michael, Thomas, 71, 73 n. 66, 74,
    75, 79 n. 96
fitz Nigel, family, 33 n. 19, 47 nn. 87,
    88, 48 n. 93, 53 n. 118, 54 and n.
    122
    Robert, 31 n. 11, 46, 52 n. 114, 54
        n. 122
        Grace, niece of, 46 n. 85
        Richard, brother of, 46 n. 85
fitz Osbert, family, 33 n. 19, 37 n. 41
fitz Reginald de Morton, family, 33 n.
    19, 38 n. 45, 45 n. 78, 48 n. 93
    William 31 n. 11, 36 n. 40, 40, 43
        and n. 72, 51
        John, son of, 43 n. 72
        Robert, son of, 43 n. 72
fitz Richard of Moreton, Walter, 42
    William son of, 42
fitz Robert, John, 35 n. 33
fitz Roger, Roger, 35 n. 33
fitz Walter de Morton, family, 33 n.
    19, 37 n. 41, 38 n. 45, 45 n. 78

Richard 31 n. 11, 37 n. 41
fitz William, family, 33 n. 19, 38 n. 45, 48 n. 93
  Otto, 36 n. 40, 38 n. 46, 45 n. 82, 46
  Thomas, son of, 45 n. 82, 46
Fleet Marston, 39 n. 47
Fletcher,
  John, 133
  Richard (I), 119
  Richard (II), 140
Flushing, 155
Foliot, family, 69 n. 46
  Peter de, 69, 79 n. 96
Folville gang, 94–5
forced loans, benevolences, 146, 161–2 and n. 75
Fordwich, 130 n. 35, 131
forest, forest law, 55
'Form of Apology and Satisfaction 157
Fors, William de, earl of Aumale, 65, 66 n. 32, 71 n. 54, 76, 79 n. 96
Foxley,
  Constance, 37 n. 41
  John, 37 n. 41, 43 and n. 71
Frampton Cotterell, 121
  Gastlings Court in, 121
France 5, 16, 89, 93, 96, 102–3, 125, 138 n. 88, 144
  Louis IX, king of, 71, 80
Fraxino, family, 33 nn. 19, 20, 38 n. 45, 40 n. 53, 45 n. 78
  Reginald de, 40, 41, 51
  Robert, of Thornborough, 41
  William de, 31 n. 11, 35 n. 33
Friars Minor (Oxford), 38 n. 45
Frome, river, 108
Frowick, Thomas, 126
  Frideswide, daughter of, 126
Fulbrook,
  Hogshaw in, 37 n. 41
Fulbrook, family, 31 n. 11, 33 n. 19, 37 n. 41, 45 n. 78, 47, 48 n. 93
  Walter de, 31 n. 11, 35 n. 33
  William de, 37 n. 41, 44

Gascony, 73 n. 66, 74 n. 67
Gentlemen Pensioners, Band of, 150

Geoffrey, Thomas de, 31 n. 11
Germany 16
  kings of, *see* Cornwall
Giffard, family, 34
  John de, 70, 83
Glastonbury Abbey, 38 n. 45
Gloucester, 109, 117
  bishopric of, 116, 119
Gloucestershire 4, 5, 23, 46, 62 n. 17, 64, 67, 69 n. 45, 73 n. 65, 74 n. 67, 75, 108–9, 113, 114, 116, 121
Goldington, Peter de, 46 n. 82
  Isabella, daughter of, 46 n. 82
Gorges, Edmund, 120
Goring Priory, 38 n. 45
'Great Contract', the, 145–6, 155–6
Great Woolstone, 41 n. 57
Greencloth, Board of the, 147–9, 153 n. 31, 154–5, 157–8, 160
  messenger of, *see* Kite
Grendon, Robert de, 62 n. 14, 69
Grenville, family, 33 n. 19, 53 n. 118, 54, 54 n. 120, 54 n. 122
  Eustace, 52 n. 114
  Richard de, 31 n. 11
Grenwich, 120
Grey,
  Henry, lord of Groby, 147, 150–2, 153 n. 30, 154–5, 158–61
    John son of, 150–5, 157–61
  Henry, lord of Codnor, 19
  Lady Jane, 136
  Reginald de, of Wilton, 40 n. 53
  Thomas, marquis of Dorset, 150
Grufudd, Prince Dafydd ap, 79
Guildford, John, 140–1 and n. 113
Gunpowder Plot, the, 153

Hales,
  Christopher, 134 n. 65
  James, 126
Hamden, Hampden, family, 33 n. 19, 38 n. 45, 47 n. 87, 53 n. 118, 55 n. 126
  Alexander de, 30 n. 8, 31 n. 11, 39 n. 47, 54 n. 121, 55 n. 123, 72–3, 76, 79 n. 96, 81
  Reginald, son of, 46 n. 82, 55 n. 123

Ralph, 30 n. 8
Hampshire, 21, 39, 61, 62 n. 14, 66,
    67 and n. 36, 72, 75 n. 77
Hardmead, 47
Hareng, family, 33 n. 19, 37 n. 41, 45
    n. 78
    John, 37 n. 41
    William de, 31 n. 11
Harengod, family, 66 n. 35
    Ralph, 66 and n. 35
Harpole, 46 n. 82
Harrold Priory, 38 n. 45
Haselrigg, Thomas, 153
Hastings, 123, 130, 138, 140, 142
Hastings,
    Edward, 150
    Francis, 150
    George, fourth earl of Huntingdon,
        147 and n. 8, 150–1
    Henry, fifth earl of Huntingdon,
        11, 151 n. 24, 152–3 and nn.
        30, 31, 154–5, 157–8 and n. 59,
        159–60 and n. 70, 161
    Henry, third earl of Huntingdon,
        150
    Henry, deputy lord lieutenant of
        Leicestershire, 151–5 and n. 47,
        157, 159
    Walter, deputy lord lieutenant of
        Leicestershire, 153 and n. 31,
        155, 159
Hautein, Hamo, 69, 72, 75, 77, 80
Haverholme Priory, 38 n. 45
Haversham, Maud de, 53 n. 116
Haye, family, 33 n. 19, 38 n. 45, 53 n.
    118
    John de la, 78 n. 91
    Stephen de la, 35, 52 n. 114, 55 n.
        123
    Walter de la, 31 n. 11
Hedon, Simon de, 69, 81 and n. 107
Heigham, Clement, 140
Hendred, Nicholas de, 67
Henry I, 43
Henry III 7, 11, 59–86
    Edmund, son of, 81
    queen of, 70
Henry IV, 17 n. 6
Henry V, 23

Henry VI 8
Henry VII, 22, 25 n. 38, 110, 125
    Elizabeth, queen of, 110
Henry VIII, 27, 112, 116, 120, 125,
    135 n. 73, 136, 137, 151
    Ann Boleyn, queen of, 112
    Anne of Cleves, queen of, 135
    Katherine of Aragon, queen of, 112
    physician of, *see* Owen, George
Herbert, William, earl of Pembroke,
    142 n. 121
    John, 142 n. 121
Hereford, castle, 69 n. 45, 83
Herefordshire, 62 and nn. 14, 17, 64,
    66, 69, 72, 75 n. 77, 77, 82, 83,
    101
heresy, 110–1
Hertford,
    Lord of, *see* Valence
Hertfordshire, 41, 62 n. 17, 66, 67, 71
    nn. 54, 58, 74, 77
Hilsey, John, 111
Hockliffe, 45 n. 82
Hogshaw, 44
Holbeche, Henry de, 112
Holderness,
    sheriff of, 66 n. 32
Holles, John, 156
Holmes, John, 140
Holyman, John, 119
Holy Roman Empire, 25
Holy Trinity Hospital, 38 n. 45
Horsey, John, 119
Houghton, family, 33 n. 19, 21, 36 n.
    40, 38 n. 45, 48 n. 93
    Simon de, 46 n. 82
        William, son of, 46 n. 82
    William de, 31 n. 11, 46 and n. 82
Howard, family,
    John, 19
Hubberdyne, William, 111
Hughes, Richard, 115
hundred rolls, 65
Huntingdonshire, 31 n. 11, 33, 44 n.
    73, 62 nn. 14, 17, 69, 70 n. 49,
    72, 75, 77 n. 89, 81 and n. 107,
    82, 101–2
Husee, John, 134 n. 63
Hythe, 123, 139, 140, 142

Iffley, 46 n. 85
Inkpen, 42
Insula, Robert de, 77
Ironside, Gilbert, 119
Isle of Wight, 115
Italy 16
Iveri, Roger de, 34

James I, 145–6, 156, 160–2
Jews, 45, 48–50, 60
  justice of the, 80
John, Ralph fitz, 31 n. 11
juries, grand assize, forest inquisitions,
    presentment, trial, 30, 32 and n.
    13, 33–5, 54, 56, 64, 98, 100, 102
justices of assize, 24, 102 and n. 71,
    104, 124, 159
justices of gaol delivery, 68, 102 and
    n. 71
justices, commissions of the peace 11,
    20–3, 54 n. 123, 56, 79, 87–106,
    149, 152–3 and n. 31, 158–60

Kene, John, 112
Kenilworth, 70 n. 49
  battle, 80
  dictum of, 79–80, 82
Kent 3, 4, 5, 21, 62 and n. 14, 69 and
    nn. 45, 46, 71 n. 58, 72, 75, 77 n.
    89, 82, 103, 125–6 and n. 12, 134
    and n. 134, 139–40, 144, 147 n. 7
  lathes in, 32
Keynes, family, 33 n. 19, 38 n. 45, 48
    n. 93, 49, 50, 53 n. 118
  John de, 49, 55 n. 123
  Luke de, 31 n. 11
  Nicholas, 49
  Robert de, 49
    Margaret, daughter of, 49
Kimble, 40 and n. 53, 46
Kingsey, 40
Kingston in Aston Rowant, 39 n. 47
Kingswood, 121
Kingswood Abbey, 113
Kite, Mr, 148, 154
knights, knighthood, 33, 36, 52–3, 56,
    57
  belted, 29, 32
Knights Hospitaller, order of, 44

Knights Templar, order of, 38 nn. 45,
    46

Labourers, ordinance of, 105
La Couture Abbey, 41 n. 57
Lancashire 2, 4, 67, 70, 71 n. 58, 73
    n. 65, 103
Lancaster,
  Duchy of, 22
    receivership of, 151
  earls of,
    Henry, 93
land, market in, 39–45, 47–8, 50–1, 57
Langetot, family, 33 n. 19
  Ralph de, 31 n. 11
Langport, 38 n. 45
Langport, family, 33 n. 19, 38 n. 45
  Ralph de, 31 n. 11, 55
Lathebury, William, 141
Latimer, Hugh, 111–2
Latymer, William le, 65, 66 n. 32, 81
    and n. 109
Lavendon, 37 n. 41, 41 and n. 57, 42
Lavendon Abbey, 38 n. 45
lawyers, 48, 95, 101, 104–5, 131, 138
Layton, Richard, 113
Leicester,
  castle, 159
  corporation, 150, 152, 160 n. 70
Leicester Abbey, 38 n. 45
Leicestershire, 6, 11, 33, 37 n. 44, 54
    n. 123, 62 n. 14, 69 n. 46, 72, 78
    n. 94, 81, 146–62
  lord lieutenancy of, 151–2
  deputies, *see* Cave; Hastings; Turpin
Leicester forest, lieutenancy of, 151
Leigh, *see* Abbots Leigh
Lenham, 135
Lewes, 138
  honour of, 44
Leyburn, Roger de, 80
Lilligstone Dairel, 37 n. 41, 39, 43, 54
    n. 120
Linch, Simon, 141, 142 n. 122
Lincolnshire, 62 and nn. 14, 17, 72,
    75, 77, 101 n. 68
Liscombe in Soulbury, 41 n. 57
Lisle, lord, *see* Plantagenet
Lisson Green, manor, 38 n. 46

Llywelyn, prince of Wales, 66
Lollards, 110
London, 34, 105 n. 89, 111, 157
    Fleet prison, 11
    Marshalsea, 141
    Tower of, 112
Low Countries, the, 97–8
Long Crendon, honour of, 34
Lucy, Geoffrey de, 35 n. 33, 44
Luffield Priory, 38 n. 45, 40 n. 53, 41, 44
Lusignan, Lusignans, 60
    Aymer de, bishop of Winchester, 67

Magna Carta, 157
Maid's Moreton, 37 n. 41, 41 n. 57, 42, 43 n. 72
Maidstone, 21
Maleherbe, Lucy, 45 n. 82
Malet, family, 48 n. 93, 53 n. 118
    Hervey, 31 n. 11, 33 n. 19, 35 n. 31, 38 n. 45, 47 n. 87
    Ralph, 31 n. 11, 33 n. 19, 38 n. 45
    Robert, 31 n. 11, 35, 44 n. 73, 47–8, 49 n. 95, 54 n. 123
Mansel, John, 74, 81 n. 108
Manwood, family, 142 n. 125
    Roger, 130
    Thomas, 142 n. 122
Marchers, 69 n. 47
marriage, 30, 45–6, 50
Marteval, Martival, family, 69 n. 46
    Anketil, 68, 70 and n. 49, 73 n. 66, 82 and n. 119
Mary 12, 120, 132–3 and n. 59, 136 and nn. 79, 80, 137, 140–1 and n. 115, 142–3, 151
    Philip of Spain, husband of, 131–3
    Vita Mariae Reginae, 151 n. 20
Master, John, 142 and n. 122
Maunsel, family, 48 n. 93
    Geoffrey, 37 n. 41
    Henry Dairel, 37 n. 41
    Henry fitz Henry Dairel, 37 n. 41
    John, 31 n. 11, 33 n. 19, 37 n. 41, 38 n. 45, 42
        Henry, son of, 42
    Thomas, 31 n. 11, 33 n. 19, 36 n. 40, 38 n. 45, 49, 52 n. 114

Mediterranean, 1
Meisy, Robert de, 64, 67, 69 n. 47, 72, 73 n. 66
Melton Mowbray, 148 n. 9
Menys, Thomas, 130, 141–2 and n. 125
Merston, Ralph of, 42 n. 62
Merton Priory, 38 n. 45, 48
Middlesex, 126
military service, 2, 54
Milton Keynes, 49
Missenden Abbey, 38 n. 45, 48
Moine, John le, 70 n. 49
    William le, 70 n. 49, 73 n. 66, 81 and n. 107
Mohun, Reginald, 142 and n. 121
Monkton up Wimborne, 120
Montacute, William de, 44
Montfort,
    Peter de, 66 and n. 34, 68, 78 and n. 94
    Simon de, 52 n. 114, 59, 61, 67 n. 36, 70 and n. 49, 77, 78 and n. 94, 79 and n. 97, 80–4
Monynges, John, 130, 135 and n. 74, 140
More, John, 138
Mortimer, Roger, earl of March, 92–3
Morton,
    Nafford, Henry de, 31 n. 11
Morton Abbey, 126 n. 12
Mottisfont Abbey, 38 n. 45
Mulcaster, Robert de, 66, 71 n. 58, 76, 82
Mulcheney, 118
Munchensi, Hubert de, 67 and n. 38
Mursley, 46 n. 85

Nafford, family, 33 n. 19, 38 n. 45, 48 n. 93
    Henry de, 51
        Denise, mother of, 51
Neirenuit, family, 31 n. 10, 33 n. 19, 35 n. 31, 38 n. 45, 39, 47 n. 87, 49, 52, 53 n. 118, 55
    Geoffrey, 39 n. 47, 49
    John, 49, 54 n. 121, 54 n. 123, 55 n. 126
    Miles, 30 n. 8, 31 n. 11, 54 n. 123, 55 n. 126
    William, 30 n. 8

Neville, family, 135 n. 73
Newcastle-upon-Tyne,
    castle, 66 n. 32, 75
New Romney, 123, 129, 130, 138–41
    and n. 119, 142 and n. 121
    jurats of, 129, 130
Nicholas of the Tower, ship 8
Noers, family, 33 n. 19, 21, 22, 38 n.
    45, 46 n. 82, 53 n. 118, 55
    Amory de, 31 n. 11, 54 n. 123, 55
        n. 126
    William de, 46 n. 82, 54 nn. 121,
        123
Norfolk, 4, 6, 21 and n. 20, 22, 23,
    41, 62 and n. 14, 69, 71, nn. 54,
    58, 74, 82, 116, 146, 160–1
Northampton, 52 n. 114, 97
    battle, 80
    castle, 69 n. 45
Northamptonshire, 33 and n. 22, 39,
    54 n. 123, 62 n. 17, 69 and n. 45,
    72, 75, 76, 82, 103
Northumberland, 30, 35 n. 33, 62 n.
    14, 66, 74, 75, 77 and n. 89
    dukes of, *see* Dudley
Norton, George, 120
Norwich, 18
Norwich, Simon de, 43
Nostell Priory, 38 n. 45
Notley Abbey, 38 n. 45
Nottigham, 91
    sheriff of, 17
Nottinghamshire 5, 23, 32, 62 n. 14,
    69, 71 n. 58, 73 n. 65, 75 n. 77,
    76, 81 and n. 107, 102, 156

Oketon, John de, 66 n. 32, 72 n. 58,
    73 n. 66, 74 and n. 67, 81 n. 108
Old Sarum, 77
Oliver, William, 112
Olney, family, 33 nn. 19, 21, 38 n. 45,
    47 and n. 87, 53 n. 116
    John de, 33 n. 22, 53 n. 116, 54–5
        and n. 123, 56 n. 128
    Simon de, 31 n. 11, 35 n. 33, 47
Osbert, Richard fitz, 31 n. 11
Oseney Abbey, 38 n. 45, 41, 44
Ouse, river, 34
outlawry, 100

Oving, family, 33 n. 19, 37 n. 41
    Peter de, 31 n. 11
Owen, George, 116
Oxenden, William, 140
Oxford,
    bishopric of, 116
    university, 119
Oxfordshire, 31, 33 and n. 21, 39, 41,
    44 n. 73, 46, 47, 54 n. 123, 56, 62
    n. 14, 67 and n. 36, 69 n. 46, 71
    n. 58, 73 n. 65
oyer and terminer, 92, 100

Padyham, Simon, 140
Paget, William, 136
Paris, Matthew, 41
Paris, William de, 44 n. 77
parliament 5, 10, 15, 29, 137–43
    burgesses in, 137–42
    commons in, 20, 54, 56, 88–91, 94,
        96–7, 99–106, 135, 145–6, 149,
        156–7, 160, 162
    elections to 19, 137–43 and n. 130,
        150
    lords in, 100, 120
    private petitions to 19–20, 99 n. 58
    acts, statutes of,
        Bishoprics Act (1539), 116
        County Council Acts (1888,
            1894), 15
        of Labourers (1351), 105
        of Northampton (1328), 93 and
            n. 25, 95–6, 102
        of Winchester (1285), 95
        Quo Warranto (1290), 129 and
            nn. 32, 34
Parliaments,
    (1258), 64
    (1305), 90
    (1307), 9
    (1327), 91
    (1328, April), 92–3
    (1330), 94
    (1332, March), 95
        (September), 96
    (1333), 90 n. 12, 96
    (1334), 90 n. 12, 91, 96
    (1337), 90 n. 12, 91
    (1339), 91

(1341), 99
(1343), 100
(1344), 101, 104
(1346), 102
(1348, January), 103–4
    (March), 103–4
(1351), 105
(1352), 104
(1353), 104 n. 84
(1354), 104 n. 84
(1361), 104–5
(1362), 105
(1363), 104 n. 84
(1365), 104 n. 84
(1368), 105
(1388), 105
(1390), 105
(1529–36), 137, 139
(1539–40), 134, 137
(1542–4), 138
(1545–7), 137
(1547–52), 120, 137–8
(1553, March), 131, 137, 140
    (October), 140–1
(1554, November), 141
(1555), 141, 142 n. 121
(1558), 125, 141, 142 n. 121
(1601), 150, 154
(1604–10), 145–6, 154, 155–7, 161
(1621), 148 n. 8
Partridge, Miles, 116
Passelewe, family, 33 n. 19, 38 n. 45,
    53 n. 118
    John, 52 n. 114
    Ralph, 31 n. 11
Paston family, 22, 23
    John, 19
Paston Letters, 18, 22
Patche, Thomas, 139
Patteshull, Simon de, 69, 72, 75, 80
Peake, Nicholas, 142 and n. 125
Pembridge, Henry de, 66 and n. 33
Perrot, John, 141–2 and nn. 121, 125
Peterborough, bishopric of, 116
Pevensey, 130
Pever, family, 42–3, 52, 56
    John (I), 41, 42
    John (II), 42
    Paul, 37 n. 41, 41 and n. 57, 42–3

    Paul son of, 41
    Roger, 41
    Thomas, 53 n. 119
        Mary, daughter of, 53 n. 119
Peyforer, family, 69 n. 46
    Fulk, 69 and n. 45, 82
Peyton, John, 140
Phelips, Robert, 161
Philip, Oliver fitz, 30 n. 8
Picot, 17
Pinnock, Thomas, 138–9
piracy, 127 n. 17
Pitstone, Ralph, 30 n. 8
Pitstone Neyrnuit, 39 n. 47
Plantagenet, Arthur, viscount Lisle,
    134 n. 63
Plessis, John du, 69 and n. 45, 70, 73
    n. 66, 74, 77, 82
Poclington, Remy de, 66 n. 32
Poitou, 41
Poitevin, Poitevins, 67 n. 38
    Roger le, 68
Pole, Reginald, cardinal, 135
Popley, William, 116
Portbury, 109
Portsmouth, 132
Portway, Thomas, 140
Poyntz, family, 111
'Prebendaries Plot', 135
Preston Bisset, 55 n. 125
Protestantism, 141, 150
Provisions of Oxford, 11, 63–4, 71, 74,
    76, 84
Provisions of Westminster, 71 and n.
    54, 77
Purcell, Purcel, family, 33 nn. 19, 20,
    21, 35 n. 31, 38 n. 45
    Otvel, 54 n. 123
    Robert, 31 n. 11
purveyance, 11, 145–62
Puttenham, family, 33 n. 19, 38 n. 45,
    53 n. 118, 54 n. 123
    Ralph de, 31 n. 11
Pyrenees 1

Quainton, 31 n. 11, 47
Queenborough,
    castle, 125

Rabyan, Elias de, 62 n. 17
Randolph, Thomas, 142 and n. 121
Rastall, Rastle, John, 114–5
Reading Abbey, 50
realm, community of, the, 9
recusancy, 119, 153
Reformation 3, 12, 19, 107, 111, 117, 120, 134
regional identities 1–4, 7–10, 26
Remonstrances, 9
Renaissance, 121, 125
Richard II, 20
Richard III, 27
Rochester,
    castle, 80, 125
Rochester Priory, 38 n. 45
Rochford, Guy de, 67 n. 38
Rochford, viscount, *see* Boleyn
Romanesque, 108
Roper, Jane, 134 n. 63
        Christopher, son of, 134 n. 63
    William, 140
Rose, Robert de la, 46 n. 82
Rowland, John, 138
Russel, Russell, family, 33 n. 19, 36 n. 40, 37, 38 n. 45
    William, 31 n. 11
Russell, John, earl of Bedford, 142
Rutland, 64, 70, 82 n. 118
Rycote, family, 33 nn. 19, 20, 21, 35 n. 31, 53 n. 118
    Fulk de, 31 n. 11, 34, 52 n. 114
Rye, 123, 126, 138, 140, 142 and n. 121
    jurats of, 134 n. 63
    mayors of, 134 n. 63
    see also Birchet, Thomas
Ryve, John, 120
Ryvere, Walter de la, 71 n. 58, 73 n. 65, 79 n. 96

Sackville, Andrew, 49
Sadler, Ralph, 116
St Alban's Abbey, 38 n. 45
St Andrew's Priory, 38 n. 45
St Augustine's (Bristol), 108–121
    Burton, William, abbot of, 111–5
    Gwilliam, Morgan, abbot of, 115
    Knowle, abbot of, 108

Newbury, abbot of, 109
Newland, abbot of, 109
St Augustines Abbey (Canterbury), 126
St Bartholemew's Hospital, 38 n. 45
Saint Fey, family, 33 nn. 19, 20, 36 n. 40
    Hamon de, 31 n. 11
St Frideswide's Abbey, 38 n. 45
Saint Germain, Nicholas de, 30 n. 8
St James Abbey (Northamptonshire), 38 n. 45
St James Priory (Bristol), 107
St John's Hospital, Oxford, 38 n. 45, 40 n. 53, 41, 44
St Mark's Hospital, 38 n. 45
St Mary's Overy, 38 n. 45
St Oswald's, Gloucester, 118
St Sexburgh Abbey, 126 n. 12
Saint Valery, John, 66, 67 n. 36
Salden, 46 n. 85
Salisbury,
    cathedral, 119, 120
        prebends of, 117
    dean of, 117
    diocese of, 116
Saltwood, 139
    castle, 125
Sandford Priory, 38 n. 45
Sandwich, 123, 126, 128, 129 n. 34, 130 and n. 35, 131–3 and n. 59, 137–42 and n. 121, 143, 144
    bailiff of, *see* Patche, Thomas
    jurats of, 131–3, 141–2
    mayors of, 133; *see also* Master, John; Menys, Thomas; Stile, John; Tysar, John
Saunders, Matthew, 152 and n. 28
Saunderton, 37 n. 41, 38 n. 45, 43, 45 n. 82
Saunderton St Nicholas, 39, 45 n. 82, 46
Saunderton, family, 33 n. 19
    Osbert de, 31 n. 11
    William de, 46 n. 82, 54 and n. 121, 122, 55 n. 123, 124
Sauvage, James le, 66
Savoy Denham, 54 n. 120
Sayn, John, 142
Scaccario, family, 33 nn. 19, 22, 35 n.

31, 36 n. 40, 38 n. 45, 46, 47 nn.
    87, 90
  Henry de, 31 n. 11, 46, 47
    Ralph, son of, 46 n. 83
Scalariis, John de, 72
Scotland, 65, 92–3, 96
Scrope, Geoffrey le, 88, 95, 98
Seer, John, 138
Serles, Robert, 135
Segrave, family, 70
Severn, river, 109
Sewardsley Priory, 38 n. 45
Seymour, Edward, earl of Hertford,
    duke of Somerset, 136, 138
  Thomas, 136 n. 77, 138
Shabbington, 47
Shaftesbury Abbey, 118
Shenley, 49
Sherington, 40 n. 53
sheriffs 7, 8, 10, 11, 20, 54, 59–86, 95,
    124
  ordinance of, 63, 68, 84–5
'Ship Money', 146
Shipton Montacute, 45 n. 77
Shrewsbury, castle, 66 n. 34
Shropshire, 23, 62 n. 14, 66, 69, 71 n.
    58, 74, 75, 77 and n. 89, 81, 85
Sicily, Norman kingdom of, 16
Siffrewast, family 31 n. 10, 33 n. 19,
    38 n. 45, 48 n. 93, 50, 53 n. 118
  John de, 33 n. 22, 54 n. 123
  Richard de, 31 n. 11
    Roger, uncle of, 49
Skipwith, William, 148, 152, 154 and
    n. 42
Smyth, John, 116
Snelshall Priory, 38 n. 45
Snow, William, 118
Somerset, 62 nn. 14, 17, 67 n. 36, 69
    and n. 45, 72, 77, 81, 90 n. 9,
    108–9, 116, 160–2
Soulbury, 37 n. 41, 42
Southampton, 21, 22
Southwark,
  churches,
    St Mary Overy, 37 n. 41
Southwell, 7
Spain, 134 and n. 67
Stafford, William, 138

Staffordshire 9–10, 23, 62 n. 14, 66,
    69, 71 n. 58, 74, 75, 77 and n. 89,
    81, 85
Stalham, William de, 71 n. 54
Stamford, 91
Stanford, family, 33 n. 19, 35 n. 31, 37
  Joan de, 45 n. 82
  Roger de, 31 n. 11, 37, 46
    Emma, daughter of, 45 n. 82
Stanho, Hervey de, 71 nn. 54, 58, 73
    n. 66, 82
star chamber, court of, 159
statistics, use of, 4–5
Stewkley, 42
Stile, John, 139
Stoke Goldington, 46 n. 82
Stokes, family, 33 n. 19, 36 n. 40
  Richard de, 31 n. 11
Stow Bidun, 37 n. 41
Strange, family, 85
Stratton, Matthew de, archdeacon of
    Buckingham, 41, 43 and n. 72, 44
Straw, Jack 8
Suffolk, 62 and n. 14, 69, 71 nn. 54,
    58, 74, 82, 151 n. 20
Suffolk, William de la Pole, duke of, 8
Sulby Abbey, 38 n. 45
Surrey, 54 n. 123, 62 n. 17, 71 n. 58,
    74, 75 n. 77, 78 n. 94, 82 and n.
    118, 103
  earls of, *see* Warenne
Sussex 2, 49 n. 95, 62 n. 17, 66, 71 n.
    58, 74, 75 n. 77, 78 n. 94, 82 and
    n. 118, 97, 138
  rapes in, 32
Sutton, Robert de, 81
Swaffham, 21 n. 20
Syon Abbey, 126 n. 12

Tadlow, William, 140
Talbot, Gilbert, 66, 83
Tany, Richard de, 71 n. 58, 73 n. 66,
    74 and n. 68, 80, 81 and n. 105
  Richard son of, 80
Tattenhoe, 41 n. 57
Tattershall, Robert de, 80
Tennant, Henry, 129
Thame, 45 n. 82
Thame Abbey, 38 n. 45

Thames, river, 34
Theydon, 81
Thomas, William, 127
Thomism 3
Thornborough, 30 n. 9, 40 n. 53
Thornton, Hasley in, 37 n. 41
Tichford Priory, 44
Tickford Priory, 38 n. 45
Toddington and Chalton, 41
Tothill, family, 36, 38 n. 45, 48 n. 93
    Robert de, 52 n. 114, 54 n. 123
    Ralph de, 31 n. 11, 33 n. 19
Townshend, family, 6
topography 2–3
trailbaston, commissions of, 87–94, 96,
    98–104, 116
        ordinance of, 90
Tregonwell, John, 120
Trenchard, George, 119
Turpin, William, 152
Turri, family, 33 n. 19, 38 n. 45, 39,
    52 and n. 113
    Henry de, 39 n. 47, 45 n. 82
        Marina, daughter of, 45 n. 82
    Richard de, 31 n. 11, 55 n. 123
        constable of Wallingford, 34
Turville, family, 33 n. 19, 38 n. 45, 48
    n. 93, 53 n. 118
    Nicholas de, 54 n. 123
    Simon de, 31 n. 11
    William de, 52 n. 114, 54 nn. 121–3
Tysar, John, 141
Tythrop in Kingsey, 46 n. 82

Upton, family, 33 n. 19
    Walter de, 54 n. 121, 55 n. 123
    William de, 31 n. 11

Vache, de la, family, 44 and n. 75, 52,
    56
    Richard, 44
Valence, William de, lord of Hertford, 67
Valor Ecclesiasticus, 113
Valognes, family, 33 n. 19, 35 n. 31,
    36 n. 40, 38 n. 45, 46, 47 n. 87
    Robert, 31 n. 11
    Thomas, 31 n. 11, 46 n. 83, 47
Vavassur, 33 n. 19
    Hugh de, 31 n. 11

verderers, 55
Verli, Verly, family, 48 n. 93
    Hugh de, 36 n. 40
    Roger de, 31 n. 11, 36 n. 40
Vernun, John de, 72 and n. 58, 73
    and n. 64, 79 n. 96
Victoria, queen, 25
Victorine rule, 108
Viponte, family, 64
Visdelou, family, 36 n. 40, 38 n. 45
    and n. 78, 48 n. 93, 52 n. 113
    Humphrey de, 31 n. 11, 43, 51
        Hawise, stepmother of, 51

Wales, 65, 66, 103
    prince of, *see* Edward, Llywelyn
Wallingford, honour of, 34
Wallingford Priory, 38 n. 45
Walsh, family, 111
Walsingham, 21 n. 20
Waltham, 148 n. 9
Walton,
    Christopher, 148, 154, 157
    John de, 71 n. 58, 73 n. 66, 74 and
        n. 67, 78 n. 94, 79 n. 95, 82
Warenne, John de, earl of Surrey, 44
Warmeston, Stephen, 30 n. 8
Wars of the Roses, 150
Warwickshire 9–10, 29, 32 n. 13, 33,
    54 n. 123, 56, 62 n. 14, 66 n. 34,
    72, 81
Waterperry, 46
Watford, Eustace de, 69 and n. 45, 73
    n. 66
Wavendon, 37 n. 41, 38 n. 45, 41 n.
    57, 42, 45 n. 78
Wavendon, family, 33 n. 19, 37 n. 41,
    42, 50, 52 and n. 113
    Nicholas de, 37 n. 41, 43, 50 n. 104
        John, son of, 43
        Ralph, son of, 43
        Reginald, father of, 50 n. 104
    Roger de, 31 n. 11
Webbe, John, 140
Wedon, family, 35 n. 31, 38 n. 45, 53
    n. 118
    John de, 52 n. 114
    Ralph de, 31 n. 11, 33 n. 19, 54–5
        n. 123

Welles, Alexander, 140
Wells, cathedral, 119
Wengham, Henry de, 70
Westbury, 119
West Goscote, division of, 155 n. 47
West Kington, 111
    rector of, *see* Latimer, Hugh
Westminster Abbey, 43
    steward of, *see* Foxley, John de
Westminster, bishopric, 116
Westmoreland, 62
Weston Underwood, 41 n. 57, 42
Wexham, 37 n. 41, 42
White, Thomas, 117–8
Whitwell, 21 n. 20
William I, king of England, 17
William, Otto fitz, 31 n. 11
Willoughby, Richard, 94 and n. 35, 99
Wiltshire, 39, 62 n. 14, 69 n. 43, 71 n.
    58, 72 nn. 61–2, 73 and n. 64, 75
    n. 77, 77, 82, 83, 111, 113, 118,
    119, 162
Winchcombe, 75 and n. 76
Winchelsea, 123, 138
Winchester, 21
    bishopric of, *see* Lusignan
        warden of, *see* Pever, Paul
Windsor,
    council of, 94
Winterbourne, 114, 121
    rectors of, *see* Bush, Paul; Compton,
        John

Wintreshull, William de, 72 and nn.
    58, 61, 73 n. 66
Woburn Abbey, 38 n. 45
Wolsey, Thomas, 126
Wolverton, barony of, 30 nn. 8, 9, 44
    honour of, 34
    lords of, *see* fitz Hamo
Wood, Anthony, 119
    Robert, 140
wool staple, 98
Worcester, bishops of, 105 n. 89,
    111–2
        see also Latimer, Hugh; Fletcher,
            Richard
    diocese of, 110, 116
Worcester Priory, 112
    prior of, *see* Holbeche, Henry
Worcestershire, 64, 101, 113
Worksop Priory, 38 n. 45
Woughton, family, 33 n. 19, 36 n. 40
    Walter de, 31 n. 11
Wyatt, Thomas, 125, 136, 144 n. 132

Yarmouth, 142
yeomanry, 5
York, 105 n. 89
    archbishop of, 7
Yorkshire 4, 22, 65, 66 n. 32, 71 nn.
    58, 61, 74, 75 77 n. 89, 81 and n.
    109, 68 n. 101

Zouche, William de la, 79 n. 94